Mary Francis Cusack

The present case of Ireland plainly stated

a plea for my people and race

Mary Francis Cusack

The present case of Ireland plainly stated
a plea for my people and race

ISBN/EAN: 9783741139260

Manufactured in Europe, USA, Canada, Australia, Japa

Cover: Foto ©Thomas Meinert / pixelio.de

Manufactured and distributed by brebook publishing software
(www.brebook.com)

Mary Francis Cusack

The present case of Ireland plainly stated

SISTER MARY FRANCIS CLARE,

"The Nun of Kenmare."

THE

PRESENT CASE OF IRELAND

PLAINLY STATED;

A PLEA FOR MY PEOPLE AND MY RACE.

BY

M. F. CUSACK,

(THE NUN OF KENMARE.)

NEW YORK:
P. J. KENEDY,
EXCELSIOR CATHOLIC PUBLISHING HOUSE,
5 BARCLAY STREET.
1881.

INDEX.

Index.

Index.

PREFACE.

INTRODUCTIONS and Prefaces are generally passed over unread, but in the present case I have to ask the special attention of the reader to this Preface. I wish to explain my reason for writing this work, and the reason why I hope to add additional and, perhaps, not altogether irrelevant information to a subject on which it might appear as if there was little more to be said.

My reason for writing this work has been—that having had the distribution of a large Relief Fund, confided to me by friends of Ireland in all parts of the world, I have necessarily derived a great deal of information. A small portion of this Fund came from Protestant friends in England, and a small portion from Catholics. While I found amongst both a kind desire to relieve distress, I could not but see that there was an extraordinary and almost total ignorance as to the true state of

Irish affairs. I believe this arose partly from want of correct historical information, and partly from a want of that personal knowledge of this country which could only be obtained by a residence in it, and by a thoroughly confidential intercourse with the people.

I use the word confidential, because it is quite impossible for persons passing hurriedly through the country to know the real feelings or the real wants of the people; nor can such information be obtained even by a temporary sojourn in Ireland. For the present I must ask to have this statement taken for granted. Later, I hope to prove it.

Further, to understand why the Irish people are so seriously disaffected, needs some knowledge of the social state of the poor and middle classes in England. I believe much misery and confusion have arisen from a want of thorough information on this subject. English gentlemen naturally suppose that the Irish peasant, or small farmer, has the social advantages of the Englishman of his class, hence, they cannot possibly understand one-half the causes which contribute to make Ireland poor and discontented. The Irish patriot, perhaps, does not always give his English friends credit for their ignorance, nor, probably, unless he has had *direct* dealings with the poorer classes in both countries, will he understand it.

Besides this, I have had interviews with many gentlemen within the past few months, all holding the most opposite political and social opinions, who came to discuss these subjects. And I may add, as an evidence how much Ireland is misunderstood in England, that just before we were "proclaimed" in Kerry for our supposed social disturbance, the Marquis of Lansdowne left this late one evening, after we had held a long and most interesting discussion, and returned home unattended, unarmed, and in the dark—for in this little town we have not yet attained to the advanced civilization of gas. Further, his lordship informed me that he was leaving in the morning for shooting in Scotland; and he left his young children alone and unprotected at his place near this. Surely this confidence ought to be a sufficient answer to the cry for "coercion," and the exaggerated reports about disturbances in Ireland.

KENMARE, *October,* 1880.

THE CASE OF IRELAND STATED.

My Case is :—

1. That English people do not know the true state of Ireland. *They are ignorant of it historically*, because they only read the prejudiced narratives of English historians. *They are ignorant of it socially*, because they do not read the Irish papers, and English papers give, with few exceptions, only one side of the question.

That English people suppose the Irish to be a lawless, indolent, ungrateful race, because the English papers report "outrages" which never happened, whereas, in point of fact, there are far fewer outrages in Ireland than in England. I refer to the present work for evidence, carefully collected, the last (to this date) manufactured outrage being denied by Mr. O'Reilly, Lord Greville's agent, who said that the man said to have been shot at did not exist. The last English outrage which did happen I find reported in the *Echo*, where it is stated that arsenic sufficient to kill 200 people was placed in a haunch of mutton which was sent anonymously to Mr. Ashdown, the Duke of Cleveland's agent.

That the case of the Irish, or Anglo-Irish, landlords alone is heard in England, when nothing is heard of the manner in which so many of these gentlemen virtually break the law by compelling their unfortunate tenants to evade Mr. Gladstone's Land Bill. The English people ought to know that a law made in England for the benefit of Ireland is persistently set at defiance by the very gentlemen who are calling the Irish law-breakers, and who are calling out for coercion. Of this I give evidence in the following pages.

That the English people know nothing of the countless injustices done to the Irish tenant by "rules of estates," an arbitrary code of laws enforced by Irish landlords, from which Irish tenants have no protection. Of this I give evidence.

That the Irish are not lazy when they refuse to pay rents which are extortionate, and will not allow them to have the mere necessaries of life. Of this I give evidence.

That while the Irish people are simply asking for such laws to be made in England as will protect their lives and enable them to live in peace and on the poorest food, the landlords are clamouring for coercion, so that their tenants may be compelled either to pay rents which will not leave them sufficient for bare existence, or to drive them out of their homes and their country. Of this I give evidence.

That the present Land League agitation is simply the strike of a whole nation against unjust government; that in all strikes, acts of violence are committed, for which the leaders are not responsible; and that far fewer acts of violence have been committed in this great national strike than in any English strike. Of this I give evidence.

That those who refuse to pay more than Griffith's Valuation, are not doing so from dishonest motives, or because they are unwilling to pay any rent; but that they are doing so on the principle on which all English labour strikes are carried out; *i.e.*, contending for more to be given to the man, and less to the master—for more to be given to labour, and less to capital.

That the Irish people cannot in justice give all to the landlord, and refuse to pay the shopkeeper, who has given them credit in the Famine; *i.e.*, they know of no moral law which makes it justifiable to give all to the landlord and nothing to their other creditors. Of this I give evidence.

Lastly—I am firmly convinced that the principal cause why Irish grievances are not remedied is, because *Ireland is governed at the caprice of party*, and not as an integral portion of the United Kingdom.

In any part of England or Scotland the question is the general good. For any Irish matter the question is how it suits party politicians. Of this also I give evidence from English sources. The *Times* says :—

"What we do not find in Sir Stafford's speech is a due sense that the next Session will bring us face to face with a great national question, and that party ties must give way before the paramount claims of common state interests. If Sir Stafford will keep clear of the fourth party and its troublesome ways he may leave the Government to keep clear of the dangerous advisers whose influence he professes to be afraid of."

The *Daily News* says :—

"Sir Stafford interprets that the three F's are 'fraud, force, and folly.' In that spirit we may presume will all proposals for land reform be entertained by his party, but the hopes of the Conservatives are not in their own strength. Only a lack of thorough union among the Liberals could even in Conservative opinion give the battle into Conservative hands."

Mr. Bright says :—

"Until now, from the last hundred years, and from longer, the English Government and the English Parliament have always come to the rescue of the landed proprietors. England has done it in the past, and the question now is whether it will do it in the future."

The *Standard* of November writes :—

"Lord Salisbury is not the man to underrate the value of the occasion, but he is too apt to turn it into an opportunity for the display of rhetorical fireworks. He ought to see in the condition of Ireland a theme for something more than the invectives and satire of partisanship. It is not enough to argue, as Lord Randolph Churchill does, that Irish disturbance and disaffection are simply due to the mistakes committed by Mr. Gladstone and his colleagues. No man of sense believes this.

Sir Stafford Northcote turns the whole question into ridicule by talking of force, fraud, and folly, and is it any wonder if Ireland has wearied of government which depends too often not on justice, but on whether this or that political party shall hold the reins of statesmanship ?

"If an Englishman," writes the *Spectator*, "wishes to know what political shame means, let him read the brilliant chapter of historical review in Sir Charles Gavan Duffy's book on 'Young Ireland,' and *he will feel it for a time a burden almost too great to endure.*"

The Case of Ireland stated.

The *Echo* says :—

" There is, as might have been expected, a good deal of denunciation of the Government, because exceptional measures have not been taken to prevent crime and outrage in Ireland. But whatever is done or left undone is sure to be opposed in certain quarters. If the Government had decided to call Parliament together to suspend the Habeas Corpus Act, or to re-enact some stringent Coercion Act, they would have been criticised, taunted, and opposed, either because they had not commenced earlier, or done more, and now they have not done so they have exposed themselves to similar acrimonious comments. The truth is that it is impossible that the Government can do anything to please its opponents. The best thing then to be done is, after surveying the whole of the circumstances, to act for the benefit of the country, and not attempt to conciliate faction or to mitigate the acerbity of irreconcilables."

Just so. All we ask is, that Ireland will be governed "for the benefit of the country." But when English writers make such statements, Ireland may well be hopeless of justice. On the motion for the second reading of the Irish Land Act in 1870, Lord Derby spoke as follows :—

" I ask you whether the Irish Church would not now have probably been still on its legs but for the Fenian agitation ? I will also ask whether this bill, in its present form, would have been likely to pass through both Houses of Parliament if it had not been for long-continued agitation, supported by many most unjustifiable acts of violence ?"

The Case of Ireland stated.

Professor Thorold Rogers, writing from Oxford, December 1, 1880, says :—

"At present I am convinced that, under the guidance of Lords Cairns and Redesdale, the Upper House deliberately intended to set the English and Irish people by the ears to increase the difficulties of government and to make conciliatory legislation impossible or difficult. But I trust that the English people will see who is to blame for the present situation."

KENMARE, IRELAND, *December 8th,* 1880.

MICHAEL DAVITT.

THE CASE OF IRELAND STATED;

A Plea for my People and my Race.

CHAPTER I.

IRELAND AND PUBLIC OPINION.

On this matter [the state of Ireland] English opinion shapes itself largely in ignorance, and he does good service to the common weal who bears ever so humble a part in making known the truth.—*Daily Telegraph.*

HERE is one subject, at least, on which we cannot complain of neglect on the part of the English nation. Ireland and Irish affairs occupy so prominent a place in the public press, that it is (especially at present) impossible to take up a serial or newspaper in which there is not some article on the Irish question. Ireland is, indeed, the best written about country in the world. The press at home and abroad is full of the subject. In Paris we have the *Figaro*, the *Debats*, and the *Univers*, each with its theory or statements as widely opposite as the poles, and so in every continental country. The *Cologne Gazette* has even reproached England with her mismanagement of Irish affairs. It would seem then as if ignorance on Irish subjects could not be the cause of our chronic state of disturbance, yet that such is the case we can give ample proof. Recrimination is not argument, yet, unhappily, recrimination forms the staple ground of all this press discussion. Where do we find anything like calm, impartial discussion? and yet never was there a subject which so much needed it. Ireland, or to speak more accurately, Irish affairs, have been made too long the object of party politics.; Irish affairs have not been treated as if they were imperial affairs; and yet the Irish people are expected to exhibit on all occasions an ardent attachment to the English crown and constitution.

We have asked for centuries to be governed by English laws; we have been governed for centuries by the caprice of party politics. Might it not be well to try, at least for a time, the effects of governing Ireland as England is governed—at least until this is done, do not call us ungrateful, or threaten us with coercion acts.

It is not a little remarkable that the same policy has been pursued as regards Ireland for centuries. It has not been successsful; and might it not be advisable, even as a matter of common sense, to try a new policy?

But before any policy can be effected, it must be grounded on a thorough and personal knowledge of the state of Ireland; and unless this has been obtained, it is equally hopeless to ask or to attempt any legislation for this country.

Now, there are several subjects, the consideration of which must precede action, and yet they are precisely the subjects on which English people have the fewest means of obtaining reliable information.

English opinion of Irish affairs is based on two separate grounds—it is based on historical knowledge and current opinion. English statesmen, or, to speak more accurately, the English people, when they discuss Irish affairs, preconceive that they are correctly informed on these subjects. Never was there a more fatal delusion. Irish history has been written much as Irish news is written to-day—not from facts, but from opinions. Mr. Froude is nothing if he is not brilliantly inaccurate. He cannot write a page of the history even of the English nation with common veracity, yet he sits down with the air of a judge, from whose sentence there can be no appeal, to pronounce

on Irish affairs on the strength of having spent
a short time in Kerry, near Kenmare, where
his family acted in direct contradiction to his
theory by doing acts of kindness to the people.
He writes for a public whom he wishes to
amuse. He knows it will not criticise any
slander he chooses to write about Ireland,
whatever may be said to the romance he
offers when he writes English history according to Froude, in amusing contradiction to
English history according to fact. All this
is of very little consequence as far as English
history is concerned. English people have
truthful histories of England, and they can
very easily test his entertaining fictions by historical facts. His brilliant inventions are amusing, and on the whole harmless, because they
are known to be the aberrations of a genius.
But the more inventive he is as regards Ireland,
the more sure he is to be believed ; and, as he
is always amusing, he is read. People want
amusement; truth, plain naked truth, is not
amusing, and they prefer the fiction, of which
he is so untiring a narrator. When the truth
is known about Ireland people may read his
Irish fictitious history as they read his English
fictitious history—for amusement; but they will
look elsewhere for facts.

Yet it is from such writers that English people learn Irish history. They have then not only to learn, but to unlearn before they can form a correct opinion on Irish affairs.

Mr. Froude's " English in Ireland" is from beginning to end a series of inaccuracies. Unfortunately we have no Irish Freeman to give him the contradiction which justice demands. We can give but one sample of the fiction which he writes. His admiration for the Norman invaders of Ireland is unlimited, and in his zeal for his clients he forgets English history. A glance at *Cambrensis* would have told him the character of the men he delights to honour.

Henry II. landed in Crook, in the county Waterford, on the 18th of October, 1171.

Contemporary historians do not give a favourable character of the English king, though he purposed to have come to Ireland to improve it.

Cambrensis says "he was more given to hunting than holiness." It would have been well if he had been given to nothing worse than hunting.[1]

---

[1] He was a tyrant to the nobility ; pushed his encroachments on the holy things of God to a detestable excess, and by a zeal for justice (but not according to sense) combined, or rather confounded, the rights of the State and Church, and would make himself all in all. The

Yet Mr. Froude in "The English in Ireland" gives a glowing description of the incalculable advantages which the barbarous Celt derived from the administration of the cultivated, enlightened, and eminently humane Norman prince. As there are nearly as many false statements as there are lines in each page, it would be impossible to refute them seriatim. Mr. Froude does not appear to have read contemporary history, either English or Irish.

Some one has said that a fact is always true after it has happened. It remained for this historian to evolve a theory out of his inner consciousness, and then to compose an historical narrative to support it. The method is simple, to a person of fertile imagination it is entertaining.

The Normans were perfect, they were "qualified and gifted."[1] Contemporary writers say they were gifted—gifted with no scanty share of depravity, and qualified for any amount of impiety.[2] A cardinal pronounced Henry to be

---

revenues of vacant benefices he seized for his treasury ; and, as a slight leaven corrupteth the whole mass, while the treasury plundered the rights of Christ, the impious soldier receives what was due to the priest.—*Cambrensis Eversus*, p. 483.

[1] *The English in Ireland*, vol. 1, p. 16.

[2] John of Salisbury gives the following account of another Norman prince :—" During the reign, shall I call it, or desolating scourge of

an "audacious liar." Count Thiebault, of
Champagne, warned an archbishop not to rely
on any of his promises, no matter how solemnly
they were made. His own son thus graphically
describes the family characteristics :—" The
custom in our family is that the son shall hate
the father ; our destiny is to detest each other ;
from the devil we came, to the devil we go."

Mr. Froude has said nothing about this ; but
he evolves out of his inner consciousness a
wonderful account of how he came to Ireland,
and what his nobles did there. The Irish were
" vagabonds." " They were wild and wayward ;"[1] but they were not wayward long—at
least not in Mr. Froude's history. A mar-
vellous tranquility came over Ireland when
the Normans landed. There was a whole century during which the Irish savage had peace
and rest and justice and plenty (in the History
of Ireland, according to Froude). The poor

King Stephen, over clergy and people, there was a universal grasping
of all things; might was truly the only law of right. Many wicked
things he did ; but worst of all, his flying in the face of God and laying
violent hands upon his anointed. But the bishops, though the first,
were not the only victims of His fury. Every man on whom his suspicion fell was instantly the doomed prey of his treachery. But the
imprisonment of the bishops was the beginning of the evils of the land
in his day, that even a brief sketch of them would exceed the horrors
of Josephus."

[1] *The English in Ireland,* p. 17.

savages became " humane" and " rational," and
all because (I still quote this very remarkable
historian) the English in Ireland " did not
destroy the Irish people."[1]   They only " ham-
mered" the heads of the Celts who were unwilling to submit, and "drove the chiefs into
the mountains ;" but it is not explained how all
this hammering and driving was carried out
peacefully.   Contemporary historians, both English and Irish, give a very different account to
Mr. Froude's, but a person of fertile imagination does not require authority for his statements.

The Normans "only took the government of
Ireland," just as a man would take his hat and
cane to go out for a walk.   Let those who
doubt look at the original ; but this very calm
and just and extremely dignified "taking the
government" involved dispossessing the chiefs.
This "changed the order of inheritance into an
orderly succession," according to Mr. Froude ;
the Irish annals call it driving out the rightful
owners and putting in usurpers.   Indeed, as
much is admitted in one part of the page, for
here he says :—" The new comers rooted themselves in the soil, built castles, gathered about

---

1 *The English in Ireland*, pp. 16-11.

them retainers of their own blood, who over-whelmed and held down those whom they forced to be their subjects."[1]

In the interval, too, there was "incessant fighting and arduous police work."[2] Yet in the next breath we are assured all was done peace-fully.

Such is the fashion in which the Irish history of the past has been written, and such being the case, it is little wonder that a very large majority of those who legislate for Ireland are absolutely ignorant of the people whom they govern.

But though the history of the past forms a considerable element in the discussion of the events of the present, there are men who are quite capable of acting on present information.

But what shall be said of not merely suppres-sions of what would serve to prove the cause of the Irish tenant, but of actual and outrageous false reports.

One English gentleman, a Protestant, and, I must add, a generous benefactor to our poor, has been sending me English papers regularly every day for a year or more, with Irish out-rages carefully marked. It so happened that many of these outrages, I might say truly most

[1] *The English in Ireland,* p. 17.
[2] Ibid, p. 18.

of them, had been contradicted previously in
Irish papers. And note, these contradictions
were not made *anonymously ;* they were made
by the very persons to whom they were said to
have happened. But the lie had got the start,
and there was no one to contradict it, and thousands of good Englishmen and women were
shaking their heads over the depravity of the
Irish people, when the depravity only existed
in the wicked imagination of the original inventor of the lie. In the *Daily Telegraph* a
writer informs his readers that "to abolish
landlordism by shooting individual landlords,
these are the end and means of the Land
League." Well, if this is true, the Land
League has been a complete failure.

Ask the next person you find denouncing
Irish crimes, and talking as if the Irish people
lived in a chronic state of landlord-shooting,
How many landlords have been actually shot?
He will possibly tell you some hundreds. You
cannot take up an English paper in which you
will not find it stated, in the plainest language,
that murder and assassination and outrage is
the state of Ireland at this moment. And
what is the fact? Three landlords have been
killed during the last twelve months. And
this is how English gentlemen misrepresent

Ireland, and try to raise a cry for "coercion." Yet, if we Irish are to believe English papers, it is England wants coercion, unless, indeed, the life of landlords is so incomparably above the lives of other men that there would be no comparison between the crime of killing a landlord and the crime of killing numbers of little helpless children and aged men and women, or of murdering strong men for mere gain.

It is, indeed, a grievous thing that even one landlord should have fallen a victim to the assassin; but what of the hundreds who have fallen victims to English murderers? Is there no judgment for them? Is their crime no sin?

I know that crime in England does not excuse crime in Ireland. But it should obtain some justice in the consideration of Irish crime.

No wonder some crimes have been committed in Ireland in consequence of the cruel evictions and the cruel demands for rent from a starving people. Many of these "outrages," as we have said, are the pure inventions of unscrupulous men; but many crimes have been committed. But take them at the most and at the worst. If one is to accept the reports of the state of England as given in the English newspapers, English people ought to come to Ireland for freedom from crime and protection for life and property! When do we hear of jewel and plate robberies in Ireland, such as occur frequently in England and remain unde-tected? If such crimes took place in Ireland, what cries of righteous indignation there would be! How fearful it would be to live in such a country! Above all, how horrible for such crimes to remain undetected! Every Irishman and woman would share in the odium for not hunting out the robbers and giving them up to justice. But here in this Ireland, where we are supposed to be in a state of chronic and horrible crime, Irish gentlemen go to amuse themselves shooting in Scotland, and leave their houses unguarded, and their children in the wilds of Kerry or Connemara, as the case may be, sure that they will be safe and happy with their servants and tenants.

And can the Irish people fail to be indignant at the miserable ingratitude of this class of men, who add to their oppression of the people, with whom they knew their children may be left in safety, the most cruel calumnies on these people?

A great deal has been said about a few acts of cruelty to animals in Ireland; but what of the reports in the London papers of prosecutions for acts of the most wanton and utterly uncalled-for cruelty to dumb and defenceless beasts ? It need scarcely be said that cruelty in England to the brute creation does not excuse cruelty in Ireland ; but those who condemn the one ought to condemn the other equally. And what of the wholesale cruelty committed on human beings in Ireland, when in this famine year they were left with little concern half starving, when a pitiful dole of food, only fit for dogs, was all that would be given to them ?

Here is an English account from the *Daily Telegraph*, of a few days ago, of the state of affairs in England. Let us suppose for one moment that such a state of affairs could by any possibility be reported as happening in any part of Ireland, and what a cry there would be for " coercion," and for " strong measures," and the suspension of the *Habeas Corpus* Act, and, above all, for that exercise of " firmness " on the part of the Government, which, during the famine, was supposed too often to be the proper course to be adopted when we were starving for bread, and which is now declared to be the one thing necessary for the Government of Ireland, when those who have been supported,

or, to speak more correctly, have been enabled
to exist during the famine year on public charity, cannot pay their rents.

If " firmness " was justice to tenants and the
poor, Ireland would soon be wealthy. But
*here is an English account of the state of
England.*

We confess to rubbing our eyes, and wonder-
ing if Blackheath and Lewisham had slipped in
by mistake for Belfast and Cork. But we do
not know that an English paper has yet declared
that we are obliged to go to sleep in Ireland
fully armed.

"The good people of Blackheath and Lewisham are
already alive to the necessity of going to sleep fully armed,
and the inhabitants of that district should by this time think
no more of hearing a pistol shot in the night than they
might of the deceitful croak of the ventriloquial corn-crake.
If all this banging of firearms lately heard had led to the
arrest of a single burglar, so much gunpowder would not
have been exploded in vain. Unfortunately, the thieves
remain more free than welcome. Sometimes the police are
on the spot, and occasionally the citizen has to fight his
enemies unsupported and unsustained. About two o'clock
on the morning of Monday, Constable Mooney, 34 R, had
an exciting conflict with a couple of intending burglars at
Westcombe Park, Blackheath. The ruffians carried firearms,
which they did not hesitate to use, and the brave officer,
who was struck on the head and stunned, and whose pluck
and determination will, no doubt, have due recognition at

the hands of his official superiors, narrowly escaped being shot dead. Almost at the same time when the policeman was being shot at, in the execution of his duty at Blackheath, young Mr. Hopkins, son of a clerk in the Bank of England, was engaged in what might easily have proved a deadly struggle with a burglar, in his father's home at Lewisham. The brave lad was awakened from his sleep by hearing a noise in the room. He jumped up to lay hold of the intruder, but was suddenly seized by the throat and half strangled. Contriving to escape the grasp of his assailant, he obtained a loaded revolver from a drawer in the room, and fired it point blank at the burglar. The pistol missed fire, just as the ruffian returned the shot, and a ball passed through the young man's shirt. As the burglar retreated through the window, Mr. Hopkins fired another barrel, this time taking effect. The wounded scoundrel, however, managed to escape, leaving a gold watch behind him."

After making all possible allowance for sensational writing, which seems inevitable at the present day, and which will save future historians of the Froude stamp the trouble of drawing on their imagination, there must be an underlying truth which shows the state of England to be very dangerous. But suppose some foreign writers were to write of the state of England, even on such grave ground, in the same fashion in which English writers expatiate on the state of Ireland, with what cries of indignation they would be met!

To write sensationally of crime in England

would do no practical harm, and certainly would not affect the lives or liberties of Englishmen ; but to write sensationally and untruthfully of Ireland is a very different matter. To do this . is to help to continue a state of things in Ireland which has been denounced even by English statesmen, and it is to bring cruel suffering on a people who have already suffered cruelly.

The *Graphic* of October says :—

" Burglaries around London are as numerous as ever, notwithstanding the fact that extra police patrols and plainclothes men have been placed on duty in the various districts. The Home Secretary has offered a reward of £100 for the conviction of the recent burglaries and attempted murders at Lewisham and Blackheath, with a free pardon to any accomplices. It is said that the announcement contains a special clause excluding policemen from participation in the reward. Robberies from churches and schools have also been very frequent in the Southern suburbs, and three young men have been arrested on suspicion of being concerned in them."

And we are also informed that Mr. Gladstone was robbed of jewels at Hanbury Hall. What a state of social disorder and crime all this reveals ! It is no pleasure to record all this ; but it is as much justice to England as to Ireland to do so.

I believe the extent to which falsehood is

circulated about Ireland is not even imagined in England. And now this systematic habit of lying about Irish affairs is extending itself to the Continent. But, let England beware; to-day it gives continental writers the whole weight of its example and approbation in lying about Ireland. The lesson will be remembered; and by-and-by, when England in her hour of need and danger is met with a similar fate, she will have only herself to thank.

Once again, let me ask—is this English honour?

Is it, then, honourable to lie systematically? Is it honourable, when the lie is refuted, to refuse to admit the denial of the falsehood? We can quite understand how a false report may find admission into any paper. But when false reports come to be habitually inserted, it looks like malice and deliberate fraud. When it becomes habitual to refuse to deny false reports, there can be no question that they are deliberate. Were such reports purely a matter of accident, honourable men would *rejoice* to see them contradicted, for honourable men do not love lying.

French correspondents are now turning their attention to Ireland; and, strange to say, it is the infidel and communistic press that is all in favour of England's oppression of Ireland,

B

Happy Ireland! She secures the hatred of the
wicked. She is too good, too pure, too holy for
their foul tongues to name her, except with
scorn. Men who, forsooth, make a love of
liberty their boast, cry out for coercion for Ireland.

As I am about to reply by facts to the
calumnies published in the *Debats* by M. de
Molinari, I will say no more here. My reply
will appear shortly in the *Univers*.

A few persons may be deceived about Ireland
by these landlord misrepresentations; but the
people of Europe, the people of America—all
civilized nations and peoples see that it is to the
eternal discredit of England that Ireland should
be in such a state. England, which boasts of
her learning, and her position, and her honour!
what a discredit that she keeps Ireland for
centuries in misery; that now, in this nineteenth
. century, Ireland is as poor, as subject to famine,
as discontented as she was 300 years ago!

And foreign countries are not slow to see
where the fault lies, or to see that the only remedy offered by England, or rather by a small
and exclusive class of Englishmen like Froude
and Disraeli and statesmen of this class, is
"coercion." Coercion! why England has been
trying coercion with Ireland for 700 years, and

it has not yet effected any improvement in the country. Might it not, then, be well for England to try something else, at least by way of experiment.

When England first invaded Ireland, she tried coercion. The Irish were hunted down like dogs, sold like slaves, treated like beasts ; but all this coercion did not make the country any the more prosperous, nor did the English settlers themselves gain anything by it.

When England thought proper to change her religion, Ireland, of course, was expected to follow, and coercion was tried again and again, but to no purpose. Englishmen got no benefit by it, nor did English settlers in Ireland benefit by it. This is the first point which honest Englishmen should consider : Ireland has been governed by coercion for hundreds of years, and no good has been gained by it.

Whenever Ireland rebelled ever so little against misgovernment "coercion" was the remedy. It is as if you half-starved a man and then flogged him for complaining.

A famine came to Ireland in this last year, and because the people have complained of the causes they are to be "coerced" again. What do honest Englishmen say to this ? I know what they will say. They will say they will not allow it ; they will stand up in their power and forbid it ; they will not fling away their character for justice because a few Irish landlords will not act with common humanity.

They may indeed, for want of better infor. mation, believe all the evil recorded of Ireland in the past, but their intellect, and perhaps their hearts, are sufficiently large to let that pass, and act in the present. For such persons it is all important that they should be correctly informed as to the present state of Ireland, and yet we can show from indisputable sources that they cannot obtain reliable information from the press ; yet it is precisely to the press that such persons look for information.   And let this one point be carefully noted, for it is of supreme moment to England as well as to Ireland. Though some just-minded Englishmen may be content to let the dead past bury its dead, yet they believe Irish history as narrated by Froude and other historians of his class.   Hence, they are quite prepared to believe reports of out- rages, because they expect nothing else from Ireland.   Then, when false reports, when ima- ginary murders or cruelties are narrated with all appearance of truthfulness by the press, they are, so to say, naturally believed.   It is only what previous education has led the public to expect; the public, therefore, readily accepts as true what, under other circumstances, it would think twice before it would believe.

But in a question which involves such grave issues, surely truth should be the first object.

There is one important point besides deliberate misrepresentation of Ireland, and that is deliberate and wilful suppression of truth. To suppress truth is to act a lie, because the suppression is a deliberate act. I now proceed to give examples of actual and most mischievous suppression of truth.

The Daily Telegraph, an organ of English opinion read by thousands, perhaps by a million, of just the very class who most need to know the truth about Ireland, has articles frequently on Irish affairs. No doubt it is necessary for an English newspaper at the present day to be sensational. The *Daily Telegraph*, I must admit, is as sensational on the real crimes which happen in England as on the imaginary outrages that do not happen in Ireland. But people are only amused at the sensationalism as far as England is concerned; as for Irish affairs, Englishmen are so entirely ignorant of them that they take all this sensational outcry as true.

Thus what amuses people in the one case does a positive and most grave injury in the other case.   It is a very serious matter to write what will mislead people on a very important subject.

The *Daily Telegraph* for October 11th has an article on Ireland.   It treats of the Archbishop of Dublin, of Mr. Parnell, of the Commission, of the Land League, and I do not know what else besides.   So far good.   These are all subjects of public interest.   It commences with the bitterest attacks on Ireland, and recommends "coercion" as the only remedy, and it ends with a quite candid admission of Irish grievances, or rather of Irish wrongs. This is precisely how the more honest class of English newspapers write. They dare not say out boldly that Irish landlords are determined to prevent the enactment of laws which would prevent oppression.   So they begin their leaders with bitter taunts against Ireland, and before they get to the end, their honesty is too much for them, and they admit the truth.

The *Daily Telegraph* did incalculable benefit to Ireland in the famine by its truthful account of the state of the country.   Why has its editor not the courage now to report on the state of the Irish land laws?   Probably because he dare not be truthful, and he does not wish to be false.   The article commences with a criticism of Dr. McCabe's Pastoral Letter.

Now, here is one instance of the suppression of truth which is carried out so largely in English papers, and which is *not* creditable to the honour or honesty of England. Why should anything be suppressed if people are not afraid to tell the truth ? Why should a letter, or a leader in a paper, or a report, or a speech give some bits of extracts because they suit the views of the English people ? And why should bits be omitted that would tell strongly on the other side ?

In the condensed summary of news which is the *vade-mecum* of so many hurried English readers, a bit is given from the pastoral to tell against the Land League ; but one of the most important bits is not given—one which should be written in letters of gold and put before every Englishman as the pronouncement of a distinguished Irish prelate who condemns all agitation that seems even to hint at violence even in words. His Grace says :—

"The periodic famines with which our people are continually threatened, the insecurity of their land tenure, which paralyses the most industrious hands, and the wretched condition of thousands of families, whose domestic arrangements might test the temper of a Slave Coast African—all proclaim that our land laws require a prompt and thorough revision. On this point we are all united. All agree that if peace and security are to be firmly established amongst us, it must be by the hand which blots out those odious laws that constitute the character of oppression."

Now, this is an old story. Whenever an Irish Catholic prelate says anything which English writers think will tell on their side he is quoted with qualified approbation. The approbation in this case is qualified by strongly expressed remarks about the clerical inferiority of Irish priests. This is no new proceeding. In the year 1797 the then Catholic Bishop of Cork addressed a pastoral to his people imploring them not to join the French, who were landing in Bantry Bay, but to remain faithful and loyal to the English Government. So important was this pastoral considered, and of such immense value was it to the Government of the day, that 4,000 copies were printed and circulated by the Government.

The Lord Lieutenant notices the "useful impression" which was made by this "judicious address," in a despatch which was published in the *London Gazette* of 17th July, 1797; but we do not hear that any further acknowledgment was made of the bishop's services. But it mattered little to one who sought no temporal reward for doing what he believed to be his duty.

Lord Bantry got his peerage for being the first to inform the Government that the fleet was sighted in Bantry Bay.

The Bishop was made use of, and neither he nor his people received any consideration; nor was the matter made, as it should have been, a reason for helping the Irish people to more justice in religion or legal rights.

Now, there are four subjects on which the whole question of the state of Ireland turns. The first and most important question is, no doubt, the relations between landlords and tenants. The next is the relations between those who hold the reins of the immediate government of Ireland. The third subject is the all-important one of the general social state of the people, and it includes the very grave and very important question of Temperance. The fourth subject is the state of the industrial resources and trade of Ireland.

CHAPTER II.

LANDLORD AND TENANT.

"The Habeas Corpus Act had been suspended in the country in 1800, from 1802 till 1805, from 1807 till 1810, in 1814, and from 1821 to 1824. There were select committees upon Ireland almost every year since the Union. Whenever disturbances arose, and distress appeared, Coercion Acts were passed, and select committees appointed. Nothing more was done."—*O'Brien—Land Question.*

IRELAND is exclusively an agricultural country; hence the Land Question in Ireland has necessarily an importance which it has not in England. It is no doubt a subject of surprise to many persons in England why there is this persistent agitation about land. But land is the one object of trade, commerce, and commercial speculation in Ireland. We have used the expression commercial speculation advisedly, because it underlies all the subjects of discussion. I will not reproach England with having reduced Ireland to this pitiable extremity, and a pitiable extremity it is. In the present state of society, in our advanced stage of civilization, no country can

CHARLES STUART PARNELL, M.P.

become wealthy which depends exclusively on agriculture. Civilization, such as we understand the term at the present day, requires artificial conveniences, if not conventional luxuries, such as never existed, and therefore were never desired, in a primitive state. The earth was tilled then to procure necessary food, and cultivated to procure necessary raiment. Nature yields to our demands so far, but when we endeavour to press a further return we fail to obtain it.

Ireland, being, then, virtually a purely agricultural country, and this to a degree which is not found in any civilized nation in the world, will give a yield of ordinary food and clothing to her population ; but, if pressed beyond this, there is anarchy and disorder. A moderate return of income can be obtained from land, which will enable the toiler to live, and allow something for the proprietor as well ; but where more is demanded, then nature revolts, and the usurer suffers. Why, then, should usury be permitted in land commerce, when it is forbidden in every other commerce ?

All the laws against usury have been repealed, but notwithstanding their repeal, Courts of Equity give relief against unconscionable bargains where the parties are not on equal terms.

No civilized government will tolerate the practice of usury, because all experience shows that it is a doubtful gain to one, while it is a certain ruin to many.

But let us suppose that usury was permitted in any nation, and that only one commercial industry was open to that nation, is it not a foregone conclusion that a universal national bankruptcy must ensue.

But this is precisely what has happened in Ireland. For years, and at the present time, the practice of usury in Irish commerce exists, and until it is legally forbidden Ireland will continue poor, and as a necessary consequence discontented.

In Ireland when a man has any capital to invest commercially, he must speculate in land ; with the miserable exception of the whiskey trade, there is scarcely one Irish manufacture in which capital can be invested. Hence, usury and usurious competition in land—the ruin of the entire nation.

In a letter to the *Chicago Tribune*, the Marquis of Lansdowne, replying to an accusation made against him as to the management of his estates, says: " There are in three counties alone about 54,000 holdings, valued at or under £4 a year. Such holdings are manifestly too

29

small to support a man and his family in comfort and respectability." This is a grave statement made on very high authority. Multiply this 54,000 by five or seven, and look at the number of persons who, in these counties alone, are living in a state of chronic misery, and then say is there not cause for Irish discontent.

Then, let it be remembered, that these men are liable at any moment to find themselves still further sunk in misery by an increase of rent. For the moment we must ask you to take it for granted that such an increase of rent is not only possible, but probable; of this we can and will give ample proof. Let us suppose, what happens every day in Ireland, that one of these 54,000 men improves his land with infinite toil and labour; his rent is too often raised, and he is taxed for his expenditure of his only capital—his labour. But it will be said Mr. Gladstone's Act at once provides for this, and he will get compensation. Compensation! And what *can* compensate a man for being ejected from his home—what can compensate a man for the bitterness of his heart when he sees his years of toil taken from him, and the place to which he had become attached, even from the very anxiety and care which it gave him, passing into other hands? What is

he to do? where is he to go? He has his
choice between the workhouse and emigration,
between exile from a country to which he is
passionately attached, and a living tomb.

And all this is possible, all this happens daily
in every part of Ireland, because usury in land
is not forbidden by English law.

The landlord who evicts the tenant, whether
he be a noble lord or a country shop-keeper,
has the same object in view. He wants money.
He wants to get from the land what the land
cannot give. He wants to get what the cultivator cannot give if he is to exist, as the
Marquis of Lansdowne has said, "in comfort
and respectability."

Now, if the landlord knew that usury in land
was not permitted by law he would not do this.
He knows very well if he evicts Patrick Daly
to-day because he will not pay him a usurious
rent, that Thade M'Carthy will take the land
at that usurious rent to-morrow, and why?
Because Thade M'Carthy has no other resource, because he has no other way whatever
of speculating, because he has a growing family,
and he persuades himself that *he* will be more
successful than Patrick Daly, that *he* will make
the land pay him a profit after he has paid the
usurious rent. When Lord Lansdowne's state-

ment is remembered, it is but too clear that
Thade M'Carthy cannot do this.. But he has
tried to do it ; he pays the new rent for a year
or so, and in his turn is evicted, or lives on, a
miserable, discontented, unhappy life—now
making some spasmodic effort to pay " the rent,"
and now getting deeper into debt and nearer
final ruin.

Perhaps in his intense desire to keep the land,
a desire well known, and much, unhappily, calculated on by landlords, he gets help from some
of his " boys" who go to America, or some of
his girls who go to service in England ; but such
help, though it may silence the clamour of the
land agent, is in fact only adding to the general
bankruptcy of Ireland. The " boys" may continue the help for a few years, they marry, and
have their own families to support. The girls
go to America, and in the end either get the old
father and mother out to them, or send them
a trifle, when they are in turn evicted, to save
them from utter destitution.

How much better then would it be for the
general prosperity of the country, for the landlord as well as the tiller of the soil, if usury
was forbidden by law.

Unhappily the desire of undue and covetous
gain is not confined to Ireland. In England

the Legislature had to interfere to prevent manufacturers from over-working, from actually destroying the lives of helpless women and children. Why, then, should not English law equally protect Irish tenants?

A great deal has been said in English papers about Irish agrarian outrages. Here is their source and their cause. Remove the source, remove the cause, and you at once put an end to the outrages. It is the wild justice of revenge. The Land League is credited with doing what ought to be done by English law. Strange that this should be made a cause of complaint. The Land League is credited with organizing a paid resistance to capricious or unjust increase of rent. It is credited with inciting " outrages " on the persons of those who take farms from which men have been evicted because they could not pay usurious rent. It is credited with protecting the many against the avarice of the few, and of using, to do this, the wild justice of revenge.

Yet the whole Irish nation, with the exception of the avaricious few, are imploring the English people for years to protect them by law. When protection by law is refused, are people to be branded as rebels and rioters if they try to protect themselves. The *raison d'etre* of the Land

League would cease to-morrow, if to-morrow saw a bill passed through the English Parliament for the protection of Irish tenants.

Strange and amazing inconsistency! The Irish people are spoken of by the English people at large as if they existed only to break the law; and yet what is the fact? The Irish nation for centuries have been imploring the English nation to protect them by law!

One is almost weary of hearing it said, that History repeats itself, and, in truth, it does; but how few profit by the experience thus gained. Certainly politicians seem, of all others, the slowest to do so. The History of Ireland has repeated itself over and over again, yet the same methods which failed in the days of the Norman invasion are repeated as if they had then succeeded to admiration.

If there is no advantage to England in having Ireland in a chronic state of rebellion, surely there should be the calmest consideration of past methods, and the most careful comparison of cause and effect. But no, there is still the same fatal policy.

Whenever any public event or calamity occurs which makes Irish chronic distress more severely felt in Ireland, there is "agitation," which naturally and necessarily culminates in

c

more or less violence. To expect a people who have a serious cause of complaint, and who have had this cause for centuries, to agitate without some violence, is to expect them to act like angels rather than like men. Hence the extreme injustice of the loud outcry that has been made whenever acts of violence accompany agitation in Ireland.

Those who make this outcry forget the fearful acts of violence which, even in the present century, accompanied public agitation in England. To denounce the Irish people for acts of violence in moments of political excitement is adding injustice to inhumanity. I would ask a very careful consideration of this point. The outrages committed in England by trades unionists are within living memory. They were of a most serious character, quite as serious—indeed, far more serious—than any outrages committed during the present agitation in Ireland. They excited terror from end to end of England; but as there were no party politics concerned, when the agitation ceased, there was an end of the reproach. It was as if a few members of a family rebelled at unjust treatment from the rest. Family ties are too strong to be easily severed. But how differently is all Irish agitation treated.

Here it is not question of one family or of
one nationality, it is made a question of race
against race. The trades union outrages were,
as we said, quite as horrible as those of which
we are accused, and which have not been
committed in Ireland—more horrible than any
which have really happened here. This is no
matter of opinion or conjecture, as those who
remember the circumstances know but too
well.

Animals were cruelly tortured and were even
burned alive. By an almost inhuman device
of cruelty, needles were placed by thousands in the clay for making bricks, so that
obnoxious workmen might be injured in the
most terrible manner. Nor were women spared,
as they most certainly are in Ireland. One was
killed, another was blinded, and yet another
was saved from a fearful death by being flung
out from a window naked. The great instigator
and head of all this fearful violence, William
Broadhead, was proved to have paid a man to
murder another, and it was proved in evidence
that men who had no personal quarrel whatever
with their victims, were obliged to mutilate
them and to inflict horrible punishments.

No one thinks now of reproaching the people
of Sheffield or Manchester for those crimes,

simply because there is no political or other purpose to serve in doing so. And people came to see that bad as these crimes were, they were in some degree like the violence of fever. It was better to find out the cause, and try to remedy that, than to think too much of the excesses.

There is unquestionably a remarkable coincidence of cause between the trades union combination and the present state of Ireland. In both cases it is a revolt of labour against capital. Labour wanted its *magna charta*. In ancient times there was no law for the labourer, and to say truth, scant justice. Men were compelled to work by English law whether they would or not. Even in the time of Elizabeth every act of legislation was in favour of the master, and against the man. The law was altogether against the trades, and the trades, as an inevitable consequence, against the law. Public opinion was against the trades also, and these acts of violence did not tend to conciliate public opinion. It was on a question of the deepest gravity, and turned on the one point—had a man the right to value his own labour or had he not? In other words, was he to work under a modified form of slavery, or was he to be a free agent?

The question is precisely the one asked now
in Ireland. If the question had been settled
in England by leaving all the power in the hands
of the employers and capitalists, there would
have been a revolution in England.

The Irish labourer and farmer ask now that
justice shall be done in Ireland between labour
and capital. We heard a great deal some years
ago of this or that being un-English. Is it not
un-English to refuse the calm consideration of
such a question, to make too much of the underlying cause, and to think superficially only of
the manner in which it is pressed ?

There is one thing of which I am perfectly
certain. If the great mass of the English
nation ever realized exactly what Ireland wants ;
if they could ever be got to see the exact truth
about Ireland, they would do her justice, and I
believe this is a general feeling in Ireland.
England may be unjust to us, but we do her the
justice to believe that she errs in ignorance.

It is not a thousand years ago, nay, it is
not even a hundred years ago, since the same
bitter clamour existed, or rather was excited
about Catholic Emancipation and tithes, as
that which is excited to-day about tenant right.
The least evil that could happen, if Catholic
Emancipation was granted, was the murder of

all the Protestants in Ireland; just as to-day, the least evil that will happen, if a farmer is allowed protection against the arbitrary estate rules of a landlord, is the total extinction of landlords.

In the year 1798, the Irish people asked, as they have so often asked, for the benefit of equal laws with England. How they were then treated, and how their demands were met, is shown, not by any Irish or Catholic historian, but by a Protestant bishop and Protestant noblemen who dared to say the truth. Sir L. Parsons' account of the fashion in which "some trivial disturbances" in the west were treated, reads as if he spoke of to-day; save only, and happily, that the government of to-day has not gone the same lengths. But it cannot be forgotten that they have been urged to do so by a certain party in England, and that they risk office and popularity by not doing so.

The following notes are taken from the Parliamentary report of debates, in the *Hibernian Chronicle*, Cork, 1798. They will show that there were at least some influential and intelligent Protestants who saw and deplored the infatuation which led a powerful minority to treat the Irish like dogs, and then turn on them with relentless cruelty if they resented such inhumanity.

The Bishop of Down, after replying in firm but courteous language to the attacks made on himself, said :—

"What is the crime which has provoked such asperity? I am charged with having been amongst many highly respectable names who dared to petition our common sovereign, and lay before the father of his people the sufferings under which we labour. Of that measure I am proud. I am convinced from ocular and personal examination of the general state of that part of the country, from the general testimony of its inhabitants, and from the infallible proof which the aspect of the country exhibits, that its manufactures and its trade have suffered, almost to annihilation. The noble and learned lord, in a tone of confidence which is so peculiar to him, asserts that I went about soliciting signatures to this petition. I assert, in opposition to the learned lord, that the information which he has received on that subject is false. I deny the fact, but were it true, I see nothing in it which, either as an honest man or a Protestant bishop, 1 should be ashamed of. Is this the conduct of one professing, as the learned lord does, such zeal for the support of the Established Church? If such be his treatment of his friends, the Catholics have little reason to regret his friendship. But what is the impropriety in a Protestant bishop uniting with his fellow subjects in a petition to the Crown."

Again he says :—

"The Chancellor, in that style of interrogatory which seems to imply so much, and which really means so little, asks whether your lordships will meet treason and murder and conspiracy with measures of conciliation, with Parliamentary Reform and Catholic Emancipation? I answer, my lords, that these are the only remedies which in our present circumstances are likely to be effectual. Of Catholic Emancipation—a full and complete emancipation—an admission to all the rights and privileges which a subject can claim—I have always been a decided friend. I have always thought it was a measure not merely of sound policy, but of strict right. Nor has anything which has fallen from the noble lord to-night, or at any former time, tended in any degree to shake my confidence in that opinion. Equally convinced am I that a full and fair reform of the representation of the people is a measure of wisdom and necessity. I see nothing but this measure which can now restore in Ireland the blessings of tranquillity and content. I have some property in this country; it is not a great deal, but it is sufficient to interest me in the safety and welfare of the State; I have also my preferment in the Church. Both of these bind me to consult the peace and good order of the country; and I declare it to be my firm belief, that unless these measures be adopted, my property, and that of every other gentleman in the country—nay, the country itself—is gone!"

Lord Dunsany said:—

"I shall take leave, therefore, though it is with much reluctance I enter on so painful a task, to supply, in a small degree, this omission, by recalling to the recollection of the house a few of the many enormities which your lordships must have known to be committed. In the County of Westmeath alone—and from the sufferings of this ill-fated county, noble lords may, without fear of being mistaken, infer those of the other counties of Ireland exposed to military execution—in this county alone, it is an incontrovertible fact, that several villages were destroyed by fire, without legal inquiry, trial, or ceremony of any kind. Three men were dragged from their houses, and shot on the fair-green of Baltimore, equally without any form of trial whatever, and time being scarcely allowed them to make their peace with heaven by saying a few prayers. After the bodies of the unfortunate victims had been exposed all the day (no friend or relative daring to approach them) the military had them tied on a car, and brought at a late hour of the night to the house of the parish priest, whom they forced to get up, and threw the dead bodies into the house, as if the murder of the dead was too little, without adding to it such an outrage on the feelings of the living.

"Look now, my lords, to another frequent and favourite mode of summary execution. Is it not notorious that several hundreds of his Majesty's subjects have been transported without any show of trial, or legal proofs of any kind? And are not these grievances? And will you, my lords, by your vote this night, countenance such cruelties, and become, by such countenance, accessories after the fact? If you do, consider how you are to answer it to God, your king, and your country.

"The noble and learned lord on the woolsack has been pleased to say that a burst of loyalty took place in the south at the time the French were on our coasts. He does the Catholics of the south but justice in the observation, a justice that prejudice itself cannot deny them. Is it, then, for that burst of loyalty the noble 'and learned earl now opposes their total emancipation? This would be, indeed, a strange return for loyalty, a strange mode of strengthening attachment, and invigorating affection. My lords, I must state it as my decided conviction, that if conciliatory measures are not immediately adopted,. this country is inevitably lost."

"Sir L. Parsons brought on his promised motion. He prepared by deprecating the most remote desire to say anything on this subject which could in the most distant degree increase the irritation which unhappily existed at present. Nothing could be more far from the wish of his heart than to add to that alarming discontent, which no man in the country could lament more sincerely or deeply than he did. On the contrary he was impelled to come forward on this occasion from the irresistible impulse of that duty which he felt called him, to submit the measure he was about to propose, for the purpose of allaying that discontent, and introducing a system which-should teach the people of this country they had a legislature who were capable and inclined to attend to other measures than those of punishment or extermination. But before he entered into any reasoning to prove the necessity of such a measure as he should propose to the House, he thought it necessary to vindicate the people of Ireland from the heavy charge which had been made on them, as if they were a people whom kindness could not attach, whom unlimited concession could not conciliate. The British Minister at that time (1778) governing Ireland, felt that there was a principle of discontent growing into vigour, which the usurpation of Great Britain had given birth to, and he thought it necessary to appease it, and how did he do it? By granting liberty to Ireland to cultivate tobacco, a plant which would not grow in the island. The people of Ireland, therefore, now began to complain that the manufactures suffered by the unequal terms on which they were obliged to contend with the manufactures of Great Britain, etc. It was remembered that while a yard of Irish cloth could not find its way into England without paying a duty of forty shillings, which amounted to a total prohibition, the cloth of Great Britain was admitted into the different ports of Ireland at a duty of only sixpence. This inequality between the established manufacturer of England and the languid infant manufacturer of this country was loudly complained of.

"What was the next measure of irritation to the people? Some trivial disturbances had taken place in the west—disturbances, which, if they did exist, were excited by the recall of that nobleman—gave an occasion to government to send thither a military force, commanded by a noble lord, no longer in this country. What was the consequence of that measure? The laws were violated in every instance where there could be an example made. The gaols were delivered, not by legal trials of the prisoners, but by the visits of a military officer, who, when there was not sufficient proof against the prisoner to commit him, transported him on his own authority; and mere suspicion of guilt was considered sufficient to transport a man for life from his country. Then for the first time (?) did the government of Ireland hold forth to the people the dangerous example of violating the law; and from that time may be dated all the atrocities which have been since committed by the people, and brought a disgrace on the national character. It was then that the populace of Ireland were for the first time brought to believe they were not within the protection of law, (?) and then it was that they ceased to respect the law. Let gentlemen consult their own feelings—for the poorest peasant has his natural feelings as sensible and as strong as those of any gentleman who heard him— perhaps his social feelings are stronger, as he is not diverted from his family or his cottage by the distractions of dissipation. When the house of the peasant is burned, even if he be guilty of the crime charged—which is generally no more than that of having concealed arms—when his house is burned. and his

decrepit parent is sent wandering for shelter about the
country, what story does he tell? Will not his appearance
—his houseless poverty, and his grey hairs, speak at once
his sufferings and his innocence? Will not the impression
which such an object makes, into whatever cabin he comes,
be that of irreconcilable hatred against the government
which inflicts sufferings such as these on harmless and helpless age? If the lower order of the people have as strong
a sense of injustice, as deeply rooted an antipathy to
oppression as the gentlemen of that house, will not the
houseless children and forlorn wife of the suffering peasant
rouse those feelings wherever they come, and create a wide-
spread aversion of laws which show themselves only in such
effects? What in fact has been the effect of these severe
laws that have given occasion to such enormities? It is
said the North is tranquilized—it may be so, but what kind
of quiet have they introduced? They have smothered the
flame, but they have not extinguished it. They have made
the North a sleeping volcano, which is every moment ready
to burst out and throw forth a torrent of destruction over
the land. But if the North had been rendered quiet
through the presence and immediate terror of a military
force, what has happened in the other parts of the country?
Until within these five months the south of Ireland had remained undisturbed. How was it now? If the enemy
were again to appear upon the coasts, would the peasantry
of the South now stretch forth the hand of affection to the
king's troops—would they share their scanty food, and give
up their bed to the weary soldier? Would they now, as they
did when last the presence of the enemy called forth their
loyalty and zeal, labour from morn till night in cutting through
the frozen snow a passage for the artillery? Would they yoke
themselves like beasts of burden, under the cannon, to ac-
celerate the business and lighten the fatigues of the army?"

Some one has said that History is philosophy teaching by experience, but in truth there are few persons whose philosophy is so perfect as to enable them to learn from history. Irish Protestants were not all destroyed when Catholic Emancipation was granted, and as if to show the utter failure of the prophecy, it is an Irish Protestant gentleman who is leading that very movement to-day which is causing such utterly groundless alarm.

When tithes were abolished, the Irish Protestant Church was to fail utterly; yet, though it has been disestablished by the act of an English Protestant Parliament, it is just where it was before. Indeed, so far has the old bitterness died out, that Protestant rectors and Catholic priests have united together in this famine year in perfect harmony.[1]

One of the great misfortunes of England has

---

[1] I have myself to testify to this harmony. I have in my possession many letters from Protestant clergymen thanking me for the help I was able to send the priests of their district. In one case, never to be forgotten, the Protestant clergyman of a large parish in the south of Ireland wrote to me to say the Catholic children had been prepared for Confirmation, that the Catholic bishop was coming to confirm them, but they were so *utterly destitute* of clothing, common decency would not allow their appearance in a church. I was happily able to send him money for clothing at once, and thanks to the energy and zeal—rather I should say to the great-hearted charity of this good clergyman—the Catholic children were clothed in time for Confirmation.

been that she has treated Ireland as the shuttle-cock of party politics. Whenever the game runs high, Ireland inevitably suffers; above all, if there is no special political foreign fiasco to distract attention. Lord Lansdowne has recently se-vered himself from his political party, and his management of his Irish property is receiving a good deal more attention than he cares to have ; but it is not so many years ago since the same Lord Lansdowne called the then English Go-vernment to account pretty sharply for their management of Irish affairs.

Would it not be wise, would it not be more just, to treat Ireland as, say, Devonshire would be treated ? Gentlemen who represent political interests, or who meet their constituents in recess, must have something to say; and men who have no marked ability can dilate with most advantage to their limited power of thought or of expression on a burning ques-tion. Hence Irish " outrages " form a subject at once attractive and easy of discussion. No one asks, are these outrages true ? And take it at the worst, admit that they are all true, who asks calmly and carefully, is there cause—must there not be something wrong in the govern-ment of a country which is perpetually in more or less open revolt ?

And if there is cause, would it not be wiser
to remove the cause than to try and put out the
flame for the moment by Coercion Acts?

Now, it is a hard statement to make, but it is
unhappily true, that Irish landlords are getting
up all this cry for coercion, simply because they
are afraid the light will be let in on their conduct towards their unfortunate tenants. They
are afraid, if the truth was once known, that
the English voter would exact a pledge from
every gentleman to whom he gave his vote, to
do justice to Ireland ; and justice is precisely
what they do not want. They want liberty to
practice usury, and the only way to obtain a
continuance of that liberty is to raise a cry
against the unhappy victims of their cupidity.
Why otherwise are they so desperately afraid
of having their dealings with their tenants regulated by law? This is all the Irish people ask.
Why do they utter these hysterical cries about
the rights of property? Why all that is asked
of them is that they will respect the rights of
property.

There is a time in the history of most nations
when the demand for equal justice between
rich and poor is refused. There is a time
when the compliance with such a demand would
satisfy the populace. But *quem deus vult*

perdere, prius dementat. The aristocracy refuse to grant justice to the plebeian, and they
forget that power is with the multitude, and
with a multitude who are apt, when justice is
refused, to ask for something more, and to take
somewhat short methods of asserting their
demands.

If one must judge from the tone of some
English papers, it would be supposed that the
Irish people have no cause of complaint whatsoever. It is forgotten, conveniently, that there
are Englishmen who admit that Ireland is
governed unjustly, and who admit this from
personal knowledge and experience of the state
of the country.

But for the sake of those who wish to know
the true state of Ireland, I must again allude to
the miserable influence of English political agitation. I take an example of it, as a caution to
those who wish to treat Ireland, not as a
political play-toy, but as part of their own
country.

The *Pall Mall Gazette* having changed
hands politically, has changed its opinions about
Ireland. Surely those sudden changes of opinion in an important English paper ought to
convince any man with common sense that
there *are* two sides to what is said of Ireland,

and that he ought to consider, not which opinion his party maintains, but which opinion is true.

The *Pall Mall Gazette* of October, 1880, writes thus of Irish affairs :—

"Now it is easy enough to talk of silly misguided peasants urged on by unscrupulous agitators to believe themselves half-starved, miserable, and oppressed, when in fact they are fat, well-looking, and the freest of the free. That may be all gospel truth, though tracts somewhat tend to show that wily, misguided peasants have at least capacity enough to know whether their bellies are full or empty, whether their landlords are tyrannous and unjust or just and sympathetic. But—and that is the matter for us just now—there are some millions on both sides of the Atlantic who don't believe it. They do not believe that the wholesome deportations of 1847 and onwards were conducted in the true spirit of Christian charity, nor for the matter of that, that the Marquis of Lansdowne's estates have been managed in the humanitarian fashion which that able supporter of "freedom of contract" represents in his letter to the American newspaper. They hold that they, as well as their friends and relations now in Ireland, have been shamefully used by the landlords and by the English Government which supported those landlords in the maintenance of a system of land tenure that no single human being who has not interests of his own to serve by doing so can be found to advocate for a moment. Thus thinking they mean some day to fight—partly for revenge, partly for the future of the country that, to do them justice, they love only too well. Now what we want to ask is this. Is it worth while to shut our eyes to this bitterness of feeling, and to laugh at the idea of

D

Ireland being a heavy handicap to us in the event of serious foreign war? We have tried the game of coercion in the interests of a small minority over and over again. What has it benefited us the English people? What indeed! Might we not now try a little steady justice on both sides? Irishmen go out to America, they go out to our colonies—nay, they come to our own cities, and work hard enough. In America, too, they earn enough money to be more liberal to their own kith and kin than any other emigrant race."

What a policy for Ireland! One wonders that English gentlemen who pride themselves on their honour and conscience can stoop so low. It is calmly admitted in a leading English paper, generally credited now with being the organ of a Liberal Government, that *England has tried the game of coercion in the interests of a small minority over and over again.*

And this is stated deliberately by one of the most important organs of English opinion, and yet we are told that the Irish people have no grievances, that they are a discontented, lazy, thankless race; always returning good for evil to their beneficent and long-suffering masters, their landlords.

And then the writer asks the very pertinent question, "What has it benefited us the English people?"

Let us hope, when such a broad gleam of

light has come to rulers of Ireland that they
will cease to do the evil which they admit that
they have done so persistently, and that they
will begin to do the good even if they only do
it from the lower motive of benefit to England,
instead of from the high and glorious motive of
eternal justice.

Are there no men in England who love
justice for its own sake, and who will rise
in their might and see justice done because it is
justice?

The truth is that it has been found on the
whole less trouble to govern Ireland on the
politics of the moment than on the politics of
principle. Whenever the support of the multitude was not necessary, Ireland was governed
on the principle, or on the want of principle,
indicated above. The "small minority" were
allowed to coerce as they pleased. How they
coerced, we shall show presently from the
speech of another Englishman. But where
there was fear lest the help of the multitude
might be needed, or lest the hindrance of the
multitude should embarrass, then, indeed,
England becomes afraid lest Ireland should be
"a heavy handicap" to her in the event of a
"serious foreign war," and so some show of
justice must be made.

And English gentlemen talk of the honour
of old England and her love of justice, and
they write and read such words, and act thus ;
and let it be remembered that if these things
are written in England they are read in Ireland.
Can it be wondered then if the Irish people are
not very devoted subjects of the English nation ?
But another English writer hás even a stronger
case to put for Ireland.   The editor of *Truth*
says :—

"The Irish occupiers may be said to have a far stronger
moral right in their holdings than must English occupiers.
After several bad harvests they ·   able to pay their
rents. Their means were exhau   they claim that if
the land produces nothing, 'hey ought not to be ejected
because they do not pay rent in their landlords. The letter
of the law is v   the landlords, but the spirit of the law, if
law be equity, is with the occupiers."

In 1048 Gavan Duffy wrote- -

"Where Frank and Tuscans spend their sweat,
    The goodly crop is theirs ;
If Norway's toil makes rich the soil,
    She eats the fruit she rears.
O'er Main's green sward there rules no lord,
    Except the Lord on High,
But we are serfs in our own land—
    Proud masters, tell us why ?"

The English writer quoted above gives a
practical reply:

JOHN DILLON, M.P.

CHAPTER III.

THE TRUE CONSIDERATION OF IRISH AFFAIRS
HINDERED BY PARTY OPINION.

"No one has heard of outrages upon the estates of the families of Devonshire, Powerscourt, Fitzwilliam, Downshire, Portsmouth, Bessborough, amongst many others. I am loth to write anything that would bear even the semblance of apology for outrage, but truth compels me to say that the scenes of most outrages have been previously associated with harsh and unjust landlord management."—Mr. Russell, M.P., letters to *Daily Telegraph*.

BUT, unhappily, there is the political side of the Irish question, which to-day interferes with justice to Ireland, as it has done for centuries.

If the *Pall Mall* and *Truth*, representing the opinions of a certain class, speak fairly of Ireland, the opposite political party are obliged, in defence of the political acts of their party, to speak in precisely the opposite fashion.

The one rule for all Conservative government of Ireland has been coercion. It has at least the merit of simplicity. If the people complained, when more than usually excited by more than usual suffering, they were to be met with coercion. The policy so aptly des-

cribed above of coercing the majority for the
benefit of the few, was at once put in practice.
If a time of comparative prosperity came, and
the people did not express their demands with
any violence, it was said that they did not want
anything, and therefore it was useless to make
Land Acts.

Sir M., Beach, in his speech at Cirencester,
referred 'in this style to the state of Ireland,
which he characterised as " more dangerous
than anything in the East of Europe." A
political necessity again. His party have involved affairs in the East in a perilous manner ;
it was obviously his business to direct attention
from that matter, so Ireland must be the official
scape-goat again. He then continued :—

"Disorder and crime reigned in many parts of Ireland
to an extent which, he feared, had hardly been known for
the last half century. He had said that his experience in
Ireland had taught him one lesson ; it had also taught him
another. They must not believe all the exaggerated reports
they had heard ; they must not consider as true of the whole
of Ireland what might be true of one or two small parts of the
country. It did not follow that because murder had been
committed in the West that, therefore, the City of Dublin
was not as safe as the town of Cirencester. He feared
that Press correspondents, anxious, no doubt, to gratify the
desire of the public for news, were not always particular in
the kind of news they supplied, and certainly the Press
correspondents in Ireland were not more particular than

their brethren in England (hear, hear, and cheers). Therefore he had at first been disposed to regard the stories of disorder in Ireland as exaggerated, but when he saw that a deputation representing the Irish landlords of every creed and class and political opinion waited upon the Lord Lieutenant and Chief Secretary, at Dublin Castle, and when he saw the reply of Mr. Forster, that they were putting law in force, and that it was feared the statements were true, then he began to think that there was really something serious, and something, he was thankful to say, in these times unique in the state of Ireland."

If ever there was an evidence of the utter unreliability of *party* opinions on Irish affairs, here is one. I use the word party advisedly, for it is evident from the whole tenor of the speech that it is made in the interest of the Conservative party and policy.

Nor do we intend by this to condemn Conservatism *per se*, or to exalt Liberalism. Our question is not whether the one policy or the other is best in the abstract; we desire simply to show that Irish affairs are not, and cannot be discussed justly when they are discussed from the standpoint of party.

Observe in what a tissue of contradictions this gentleman is involved. First he announces to an audience quite unable to contradict his assertion, that the state of crime and disorder is worse in Ireland than it has been for the last

half century. Irish people will ask in amazement *where* this extraordinary state of things exists. He admits, however, that Dublin is "safe."
Well, if he had taken the trouble to ascertain facts
before he put forward fancies, he might have
ascertained easily that Dublin, on account of its
mixed population, was the only place in Ireland
where there was anything like the amount of
crime that is found in every English town.
But he has the candour to say that the Press
cannot always be relied on. We have shown
how utterly fallacious are its reports when Ireland is concerned; but he says the "landlords"
have convinced him.

Was ever logic more absurd! He asks the
persons who have the strongest possible interest in making it appear that the country is
disturbed, and accepts their opinion. As well
might he ask the criminal in the dock what he
thought of the testimony given by the witness
of his crime.

In the year 1851, even after the Famine,
there were 351,000 people in the county
Tipperary. In the year 1871 there were but
230,000; in that short twenty years of landlord
government of Ireland, over one hundred thousand people were driven out of their native
county by the misrule of Irish landlords, and

yet we are told that to continue and uphold this misrule is the one thing necessary for Ireland.

But if we turn to Irish political opinion on Irish affairs, we find the same hopeless confusion, even where there is an apparent desire to act fairly.

The Protestant Bishop of Cork has been addressing his clergy on the subject, which is certainly a question of the most momentous importance to every man, woman, and child in this country.

After the usual platitudes about the condition of Ireland being a puzzle to statesmen, his Lordship has the honour and manliness to admit that religion is not the cause of all the ills of Ireland, though that, he says, "used to be said."

Another proof of what we have said, that one generation condemns what the previous generation has done; and that the truth about Ireland, social, political, and religious, is the subject of bitter and acrimonious dispute to-day; and to-morrow it will be admitted that the Irish claims so disputed were, after all, not so unfair.

To act on party politics in questions of foreign policy may not be a matter of serious moment;

to act on them where the interests of home
government are in question, is to inflict a deadly
injury on one member of the body politic to the
equal hurt of the whole body.

Here is what an Irish Protestant landlord,
who is neither Home Ruler nor Land Leaguer,
says :—

"Our manufactures and our trade in raw materials were
destroyed to please English monopolists. Smuggling per
force became the national industry, and did not tend to
make a law-abiding people. The Volunteers extorted some
concession, but manufacturing traditions had perished irre-
trievably ; a craving for independence succeeded the desire
for Union, and Pitt's offer of a commercial partnership was
refused as tending to tighten the bond between the two
nations. When Union came at last, it was unaccompanied
by religious freedom, and earned no gratitude. Until 1782
the English Council had a veto on Irish bills, and during
that period all the worst laws were passed. The Constitution of 1782 was unworkable, but the Irish House of
Commons, though elected and managed in the worst way,
did what it could (not always wisely or well) to foster trade
and lighten Catholic fetters. After the Union power
returned to England, and it took thirty years of agitation to
gain religious freedom. which was only granted when the
Duke of Wellington could no longer see how the King's
Government was to be carried on. The Church Establishment survived forty years more, and was then destroyed in
deference to an agitation which had culminated in rebellion.
. . . I am no Home Ruler, seeing the impossibility of
that platform, feeling that our best hope lies in strengthening
the tardy and imperfect Union. But, before God and man,

England is responsible for Ireland. Enlightened British opinion must be the final judge in this cause. I appeal from the England of test acts and protection, to the England of free trade and the conscience clause. Englishmen who would understand our case must know our history as they generally know their own. Mr. Froude and Mr. Leckey are in every library; let them correct one another."

The opinion of Irish gentlemen, like Mr. Bagwell, should have weight in England. But unhappily the opinion of such men is not known there, and there is therefore a general and most untrue impression that all Irish land-lords desire the continuance of a state of things which leaves the tenant at the mercy of caprice, instead of placing him under the protection of law.

CHAPTER IV.

DISCUSSION which is carried out on the platform of mutual recrimination does not tend to the advancement of truth. Unhappily we have had far too much of this kind of discussion when Irish affairs are in question; but it is neither statesmanlike nor patriotic. A statesman who would sacrifice the well-being of any portion of the empire to party politics is not worthy of his manhood, and is no friend to his country. The purest patriotism is that which desires the well-being of all.

Now it is but too obvious that the "state of Ireland" has always been made a crucial difficulty in the discussion of Irish affairs; and it cannot be doubted that to ascertain the truth on this point is of the utmost importance.

Now, it is impossible to take up any English paper without finding it full of the most terrifying reports of the state of Ireland. We have

1

T. D. SULLIVAN, M.P.

already shown that to publish such reports has been a regular practice for centuries. We shall proceed to show that at this very time the very same practice is continued, with the very same result. Now, as I can show that "outrages" are largely and deliberately manufactured, I trust to the high honour of English readers that they will condemn such mischievous, such miserable policy, and assuredly when they know that outrages are invented by the press they will use their common sense, and distrust many of such reports. When this is done sytematically, must there not be some cause for it. And they will then ask what is the cause, and who gains by all this malicious lying.

We fear there can be only one reply. The people ask for English laws to protect them in their farms and houses. The demand is so reasonable and so just, that it would certainly be heard if it was allowed to reach the ears of the British public. But the landlords, and land agents also, are interested in keeping up the social disorder which they cause by their arbitrary power of eviction, and try to drown the voices of the people. The safest, truest, and quietest way to do this is to manufacture outrages. It may seem a hard thing to accuse gentlemen of doing this, but that it is done, I shall prove,

and since it is done, who can do it, and would
care to do it, save only those who have a special interest in the doing of it.

Now, I ask English readers is *this* justice to
Ireland ; rather, I would ask, is this justice to
themselves ?   Falsehood may triumph for a
while, but even in this world it never succeeds
in the end.   Besides, do people wish for facts or
for falsehood ?   As I have said before, Irish
people are perpetually reproached with a want
of truthfulnesss.   There is, or I should rather
say there was, no more constant accusation
against us, and, of course, it was all the fault of
our religion.   But what of this English want of
truth ?   Is it any the more honest because it is
English—any the more honourable because
those who promulgate these falsehoods are Protestants ?   Then we are repeatedly told in the
English papers that the Irish are lazy, that they
will not work, that their poverty is all their own
fault.   For that calumny, too, I have an answer,
in the very words of landlords who have been
betrayed unintentionally into strong admissions
of the industry of the Irish people, though the
vast majority of landlords deny the industry of
the people, even while they are living on it.

Some of the statements made by papers
which circulate only amongst the upper class of

English Protestants and Catholics have observations on them which actually contradict themselves, and would strike anyone not anxious to
believe them with their utter absurdity. In one
paper it was said that a party of armed men cut
off a man's ears while he was in bed, but not
being able to get into the house (!) contented
themselves with digging a grave outside the
door! The statement was contradicted in the
Irish papers—but what did that matter? and
what did it matter to a certain class of English
readers whether the whole story bears on its
face the marks of a palpaple calumny or not?

A gentleman—Mr. Barry—wrote to contradict the statement of an outrage said to have
been committed on him. He denied the whole
story, and added that the only foundation for it
which he could imagine, was the work of a too
enterprising pig, which had attempted a raid
upon his hen house! And yet the contradictions
of these outrages are *never* given in English
papers; and if any one attempted to write to an
English paper denying them, even on personal
authority, their letters are refused insertion.

*Are there no Irish outrages? Certainly there
are.*

We are not yet living in Paradise, nor are we
all fit to be canonized saints. But there is one

question I would like to have asked by every
one who hears Irish outrages made the subject
of conversation.   Is it worse to commit a
murder in Ireland than in England? and is
there any difference in the sight of God between
the murder of a gentleman, and the murder of
a poor man, or woman, or helpless little child?
   For the sake of her own interests, let England beware.   She is not wanting in men of
honour and of conscience, and amongst some of
her so-called middle classes there is a deep and
true spirit of religion.   The poor understand
the poor.   Men who have suffered themselves
know what others suffer practically, and there
is no knowledge like practical knowledge.   In
England there is a very large, and very influential, middle class far above the poor in worldly
position, yet who are not blinded by the temptation of excessive wealth or high rank.   If this
class of Englishmen were once convinced of the
true state of Ireland, the Irish question would
soon be settled.   But how are they to know
the truth?   Every English paper that is published is full of the most lying reports of Irish
outrages which have never happened, and contain the grossest misrepresentations of everything Irish, while anything that would go to
show the true state of the country is carefully

suppressed. Certainly it is difficult to see how
the suppression can be otherwise than deliberate
since it is persistent. It is carried on on a very
large scale, and no sign--not even the very least
sign—of reparation is ever shown.

For example, I find the following paragraph
in the *Cork Examiner* of Oct. 14 :—

"The *Times* has been furnished by a correspondent, who
dates his communications from Cork, with the following
description of the state of society in the barony of
Duhallow : 'The lawlessness which was exhibited in the
neighbourhood of Kanturk a few weeks ago has been
followed by fresh acts of violence. Organised gangs of
men are permitted to prowl about at night, committing
violence and outrage, avenging imaginary wrongs, and
carrying terror into the hearts of well-disposed men.
Ribandism in its worst phases appears to be rampant, and
the legitimate exercise of men's rights is opposed and
thwarted.' It is much to be deplored that statements of
this character should be foisted day after day upon the English public by its leading organ to support the clamour for
coercion laws. In nine cases out of the ten the *Times'* reports of outrages in Ireland are simply wicked inventions."

What a tremendous responsibility rests on
men who deliberately and persistently write
what is utterly false of a whole nation ! They
do well to talk of the honour of England, and
they do well to deny God, and to claim their ,
descent from the lowest types of the brute
creation. But a time of reparation will come

E

most assuredly, not only in the world to come,
but in this world. If the English press lie
about Ireland, other nations will lie about
England. If the English people allow their
representatives to treat Irish wrongs with indifference, and Irish grievances with contempt,
they may well tremble for the consequences.
It is not man who will judge them—it is God.

The heathen had a saying : " The mills of
the gods grind slowly, but they grind exceeding
small." The Divine books tell us with what
measure ye mete it shall be meted to you
again. Sooner or later, even in this world,
every outrage against justice is punished,
because an outrage against justice is an outrage against God.

It is curious to find History repeating itself,
and if the subject were not so serious, it would
be amusing. We have already shown the panic
which beset and bewildered the lords and
magistrates of Bantry and Bandon, and their
consequent wild cries for coercion in 1798.
We have shown also how they were answered,
and how the panic was shown to be of their
own causing by a Protestant bishop and Protestant gentlemen. To-day there is the same
causeless panic, the same cry for coercion and
troops ; yet I find, in the *Cork Examiner* of

Oct. 30 (1880), letters from three parish priests denying that there is any disturbance or any need for extra police or soldiers. The Rev. Mr. MacMahon writes from Boherbee, County Cork :—

"Your informant would seem to wish to leave the public under the impression that danger and insecurity prevailed in these parts. But I unhesitatingly affirm, that life and property are safer in this locality than in London and its vicinity. There armed burglars commit their depredations night after night, often delivering and receiving fire, and their operations are treated by the English Press as only the ordinary incidents of English life. What a howl they would raise if those outrages had taken place in Ireland. Let us hope that our own journals will not furnish these foul and malignant slanderers with pabulum for their diatribes against our wronged and sorely-tried people, by giving undue publication to, or attaching groundless importance to, those wretched threatening letters, which are obviously the production of idiots or enemies.

"Faithfully yours,

"P. MacMahon, P.P."

The next letter is from the Rev. M. Shinkwin, of Bantry, contradicting an account of an outrage on a "paralysed farmer," and simply saying that no such person existed. The third letter I give more at length :—

"To the Editor of the 'Cork Examiner.'

"Dunmanway, 28th October, 1880.

"Dear Sir—I have read with much surprise in this day's *Examiner* that a certain number of magistrates of the county assembled in the County Courthouse in Cork yesterday, passed resolutions calling on the Government to suspend the *Habeas Corpus* Act, and to garrison Bandon, Skibbereen, Bantry, and Dunmanway, with British troops.

"As no reporter was admitted to the meeting, I am slow to believe that such resolutions could have been passed by gentlemen who live in the midst of the people, and must know how peaceful and quiet they generally are.

"Nothing certainly has yet occurred, nor does there appear reason to apprehend the occurrence of anything to justify so extreme an interference with the civil rights and liberties of the whole community as the suspension of the *Habeas Corpus* Act. And as regards Dunmanway in particular, with which I am more intimately connected and more fully acquainted than with the other parts of the county, I feel bound in justice to its most peaceful people thus publicly to state that it would be a gross injustice to their character to represent them as a lawless people, or such as needed to be kept in order by the presence of a British garrison.

"That you were misinformed as to Dunmanway being included amongst the places needing a 'British garrison,' must appear evident from the fact that no less than four magistrates who reside in the parish of Dunmanway are reported as present at the meeting. They, from their constant residence among the people, and from their experience at Petty Sessions, know full well that the people of this part of the country were never more peaceful than they are at the present time; that they are quietly and industriously attending to their own ordinary business, and in no way conspiring either against the public peace or individual rights.

"In the fulness of conviction, I venture to affirm that in no county of Ireland and in no shire of England are the people more law-abiding than the inhabitants of Dunman-way. Even during the present great national movement to abolish unjust and cruel laws, they have not been carried away by any violent agitation; they have even generally stood aloof from the Land League; not indeed from any indifference to the great and necessary reforms needed in the land laws of the country, but from their disapproval of language used, and of principles propounded by prominent members of the League. They rely on peaceful and con-stitutional means to obtain the long delayed redress of their patiently endured grievances. They anxiously, but peace-fully and hopefully, looked forward to the meeting of Parlia-ment, when they expect that those really great and truly liberal statesmen, Gladstone, Bright, and Forster, will make such a wholesome change in the land laws of the country as will ensure the proper cultivation of the soil, the reclama-tion of the vast waste lands, and the much-needed protec-tion and encouragement to the hard working and badly requited farmers. Such people have not forfeited their con-stitutional rights, nor need they be ruled by a British garrison.—Yours truly,

"JOHN COTTER, P.P."

I will not do the common sense of English readers the injustice to suppose that these letters will carry less weight because they are written by priests. I will only again recall to their attention how a similar, and certainly a more excusable panic, was met nearly a century since by Protestant gentlemen who did not allow their religious opinions to render them unjust to their fellow-subjects.

But here is another specimen of outrage manufactured in the County Limerick :—

"MANUFACTURED OUTRAGES.—Much indignation has been evinced by the farmers in the neighbourhood of Drumbanna at the publication of a paragraph in a contemporary relative to the serving of threatening notices, for which it is stated there was no foundation whatever. The following has been handed to me, with a request that it may be published in the *Examiner* :—' At Drumbanna, about two miles from Limerick city, a number of threatening notices were discovered posted early yesterday (Sunday) morning, to the effect that unless a farmer surrendered up a farm of which he had lately got possession an untimely fate awaited him. On the notices was the rude sketch of a coffin. It is alleged that the man has lately taken over a farm from which a farmer has been evicted for non-payment of rent, the latter, however, obtaining £50 for his good-will of the place, a holding of some sixty acres, and the incoming tenant paying some three years' rent due.' The foregoing is substantially a fabrication from first to last. Not a single threatening notice was found on the day mentioned, nor any other, for the best of reasons, that none were posted or written at all. There was no occasion, nor any reason. The late tenant left the farm entirely of his own accord, and was glad to obtain the terms which the incoming tenant, a most respectable Catholic Irishman, afforded. He paid not only £50, but altogether, for rent and interest, up to £400 ; and it is a fact that he and his predecessors parted as best of friends."

But I might occupy the entire of the present volume with cases of reported outrages which have been *proved* false. Unhappily, however, the proof of the falsehood never extends beyond the local papers, while England and Europe are left to stare aghast at crimes which were never committed.

A most terrible outrage was reported and much commented on in the English papers, as having been committed at Kanturk, where it was said a man's ears were cut off. Doubting the whole story, I wrote to a gentleman there, and ascertained that there was not one syllable of truth in the whole story.

The *Times* had the following statement last month :—

"At Macroom yesterday a steward in the employment of Mr. Massey, J.P., observed three men lurking about the plantations. Finding that they were watched, they attacked and violently assaulted the steward, and cut his throat. It is stated that he was seriously wounded."

But what are the facts? The man was not Mr. Massey's steward; but it adds to an outrage, to some minds, to connect it with landlords. He did not see three men, and he was not assaulted. The whole affair was thus dressed up for English readers. But what was the fact? A poor farmer's son attempted suicide in a wood, and not for the first time. No doubt some future historian will write a chapter on this supposed outrage, and know nothing of the real facts.

In a recent leader the *Times* says :—

"Englishmen always like to know the worst about themselves. If a battle has been lost, or a job perpetrated, or if unsoundness is suspected in any department, the demand is for the full facts. There must be no concealment, no half inquiry, no shrinking from publicity. The revelation may be a shameful one, but it must not, therefore, be withheld. Out the whole thing must come into broad daylight, and must be seen, and judged, and remedied. This national characteristic is put to a good test by the reports which reach us daily from the election commissions now sitting. Disgraceful they are in the very highest degree. No Englishman can get through his morning paper without shame at its contents. The Commission Reports are one long record of the most naked and unabashed corruption. A novelist would never have dared to introduce such stories. They are too incredibly bad for fiction."

And so on. Let us hope that Englishmen will show now this highly honourable point as regards Ireland, and when they know how they have been deceived, that they will act accordingly.

It is especially in the matter of murders that these false statements are so rife. It scarcely answers to venture on murdering any prominent Irish nobleman or gentleman in print, as the case would be too flagrant and too easily disproved. . The only way in which misrepresentation on this point can be carried out well is by what Americans call " tall writing." This impresses the public very much. When they are told that gentlemen are obliged to go to balls fully armed, that there is a reign of terror, that landlords are afraid to remain on their estates and are obliged to fly to England, that priests are obliged to get their whole congregations to kneel down and swear they will not murder some particular land agent, to answer all the purposes of fact.

It was said that Lord Ardilaun was obliged to leave his Irish estates in consequence of threatening letters, that he had packed up all his household goods never to return, and a parallel was drawn therefrom as to the baseness and ingratitude of the Irish, who could never be satisfied, and who turned even on their most generous benefactors. But what was the truth? Simply that Lord Ardilaun never had the least intention of leaving Ireland. But the lie answered the purpose all the same. Lord Muskerry was also held up as another useful example of how good landlords were compelled to fly the land, but Lord Muskerry had the good sense to write himself to the Irish papers

denying the report.   Whether it was denied in
any English paper or not I have not been able
to ascertain, but, to the best of my belief, it was
not.

Indeed, Irish gentlemen, if they wish to deny
such reports, get little thanks.   Another Irish
landlord, who wrote to a "society" paper to
contradict a report that he was in bodily fear of
his life, and who said he had always lived most
happily with his tenants, was told that he was
an exception, not to the general rule, but to the
invariable rule ; and, it was added, with a sneer
of contempt, that such tenants were not to be
found in all Ireland.   The writer of this remark
had probably never visited Ireland, or, if he
had, knew nothing whatever of the relations
between Irish landlords and tenants.

Let the English reader who thinks and who
is not actuated by prejudice, ask himself this
one question, and the reply will soon settle
this part of the Irish question.   *

If it is true that Irish landlords live in mortal
fear of their lives, that they are always at war
with their tenants, and that they never, or rarely
ever, can get their rents paid, how is it that they
are so anxious to retain possession of their Irish
estates ?   If one-half the stories were true
about the bad character of Irish tenants, might

you not be assured that Irish landlords would
not only accept, but would even press on the
government a scheme for the purchase of their.
estates.

Is is not enough to alienate a warm-hearted
and faithful people, who have made such
struggles, as will never· be known to pay their
rents, even in times of famine. Let the truth
be told about the state of Ireland. We ask no
more. And we demand in justice to ourselves,
as Englishmen would demand in justice to them,
that the truth, and that alone, should be told.

Even on this very day, or while I write, the
Irish papers had reports of terrible crimes in
England. Amongst others, a painful tragedy
at Chiselhurst, where a head game-keeper and
his wife were killed, and quite a lot of other
outrages. But they are told simply as public
news, and are not made the subject of writers
on the general depravity of the English people.

But there is another form in which false reports are made about Ireland which is scarcely
less injurious than that to which we have already
alluded.

An Irish landlord, especially if he be a nobleman of any influence, can very easily get a
paragraph in the *Times*, or in a society paper,
which will represent him as a model of benevo-

lence. Sometimes these statements are made as reports of public affairs without any action on the part of the landlord, but all the same they are utterly misleading and extremely mischievous.

In the early part of this year when the distress here was at its height, there was a public dinner of the St. Patrick's Society in London ; what this society does to deserve its name I know not, but let that pass. Two or three Irish noblemen were present, and complimented each other very liberally—one of these gentlemen, the Duke of Devonshire, I think, for I write from memory, complimented the Marquis of Lansdowne very highly. This nobleman, he said, had at once flown to his Irish estates when the distress appeared, to see what he could do for his tenants. He blamed himself by implication as he praised his friend, and those who read the report must naturally have concluded that extraordinary exertions had been made by Lord Lansdowne for his tenantry. But what was the fact, beyond the gift of £20 to the fund, which we had collected, Lord Lansdowne did actually nothing for his tenantry. What he did was wholly for his own benefit, and it will perhaps be scarcely credited that the only action taken by him was to improve his property at the permanently increased rents of his tenantry, and this in the Famine year.

This subject is too long to enter upon here, but I shall do so in the next chapter.

Again, it was announced far and wide in the Press that Lord Lansdowne was providing his tenants with seed potatoes. It was left to be inferred—we must fear it was intended to be inferred—as otherwise why should it have been inserted in so many papers as a Press notice, that the potatoes were to be given to his tenantry. But what was the fact? The potatoes were all sent down at the full market price. If the people thought that this was done more for the sake of securing Lord Lansdowne's future rent than for their benefit, they can scarcely be blamed.

Lately his tenantry were not a little amused at a paragraph quoted from a county paper announcing that he was "packing up his traps" (sic), to exchange Bowood, one of his English estates, for Kenmare, and loudly praising his "generosity" and his "unselfish example of duty," holding him up in fact as a social martyr to the good of his Irish tenants. But what was the fact? Lord Lansdowne was just leaving Kenmare for his shooting in Scotland.

These may seem trivial matters, but they are

not so when they affect and help to prove opi·
nions on very grave subjects—on subjects which
affect the well-being of some millions of our
fellow-creatures.

"Some time back we had an 'outrage' in the shape of
a very neatly made coffin, covered with crape and adorned
with a breastplate, left at the Hon. Captain Chichester's
gate. He is brother and agent to Lord Templemore. Now,
it is absolutely certain that this 'agrarian outrage' was
not agrarian at all, and that the individuals who perpetrated
it have no connection whatever with Lord Templemore's
estate, nor with as much land on any other estate as 'would
sod a lark.' There are two opinions on the subject. The
first is that it was done simply as 'a lark'; the second,
that it was the act of certain individuals, not at all connected with the estate, who thought if they could frighten
away the captain they could more effectually advance their
personal interests, on the principle, 'in the cat's absence the
mice can play.' "

"KNOCKDRIMMIN, Oct. 29th.—I regret to have to inform
you that a pug-dog belonging to Lady Balragget was very
badly bitten on the public road in this neighbourhood, some
days ago by a dog of mongrel breed, and said to be un-
registered, who lives with a tenant named Bryan Sweeny.
There were several dogs mixed up in the row, concerning
the origin of which there are conflicting accounts, but the
interference of her ladyship's pug appears to have been
specially resented by several of them, evidently for no other
reason than that he belonged to one of the better classes.
A branch of the Land League has lately been established in
this parish, and there can be no doubt that to its malign
influence we may trace the disgraceful occurrence we have
mentioned."

Letters such as those of Lord Lismore and the Rev. W. B. Wright, which are appended below, show also that there is not quite such a social upheaval as English politicians like to assert.

There is one point of view in which such matters as threatening letters 'and the very few murders which have occurred in Ireland should be considered. In a state of general excitement, the temptation to and the opportunity for revenge for personal wrongs arises more easily. Moreover, many of the acts which have been credited to agrarian excitement, have had nothing to do with it. Those who would have feared detection if they were guilty of the crime of avenging a personal wrong, have the temptation of comparative safety when there is public excitement. It was commonly believed in the North that Lord Leitrim's murder had nothing to do with agrarian causes. There is one crime more detested in Ireland than any eviction, and for that men will take vengeance in their hands when no other cause would move them to do so.

And it should be remembered that while sympathy on false grounds is excited in England, the truth is known well in Ireland, and it does not tend to promote feelings of amity when men are held up as models of virtue when they are well known to have been simply detested for their vices.

The *de mortuis nisi nihil bonum* theory is carried too far when the dead are praised at the expense of the living, and to the injury of national peace.

The following will give further proof how persistently outrages are manufactured :—

"THE LAND AGITATION.

"TO THE EDITOR OF THE 'FREEMAN.'

"ATHLEAGUE VICARAGE, ROSCOMMON,

"*Nov. 1st.*

"SIR,—My strong feeling on the subject urges me to enter my earnest protest against aggravating the trouble now existing in Ireland by the introduction of the religious element, so as to connect the one in any way with the other. That there is no reason for doing so my experience leads me implicitly to believe. I have been for nearly ten years resident in the west of Ireland, and I declare with great pleasure that I have never met anything but extreme kindness and courtesy from my Roman Catholic fellow-countrymen, lay and clerical. Religion has nothing to do with the present disorder, the cessation of which is earnestly desired by all peaceable citizens—by Roman Catholics as much as by Protestants.—Yours faithfully,

"W. BOURKE WRIGHT, Vicar of Athleague.

'I have sent a copy of this letter to the *Daily Express.*"

Here is another instance of manufactured outrages :—

"A MANUFACTURED 'OUTRAGE.'

"FROM THE 'FREEMAN'S JOURNAL.'

"BALLINASLOE, *Saturday.*

"J. Caulfield, Esq., Sub-Inspector R.I.C., Ballinasloe, visited Lismany to-day to ascertain the particulars of the threatening notices which Mr. Pollock and his gamekeeper were reported to have received, and found that there was not a word of truth in the reports which were circulated in Friday's papers. Much indignation is felt at this quiet locality being groundlessly aspersed."

"THREATENING LORD LISMORE.

["SPECIAL TELEGRAM.]

" Last evening the Mayor of Clonmel received the following letter from Lord Viscount Lismore, with reference to the proposed public meeting to be held in Clonmel condemning the outrage committed on his lordship :—

"'31 OLD BURLINGTON STREET, LONDON, W.

"' *November 1st,* 1880.

"'DEAR MR. MAYOR,—I see by this morning's Clonmel papers that many kind friends propose to have a meeting called to give expression to their feelings in respect to the letter I received. Although most grateful for the kindness which prompted them, I think that such a meeting, in the present state of our county, would not be advisable. I have always been jealous of the good name of our county, and was proud to be able to repeat at our agricultural dinner

F

last August, that Mr. Forster in Parliament had called it
the model county of Ireland.   After all, it is possible, and,
I think, most probable, that the letter never came from
Ireland, and it would be a great injustice to the people of
our country to accuse any of them of having written such a
letter to me without positive proof.   A meeting such as I
see proposed would be complimentary to me, but not to the
country.   Do not think that I am insensible or ungrateful
for all your kind wishes, as so plainly expressed.   I hope
and trust, as long as I live, to continue in the future what I
have attempted in the past—the development of the agricultural and other interests of our country.—Faithfully yours,

"'LISMORE.'"

J. G. BIGGAR, M.P.

CHAPTER V.

THE CAUSE OF IRISH OUTRAGES.

"There is no real bargain when one side cannot afford to refuse whatever terms the other side sees fit to propose."—Lord Sherbrooke's article in Fortnightly Review.

BUT, it will be said, are there no Irish outrages? Unquestionably there are; and if they were better known in England, the Irish question would soon be settled. Unhappily public speakers and public writers carefully suppress the facts, whilst making the most of the circumstances. In the first place, no one will deny that, with rare exceptions, Irish outrages are all connected with land. There are few murders in Ireland from other causes, which is remarkable, since unhappily, there is much drinking in some districts; wife-beating is unknown; child-murder is so rare as to be almost unheard of, and our worst enemies admit the singular purity of our people. As a matter then even of social science, as a question of the philosophy of jurisprudence, would it not be a matter of

interest to inquire into the causes of agrarian
crime? And when a people are otherwise so
free from crime, is there not a presumption in
their favour that there must be grave cause for
crime in this case?

There are two points with regard to the
Land Question in Ireland that should be thoroughly understood before the question can be
argued on with any degree of justice. First, it
should be perfectly and clearly understood that
there is no freedom of contract; and secondly,
that there is no other source for the investment
of capital.

A man must either take a farm at the rent
which the landlord chooses to name, or he must
continue the occupation of a farm of which he
is in possession at an increased rent, or else at
once emigrate, or go to the workhouse. Having
absolutely no choice, he takes too often the
former alternative in a modified form. He takes
or continues the farm at a rent which is so high
that he can only maintain existence in a condition of semi-starvation. Is it any matter of
surprise that a man should commit an outrage
on landlord or land agent when the very conditions of existence have been made almost
impossible to him, toil how he will?

Let it be remembered that we have already

stated, on the high authority of the Marquis of
of Lansdowne, that there are 54,000 families in
three counties alone who cannot live either in
decency or comfort. On Lord Lansdowne's own
estate, and he is no rack-renter, and as regards
rents, is probably one of the most reasonable landlords in Ireland, there are numbers of families in
this unhappy condition. The remedy for all this
is another question. At present I am dealing only
with facts, about which there is no dispute on
either side. Here is what Lord Sherbrooke
has said on this question; and let it be remembered he is now by no means favourable to Ireland. And here is what the *Times* says on Lord
Sherbrooke's article, both showing that extraordinary inconsistency between facts and conclusions which characterises every English writer
about Ireland.

The *Times* says :—

" The odd thing is that Lord Sherbrooke himself admits
in one paragraph that the supposed contracts between landlords and tenants in Ireland are not contracts at all. ' If
we will look the matter fairly in the face, the truth is that the
small Irish tenant is too poor to enter into a contract, which
presupposes equality between the two contracting parties.
In England the tenant can afford to bargain. In Ireland,
as far as the contract goes, and speaking about small farms,
the landlord lays down the rule, and the tenant submits to
it . . . The very idea of equality is banished from

such a proceeding. There is no real bargain where one
side cannot afford to refuse whatever terms the other sees
fit to propose.' Here we get something of a touch of fact ;
but Lord Sherbrooke makes no use of the truths he seems
to have in his grasp. Surely, if his description of the position of the small tenants in Ireland is right, all his reasoning
about non-interference with contract vanishes. The Land
Act of 1870 was based on the principle that the relations of
the tenants of Ireland with their landlords are more accurately regarded as relations of *status* than as relations of
contract ; and it was in the recognition of this view that its
provisions were framed. It is, of course, possible that what
was then done may require amendment. It was a great
experiment, and it would be strange indeed if it were perfect
at the first draft. But if anything more is necessary, it must
be conceived, we doubt not, on the principles of the Act of
1870 and in the same spirit."

So far for the question of contract. There is
no freedom of contract. But there is another,
and a most important point : there is no other
source for the investment of capital ; yet,
curiously enough, Lord Sherbrooke overlooks
this, and his remarks on this point are thus
noticed by a writer in the *Standard :—*

" In Lord Sherbrooke's paper ' On Legislation for
Ireland,' in the *Nineteenth Century* for November, he
remarks :—' The Irish mind is far too extensively given to
the cultivation of land, to the neglect of safer and more
profitable industries.' Lord Sherbrooke ignores the fact
that Irish manufactures were prohibited in the interest of

English trade, with the exception of the linen manufactory, ofwhich England had none."

Now no English writer denies that every Irish industry was crushed by England. We are often told to forget the past, to let bygones be bygones. But when the past seriously and materially affects the present, it is no charity to ignore it.

These two points are the whole source of Irish outrages. Men commit outrages when they find rents demanded from them which they cannot pay even if they starved. Men commit outrages when they find that the want of any other source for investment of capital except land, leads some one else to take the land at a rent which the former tenant could not pay and live.

One cannot help asking then who is to blame for these agrarian outrages. Are they all the fault of a singularly oppressed people? It is a question for thoughtful minds, and we ask a very careful consideration of it.

No doubt it is very foolish and very unpatriotic to take a farm from which a farmer has been evicted because he could not pay usurious rent. But to the end of the world there will be men to do this. John has, perhaps, £200 in hand, his little all. He sees no other way of using his capital. Peace, Lord Sherbrooke! there is no other industry open to him, safe or unsafe. And so he unwisely invests his all, only to lose it, or to live out an existence of yet greater misery than that of James, whom he has succeeded. No doubt if Irishmen had the good sense and the patriotism to refuse to take a farm from which a tenant had been evicted for being unable to pay excessive rent, the Irish question would be settled very speedily without legal intervention. But since there will always be persons who will speculate unwisely, if not ruinously, legal intervention is a necessity.

The Land League has tried to effect by public opinion what should be effected by law. Now, if the outrages which have occurred in Ireland this year are carefully examined, they will be found to have arisen from this one cause.

But since nothing can be more ruinous to the morals of a people than to take the law into their own hands, however just may be the grounds on which they do so, it is the first duty of Government to protect the people by law from this demoralising course. A Government which fails to do so is neither just nor paternal.

The state of the country with regard to excessive and usurious rents will be shown by the results of the present Land Commission, in a way that will simply amaze the people of England. Instead of expressing horror at the few outrages which have been committed in consequence of this state of things, they will be amazed that these few outrages were not multiplied by hundreds.

The evidence taken before the Land Commission is not yet published, but by permission of the gentlemen who are examined a report can be obtained for the press. The following extracts from the Report of the Commission which took evidence at Killarney in October (1880), I add here. No words are needed to enhance its importance :—

"Rev. Father O'Connor, whose name is so well known in connection with the Harenc tenantry, said that the Government valuation was, generally speaking, a fair rent. The disturbed state of the country at present, he said, was owing to the high rents the tenants were asked to pay, and withal they had no security. He was in favour of a peasant proprietary, or a system that would be virtually equivalent to it. He brought forward a number of cases of rack-renting in his district, and said that the rents were on an average double and treble the poor-law valuation. He also cited several evictions that had taken place owing to the inability of the tenants to pay the enormous rents they were charged. Father O'Connor then entered fully into the circumstances connected with the Harenc Estate tenantry, and the well-known part he took in trying to secure the farms for the tenants. Although Mr. Hussey professed to be willing to re-sell to the tenants, not a single working farmer had a chance of purchasing his holding. Father O'Connor also said that before the sale peace and harmony prevailed over the property, but at present it was a scene of riot and disorder ; and lately an extra force of constabulary had been drafted into the district to keep the peace.

" Rev. Arthur Moynahan, Adm., Listowel, in giving his evidence, said that the radius of the parish was three miles, and the number of landlords was twenty, of whom very few were resident. He gave various instances of rack-renting in the district, and as being favourable to a peasant pro prietary. He said there was no peasant proprietor in the parish, and there was not any more hard-working or indus- trious farmer to be found in the whole of Ireland. To multiply instances, he said, would be repetition. It was the same tale re-told. The landlords some few years ago seemed to compete in increasing their rent-rolls, to meet which the tenant borrowed from the banks, and the result of it all now was that the whole fabric threatened and shook to its very foundations. To pay those very high rents the farmers of the district and their children lived most sparingly—in fact, the farmers gave all to the landlords, and kept nothing for themselves. He quoted a number of instances which showed that the rent was two, three, and sometimes six times as much as Griffith's valuation, and said that beyond any doubt North Kerry was as a rule rack-rented, and the condition of the tenant-farmers was in many cases deplor able. The landlords had, for many years past, raised the rents, and sometimes in a woful manner. Several of the landlords were non-resident, and as a rule non-improving, and they seized upon every opportunity, by the raising of rent and enormous fines, to confiscate the improvements of the tenantry. No wonder, he said, the tenantry of Ireland were heartless and dispirited—the land was neglected, and the country was a reproach to its rulers. The present system was radically wrong, and the axe should be laid to the root of the evil. Father Moynahan proposed the following remedies :—1st, a peasant proprietary by every possible means; 2nd, a public means for the fixing of fair rents; 3rd, no evictions while a fair rent is paid; 4th, the right to sell, without leave, for the tenant; 5th, a measure for advancing moneys for improvements to the tenant himself without first giving it to the landlord, as at present; 6th, a measure for facilitating the reclamation of waste lands; and 7th, a tax on absenteeism. Father Moynahan, in the course of his evidence, gave the case of Widow M'Carthy, on Lord Ormathwaite's estate, where the rent was £100, and the valuation £33; in another case the rent was fourteen times the valuation; and in the case of John Feeley, a tenant of the Rev. Mr. Moore, the rent was £75, while the valuation was only £16 10s. Another matter Father Moynahan drew attention to was that in his district the landlords were in the habit of raising the rent when a farmer got married; and, worse than all, one farmer had his rent raised during the past year."

" Mr. Thomas O'Rourke, Tralee, in his evidence gave it as his opinion that the best solution of the land question would be on the lines of Mr. Butt's bill, which went in for fixity of tenure, fair rents, and free sale, which was almost analogous to the Ulster custom, with the addition of having the Bright clauses of Gladstone's Act of 1870 embodied in it, and also to have the Government purchase up the four millions of acres of waste lands in Ireland, to be parcelled out amongst cottier tenants at 1s. an acre, the loans to be repaid in thirty-one years. Labourers' cottages should also

be built on the lands at the expense of the Government ;
the loans to be repaid in thirty-one years at 1½ per cent.
Those were his ideas as to what a land bill should be that
would give peace to the landlords, peace to the tenants, and
peace to the Government. He knew of one man, of one
tenant, on the estate of Mr. Beale Browne, of Crotto,
County Kerry, whose valuation was 15s., and who was now
paying a rent of £15 ; and he was aware of another tenant
on the same property who paid £85 10s. rent, and the
valuation was only £9 5s., and this man could not record
his vote at the election of 1872 owing to the lowness of his
valuation. As regarded the way in which tenants were
compensated for improvements, he instanced the case of a
tenant named Dwyer on the property of Mr. G. D. Stokes,
J.P., who on being evicted from his holding some few years
ago got £170 compensation from the then Chairman of
Quarter Sessions ; but the landlord appealing to the assize
court, the tenant was only awarded the small sum of £27,
and the landlord got £900 fine from the incoming tenant.
Another case of hardship was that of a tenant, named Shea,
living at Ahane, on the Ballyseedy estate, of which Mr.
Hussey was agent, and a great many years ago he got a
piece of cut-away bog. He improved it and made it cultivable, and he was afterwards evicted for non-payment of
two years' rent (£20), the rent being ten times the valuation. That man and his family were now living in a kind
of hut like a wigwam. Mr. O'Rourke also instanced another
case of hardship, that of Mr. Bateman, of Deelis, Castle-
gregory, who owed £100 rent, and debts to shopkeepers.
Having been served with an ejectment process, he mortgaged his land to Mr. Patrick Bateman, J.P., Tralee, until
the debts were paid, and he (the witness) said the result
was, that the tenant was now turned out on the wayside,
although he had spent £1,000 in improving the farm. He

(Mr. O'Rourke) was in favour of the reclamation of waste lands ; there were 4,000 acres of waste lands in Kerry, and one-half of them could be improved. In conclusion, Mr. O'Rourke said he believed that if the tenants got fixity of tenure, with the right of free sale, the lands to be valued by arbitration every twenty years, it would be a fair solution of the question. He was also in favour of a peasant proprietary, and of tenant right in towns."

The Mr. Beale Browne who exacts such usurious rent demands a special notice. A few weeks since he published a letter in a Kerry paper, in which he dwelt on the perilous state of the times, and implored all the landlords in Ireland to meet him in spirit at the throne of grace, to pray for their mutual interests. But when the people of Kerry were on the point of starvation, we did not hear that he either prayed for them or gave them any practical proof of his piety. All this is especially noted by a quick-witted people.

Indeed we know another similar instance. Tralee was placarded with announcements that the land agent of a large Kerry proprietor was "to preach the Gospel" there ; at the same time he was actually preventing the Gospel from being practised on his master's estate. He denied the distress which he did not wish to relieve so vehemently, that help was actually prevented from being sent to the people.

The following extract from the *Freeman's Journal* of October 29th, 1880, will explain an allusion in this chapter:—

"The *Whitehall Review* stated last week that Mr. Hope Johnstone had been the victim of an agrarian outrage on his estates in Kerry. Mr. Johnstone writes, and gives a flat denial to the *canard*, and adds that he lives in the midst of an honest, kindly, and industrious tenantry, being on the most friendly terms with his neighbours. Mr. Legge, who is the responsible editor of the paper, and who signs the series of paragraphs entitled 'Bureau and Salon,' cannot allow the correction to pass without adding the sneer that he cannot regret the original statement, 'because it has elicited the information that there is a place in Ireland where the peasantry are honest, kindly, and industrious. Many of us might have gone to our graves, and never in our wildest dreams imagined such a thing possible.' I may point out to your readers that this is the print in which articles styled 'The Morals of Merrion Square' appeared."

Now, there is scarcely ever an Irish paper published which does not contain some such paragraphs as those given below, which show that the above is painfully untrue. How unfortunate it is for the educated classes in England that the truth is so persistently kept from them, and yet the truth is either denied or carefully concealed ; some very bad motive must exist for doing so :—

"The agent of Mr. P. Bartley, who attended at Westport yesterday, for the collection of rents, allowed to the tenants

50 per cent. on all arrears, and did not press for the payment of the gale now accruing."—*Cork Examiner, October 30th,* 1880.

"LANDLORD GENEROSITY.—Mr. Godfrey T. Baker, Fort William, County Cork, has not only made reductions of rent during the past three years to his tenantry at Crough, Knockroe, and Colligan, but even now, when the prospect of the tenant farmer is more cheering, he has allowed his tenantry a liberal reduction on last gale. Mr. Baker, accompanied by his esteemed agent, Mr. Charles Langley, visited the houses of his tenants, and both landlord and agent addressed to them words of hope and comfort."— *Correspondent.*

"TO THE EDITOR OF THE FREEMAN.

"COOTEHILL, *October* 30th, 1880.

"SIR,—It is my pleasing duty to place on record a noble act of kindness and benevolence on the part of the landlord of this town and district, Edward Smith Esq., J.P., of Bellamont Forest, Cootehill. He has given three acres of land rent free for ever, in a most eligible position, adjoining his demesne, and in the immediate vicinity of the town, for the erection of a Convent and Schools thereon. By this additional act of generosity, he has entitled himself anew to the thanks and gratitude of his Catholic tenantry. May he be long spared to live amidst a grateful people, and may every blessing descend and abide with him, his excellent lady, and family.

"Faithfully yours,

"FRANCIS O'REILLY, P.P., V.G."

CHAPTER VI.

WHAT IS COMMUNISM?

"The privilege which of all others Ireland most desires is that of being permitted to work and to cultivate her own vast wilderness."— J. H. TUKE, *Nineteenth Century, August*, 1880.

ONE of the great difficulties of dealing with any vexed social question is that recrimination so often takes the place of argument. Until this ceases, it is hopeless to expect an intelligent attention to either side of the question. And yet the question may be one touching the very foundation of the whole social state of a nation. But, strange as it may seem, this very disposition, which incapacitates men from the fair consideration of an important question, is most frequently found amongst those who, by their position, by their education, and not unfrequently by their intellectual ability, are precisely those who might be expected to consider every subject dispassionately.

I do not possess any special gift of eloquence or persuasion, nor have I any position, social or otherwise, which can entitle me to a special

MISS FANNY PARNELL,
Financial Secretary of the " Ladies' Land League."

hearing. But I ask each reader of this work, not on my account but on his own, to give a calm and thoughtful attention to each side of this most important question now before the public. He is bound to do so as a Christian desiring the benefit of all his fellow-Christians. He is bound to do so as a man, for he is unworthy of his manhood who allows himself to be influenced by passion or prejudice. He is bound to do so as a patriot—I venture to use the much-abused word—for a man who does not love his *patria*, his country, his fatherland, is not worthy of it; and such a man, most assuredly, has no right whatsoever to take a part in the government of that fatherland.

Let us, then, cast aside recrimination, and send prejudice to the nursery, its proper abode.

It cannot, I think, be denied, that the great majority of Englishmen of all social classes and of all creeds, had a very strong prejudice against Ireland. This was caused, as we have said, by historical inaccuracy; they naturally believed what was said about Ireland historically, and were prejudiced; they came to certain conclusions as to Irish character and habits, contrary to fact, and having formed their judgment on false premises, their conclusions were wrong—often substantially so.

G

But, undoubtedly, there is a change for the better. In the most bitterly anti-Irish articles written to-day in the glow of hot social controversy, there are evident gleams of light. Even the Conservative *Frazer* admitted an article on *Irish Land Reform*, though with the curiously significant addendum "from an Irish point of view."[1]

Hence there is a gleam of light, and let us hope the gleam is the precursor of full sunshine.

But there is the difficulty, the almost insuperable difficulty, of recrimination. It is not logical, and it is not wise. Why should Irishmen be classed with Communists when they ask for reform of the land laws? Why, the very asking for legal reform should at once protect them from such an imputation. Do those who cast at them the epithet of Communists know what Communism means?

An immense amount of nonsense, sheer, pure nonsense, has been written on this subject. Communism is not proceeding by the way of law, it is proceeding by the way of violence. But it will be said at once, and said truly, there is violence in Ireland ; and demands have been made which came very near Communism.

---

[1] *Frazer's Magazine*, March, 1880.

There has been violence in Ireland, and though it is made a subject of criminative reproach in England, one day it will be known how far more deeply and truly it was deplored in Ireland. But that time has yet to come, and we have to do with the present.

I will ask you to remember the state in which Ireland has been during the winter of 1879-80. Later I shall enter more fully into this subject. Here I offer only two English witnesses.

The special correspondent of the *Daily Telegraph* wrote thus :—

"What with smoke and the lack of openings, these cabins are almost dark even at midday. Such, ye gentlemen of England, is a Donegal cabin in this present advanced year of grace, and in such manner do thousands live within two days' journey of the capital of your mighty Empire. The fact, you will admit, is not one to boast of. I verily believe that Cetewayo would not have permitted his Zulus to be housed like these wretched people. Uniformly miserable as are the cabins, the misery of their inmates is a little diversified. In one place we find the mother preparing —what do you think?—a dish of seaweed wherewith to flavour the Indian meal obtained from the relief funds I I am not joking. God forbid. Her children have gone to the shore and gathered the stuff, and while I look on she prepares it for cooking.

The truth was the Irish famine was not half credited by England. But when it is remembered that the people of the north-west, and of part of the south and west of Ireland were in such a miserable condition, is it any wonder that there would be outrages—that men who have asked in vain for legal redress take the law into their own hands. The subject of wonder is not that there have been outrages, but that there have been so few. As a proof of this, I may add, that when Mr. Gibson, M.P., strove to excite his Orange audience in the north of Ireland against their brothers in the south, the worst, and the only case of violence towards women he could find for his text, was one in which two women's hair had been cut off.

But there is a second cause. Every gentleman who gave a vote against Mr. Gladstone's Compensation for Disturbance Bill is a cause of the present disturbance in Ireland. Now, I do not say for one moment that no outrages would have happened if that Bill had passed, but, undoubtedly, it tore the last hope of legal justice from England from the hearts of a famine-crushed people.

But it will be said that demands have been made that are Communistic. Now we come to define our terms, and ask what is Communism? It is the devil's parody of God's eternal truth.

Evil is the negation of good. Every evil is an exaggeration more or less horrible on what is good ; and the more clearly we see this, the sooner we shall clear the moral atmosphere of our thoughts.

Liberty, equality, fraternity—why, these are divine. But an enemy has sown cockles with the wheat. Liberty! Has not an English poet said :—

> "He is a freeman whom the truth makes free,
> And all are slaves beside."

Liberty! Is it not the pride of a nation, of a people, of an individual? So long as liberty remains pure it is divine; when it becomes licentious, then it ceases to be liberty and becomes evil. This is Communism. It is not licentious for a man to ask liberty—to ask laws which will enable him to live in decency and comfort in his own country.

But when such laws are refused, when the rich and powerful are protected by law; and when the mass of the people are refused redress, and left in a worse condition than the Zulus,[1] and in a normal condition which would test the temper of a slave coast African,[2] then,

---

[1] *Daily Telegraph* Special Correspondent.
[2] Pastoral of the Catholic Archbishop of Dublin.

indeed, there is a terrible fear that men may be driven by hopelessness of redress from the law to hopefulness of redress by violence.

Equality! What is this but an eternal and sublime truth, that the well-being of peer and peasant, of learned and unlearned, are equal in the sight of their Maker, and should be equally respected by all. The poor are not often envious, but when a time comes in which they find themselves left to starve with less concern than if they were brutes—for rich men care for their cattle—then there is fear lest they should demand an equality which is not divine; lest they should demand the whole of those good things of which before they only asked a little.

Fraternity! How sublime a word, and yet how often abused to the vilest purpose. Christian fraternity leads us even to sacrifice ourselves for our brethren; the fraternity of evil sacrifices all others to its own crimes and violence.

Where was the fraternity exhibited in the Famine year by the rich landlord to the poor tenant? I am certain that the truth will not be believed, and yet it is not less true. Here is what an American special correspondent has said on this subject, and let it be remembered

that this statement has been read by millions of
Irish in America who, remembering a former
famine year, but too readily believe it true :—

"The New York *Tribune* sent Mr. James Redpath to
Ireland to investigate affairs. Mr. Redpath is anything but
pro-Irish. Yet this is the information he communicates
from Dublin : 'There is an impression in America—which
I shared—that the agitation against the landed proprietors
in Ireland is an agrarian movement. It is nothing of the
sort. It is an honest effort to remove the causes of the
famine. I find that every priest of intelligence—every man
whom I have met and who has studied the effects of the
present system of land tenure—shares in the indignation so
deeply and widely felt among the peasantry against the
landlords and their land laws. The evidence is overwhelming, and comes from every county, to show that the landlords of Ireland are not contributing a shilling to the relief
funds ; but, as a class, they are mercilessly enforcing their
legal claims to their pound of flesh from their starving
tenants.' "

I know Mr. Redpath personally. He is
English by immediate descent; he came to
Ireland simply as a matter of business, as correspondent to an American paper; not, be it
noted, to an Irish American or Catholic paper.
Mr. Redpath assured me that so far from having any prejudice in favour of Ireland, he was
prejudiced against it, but facts were too much
for him.

One might as well expect a battle to be fought without murder and plunder and violence, as expect a great social upheaving of a nation to be carried through without some crime. The statesman who tries to avert the recurrence of war is wiser than the man who writes diatribes of useless invective on its evils. The statesman who calmly considers the cause of social disturbance and removes it, is wiser than the angry politician who utters a torrent of abuse and never attempts a solid remedy. Men who have honoured Garibaldi, welcomed Mazzini, and praised Bismarck, should be the last to reproach Ireland with Communism. Communism denies all the rights of property; Ireland asks that the rights of property should be protected by law. But some Irish landlords, a vast majority, we fear, wish to have the rights of property in their own hands, and not regulated by law, *hinc illa lacryma.*

CHAPTER VII.

WHAT THE IRISH NATION ASKS.

"Let not the law of thy country be the *non ultra* of thy honesty, nor think that always good enough which the law will allow or make good."—*Sir Thomas Browne.*

F what was written above some two centuries since by an English doctor and philosopher, met with more general acceptance, there would be less trouble in the world. It is Christain charity and common sense.

The Irish people do not ask for a complete, or any, subversion of law and order notwithstanding Mr. Froude's wild utterances, over which he must surely have blushed as he wrote them.[1]

"Seven hundred years have now passed since Henry the Second attached Ireland to the English Crown : for all those years successive English administrations have pretended to govern there ; and as a result we saw in the last winter the miserable Irish people sending their emissaries, hat in hand, round the globe to beg for sixpences for God's sake to save them from starving. The Irish soil, if it were decently cultivated, would feed twice the population which now occu-

---

[1] Mr. Froude in the *Nineteenth Century*, Sept., 1880.

pies it; but in every garden there grow a hundred weeds for one potato. If a landlord ejects an inefficient tenant, and gives the land to some one who will grow potatoes and not weeds, gangs of ruffians with blackened faces drive out the new-comer, or the landlord himself is shot, like Lord Leitrim, at his own door, as a warning to his kind. The Irish representatives in Parliament tell their constituents to pay no rent except when it is convenient to them, yet to hold fast by their farms, and defy the landlord to expel them; while the only remedy which the English Government could devise, since the people would not obey the law, was to alter the law to please them, and to propose that for two seasons at least the obligation to pay their rents should be suspended."

The gardens where a hundred weeds grow for every potato, must be of a very remarkable character, and we think every case of ejectment in Ireland shows that tenants are evicted, not because they do not " grow potatoes," but because they do not pay impossible rents. Irish landlords are not shot every day. Lord Leitrim was not shot at his own door. Irish members of parliament do not tell the people to pay no rent except when convenient. Irish people knowing how utterly false all this is, what respect can they have for the English nation when they find such utter nonsense stated as if it was gospel truth?

He has chosen deliberately to misrepresent the Compensation for Disturbance Bill, and, as any one, whether he approved of that bill or not, can see at a glance that it is misrepresented, we must say wilfully, unless Mr. Froude possibly may not be capable of using his reason when Irish affairs are concerned.   But all this is very well for those who know him, but he appeals to a great number of readers who, not being aware of his idiosyncracy, will take his statements for truth.

He is, however, by no means the only offender on this point, and probably he is less to blame than many.   Let me then put before the reader, who prefers fact to fiction, what it is the Irish people ask, and why they ask it.

A land meeting took place in Limerick on November 1st, to receive and honour Mr. Parnell, and at that meeting 70,000 people were present.

"Mr. William Abraham, who was warmly received, proposed the first resolution :—

"'That we demand, as a strict right from the English Government, such an immediate settlement of the land question as will save us from the capricious raising of rents and eviction, and which will ultimately make the cultivators of the soil also the owners' (cheers).

John Bright, the friend of the Irish people, had said that he could imagine such a state of things in Ireland as would make a settlement of the land question possible—namely, when Ireland was united under the Land League and was menacing England if it refused to yield.   That was their condition at present; they were united to-day, and they would remain united until the land question was settled (hear, hear)."

"Mr. Synan, M.P., in supporting it was warmly received. He said—Mr. Chairman, as the day is a day of action and not of words, I will find it necessary to be brief, and I believe I will be brief, and will also do justice to this resolution, by pointing to my acts and words for twenty years in the cause of tenant-right (cheers). The men of the County Limerick know what sacrifices I made twenty years ago, when I raised the standard of tenant-right in this county (cheers). I need only point to the existing monument of that sacrifice, which stands six miles away from the spot on which I address you, and which, I believe, every one of you is acquainted with, where my mother, at the age of eighty-six years, was evicted from a house that cost £200, by an absentee landlord, because I raised the standard of tenant-right in this county (cheers). Bad as Mr. Gladstone's Act is, and bad as I thought it always was, that injustice could not now be perpetrated (cheers). You cannot evict a man out of his house now without paying him. She was evicted out of her house without any compensation, and I had to procure another residence for her. Well, I carried out the spirit and the words of that resolution, in opposing the principle of Mr. Gladstone's Bill of 1870, as you will find in my speeches, as reported in "Hansard's Debates." I opposed it, because it was my opinion that it would lead to the consolidation of farms (cheers). It has led to the consolidation of farms.

At a Land Meeting, held at Clonmel, County Tipperary, at which 25,000 people attended :—

"Count Moore, M.P., who was warmly received, proposed the first resolution :—' that the periodical depression, deepening into famine, with which Ireland, a fertile country, is

afflicted, proves incontestibly that the laws which hamper
the cultivation of the soil are unsuited to the present state
of society, and demand radical changes.' He had, he said,
travelled a long distance to be present at that meeting, for
he felt not only that it was due to his constituents, but to
his own sympathy with every generous impulse and every
lofty inspiration that warmed the hearts of Tipperary men.
In the cause that lay at the root of all their miseries connected with the Irish land, was the absenteeism, which
drained so much of their money out of the country. Another
cause of the great distress was the harsh and inelastic Poor
Law, which never adapted itself to the wants of the Irish
poor, but, in fact, set a premium upon extermination. The
Irish land laws were not paralleled by the land laws of any
other country in the world; but now, he firmly believed,
they were on the eve of a final settlement of the land
question. Everybody—landlords as well as tenants—were
calling out for it; and he believed the landlords were only
too anxious for a fair settlement, such as fixity of tenure,
fair rents, and free sale (loud and prolonged cheering).
He wished to see the farmers of Ireland owning their own
lands, but he should say frankly that he was not in favour
of expropriating the landlords. He did not believe that
would better the condition of any class in the community.
He believed that they could and would, next session, get
from the Government a measure of peasant proprietary.
He would have free land, and by removing the restrictions
by which owners were at present hampered, and prevented
from selling. He would also have a Government department to manage the sale and purchase of properties on
behalf of the tenantry; and he would, in the next place,
offer inducements to the landlords to sell to their tenants.
He would have some pressure also applied to the absentee
landlords, who spent their money in London and Paris, and

gave no aid whatever to relieve the distress of the country. A good deal might be done in that way by putting all the poor rate and county cess on the absentees. The objection often raised to the establishment of peasant proprietary—namely, that the tenants would not pay the rents to the State—he believed to be unfounded. For the Irish people were not a nation of robbers, and they never objected to the payment of a just debt. He next warned the people not to be led astray by persons who were trying to cause dissension between themselves and their clergy, with whom they should stand or fall (applause). The people had the settlement of the land question in their own hands, and it could not be prevented, except they took to ways of violence and crime, which would estrange from them the sympathy of all honest men (applause).

"The Rev. Father Meagher, C.C., Irishtown, Clonmel, seconded the resolution, and said that in all constitutional struggles the priests would be faithful to the people, and when wanted they were irresistible. The present land agitation was perfectly legitimate, and if he thought that the Land League directly or indirectly incited to crime he would not, for all the gold in Peru, have any connection with it. They tried to remove the cause of crime in this country, and when they had done that the crime would disappear. What the Irish farmers wanted was fixity of tenure, fair rents, and free sale.

"The resolution was supported by Mr. Leamy, M.P."

At a meeting at Ballinahinch—

"The Rev. Mr. M'Keon, P.P., moved the first resolution as follows :—

"'That we declare the system of landlordism created by an immoral conquest to be the mainstay of English misrule and oppression in Ireland ; that it has been the cause of the depopulation and impoverishment of a fair and fertile land, created by God for the Irish people, and that the laws that sustain and perpetuate it being contrary to right, reason, justice, and humanity, incapable of adequate amendment, and opposed to the national aspirations of our countrymen, we demand their abolition, and the establishment of such proprietary rights in the soil as will secure to the industrious occupier the permanent possession of his home, and the fruits of his industry.'

They had not assembled for the purpose of doing an injustice, or expressing the opinion that they ought to do injustice to any man—they were there to assert their rights. Landlordism as established in this country was an oppression and a degradation placed upon the industrious farmer. They did not want emigration—they wanted the people to live at home, and they wanted from the Government that ruled them strongly but not well, nothing else but a recognition of the right to live in Ireland, created by God for the Irish people."

At a meeting at Bawnboy, county Cavan—

" Mr. Baxter proposed—

"' Resolved—That as the present system of tenure of land is the cause of our country's poverty, we demand its abolition, and the substitution therefor of a system that will make the cultivator of the soil the owner thereof.'

At the plantation of Ulster the undertakers got their lands at 10s per 60 acres, or at 1½d per acre ; but in the mountains there were no rents, and since that time the improvements had been made by the farmers. In the year 1802 there was a valuation of the whole kingdom, and that barony of Tullyhaw lying between two mountains was valued at 10s. They were there that day to support that noble patriot, Charles Stewart Parnell, and the Land League in trying to have their grievances redressed, and they would resolve not to pay rents higher than the Government valuation.

" The Very Rev. Dean M'Govern seconded the resolution. There would always be unity between the priests and people of the parish. What brought them there that day?

"A Voice—' The reduction of exorbitant rents.'

" Dean M'Govern—Not any communistic or socialistic purpose, but to look for fair play (cheers)—to look for the breaking down of the grievances under which the people groaned. He had been living in the parish for thirty years, and he could safely declare that half of the people were living in a state of starvation ; they were processed and decreed and not able to clothe their little ones (true, your reverence). As Bishop Berkeley, a Protestant divine, had said, on the face of the earth there were no people so badly fed or clothed as the Irish people (cheers for Bishop Berkeley). What did he attribute this to? To the landlords who were taking away the money out of the country, and had the power of extorting it."

"A meeting was held to-day at Kilreecle, a neat village four miles from Loughrea. Early in the morning contingents poured in from the surrounding districts. A body of five hundred stalwart men from Killalaghlin, wearing green sashes. At the front of this contingent four men carried a green silk banner, on which was the figure of Erin weeping for her children. The contingent was headed by the Rev. P. Burke, Kilreecle. A contingent from Loughrea, accompanied by the brass band, headed by Fathers Egan and Cunningham. The Loughrea, Killalaghlin, and Donary contingents proceeded to meet the men of Bullane and Gurteen. The procession, with its bands and banners, at the head of which rode the Rev. P. Flanagan and the Rev. P. Coghlan, presented a grand spectacle. The procession then proceeded to the platform, in the centre of a field given by the owner,

Mr. Ryan, for the purpose. The chair was taken amidst applause by the

"Rev. P. FLANAGAN, Kilreecle.

"Amongst those on the platform were—

"Rev. P. Burke, Rev. P. Flanagan, Rev. P. Cunningham, Rev. P. Egan, Rev. T. Head, Rev. D. Coghlan, Rev. J. M'Keigue, Rev. J. Canning, Captain Dunne, Chicago ; J. Ryan, J. Burke, J. Kilmartin, D. Connor Carton ; G. Larkin, E. Kean, J. Sweeney, J. Hubon, J. Kirwan, M. Fahy, M. Egan, T. Griffin, &c.

"A Government notetaker was allowed on the platform A large force of police were present in charge of S.I. Barry.

"The following letters of apology were received :—

"'Loughrea, October 30th.

"'SIR,—My earnest desire was, and still is, to witness a settlement of the land question on principles that will secure to owners and occupiers those rights that have their sanction in the laws of justice. Less than this neither should accept. More than this neither should claim. That a crisis has come which renders an adjustment of those rights inevitable appears to be agreed by all reflecting minds. It may be that extremes on either side may mar or help to defer this adjustment. To every observer it is clear a settlement is essential to the prosperity of the country.—I am yours,

"'✝ P. DUGGAN.

"'M. Keane, Secretary.'"

"A Voice—'Three cheers for Dr. Duggan.'
"Another—'Three for Dr. Croke.'

"'Ballinasloe, 30th October.

"'DEAR SIR,—I have to thank you for your invitation to the meeting to be held. I regret the duties of Sunday will prevent me being with you, at the same time I concur with

H

the object of your meeting. I hope it shall be successful.
The ground you stand on gives evidence of the necessity of
agitation and enlightening the public mind of England on
the unsatisfactory condition of the land system in Ireland.
The beautiful plains between Ballinasloe and Loughrea are
entirely depopulated, its former inhabitants driven into exile
or perished in the workhouse. Thus the trade of the town is
paralysed, while the tillers of the soil are left on the barren
lands of the highland. It is time the hand of the victor
should be stayed, and the peasant should be secured in his
holding. Till this is done no wonder the energies of our
people should be damaged, and industry be wanting. Your
meeting, by joining in the demand for a settlement of this
question, shall have done much to bring peace to Ireland.—
I am yours,   .   "'J. K. MOLONY.'"

" Letters of apology were read from the Rev. M. Badger,
Rev: A. Griffin, Rev. J. P. M'Philipin, M. Harris, M. Ryan,
and P. Broderick."

All these and the following meetings were
held during the last fortnight of October or
first week in November.

At Cahirciveen, where the severest distress
occurred in the famine.

"At three o'clock the chair was taken by the Very Rev.
Canon Brosnan, P.P., V.G., Cahirciveen. Almost all the
clergy of the deanery were present on the platform, and the
traders of the town and the farmers of the barony were well
represented. A Government reporter took notes of the
proceedings, as did also two amateurs of the Royal Irish
Constabulary.

"The Very Rev. Chairman, who was enthusiastically
received, proceeded to say, when the cheering had subsided—

My friends and fellow-countrymen, I have to thank you for
the honour conferred on me of presiding at this great meeting—a meeting, I am happy to say, which has the sanction
and best wishes of our revered bishop. The object of our
meeting is to confer together on the great and all-absorbing
question of the day—the land question. A mighty effort,
unexampled in extent and rapidity, is, you are aware, being
now made to settle that question by a thoroughly effective
and comprehensive measure of land reform (cheers). Resolutions affecting it will be proposed here to-day for your
consideration, and, if you so think fit, for your adoption ;
and I trust the gentlemen who will address you in reference
to them will be listened to with that respectful attention
which has characterised other public meetings in this town,
and which the present great subject so eminently deserves
(hear, hear). I do, indeed, most earnestly hope and pray
that no idle or foolish remarks will be indulged in at this
meeting, nor anything unseemly occur thereat, or in connection with it ; and that when the proceedings are over
you will all soon set out for your respective homes soberly
and peaceably. Fellow-countrymen, I am most willing and
determined to further in every way within my humble ability
the great and just cause for which we are here assembled
(cheers). But you will allow me most respectfully to say
that I can do so only on condition that the movement be
peacefully and constitutionally conducted in our midst, and
that violence and outrages of all sorts in connection with it
(which may God forbid should occur) be reprobated by you
as they should ever be. Oh, my friends, what else, I ask,
could such do but mar your good cause whilst they war
against heaven ? Never, indeed, was that saying of our
great and illustrious countryman (great cheering), who drew
his first breath yonder there, truer or more appropriate than
at the present juncture of the land movement—namely, that

"He who commits a crime gives strength to the enemy. People of Iveragh, numerous land meetings have been held in various parts of Ireland ; but, I ask you, is there a spot from the Giant's Causeway to Cape Clear, or from Connemara to the Hill of Howth, where one was more needed than in Iveragh ? (Loud cries of 'no, no.') Is there any other place where poorer or more miserable, or more rack-rented, or worse fed, or worse clothed, or worse housed poor people are to be found, aye, in thousands and tens of thousands, than in Iveragh ? Look at this wretched town, the heart and centre of the barony. Look at its filthy lanes and hovels ; look at its highways and byways, its streets and its sidewalks ; look at the country south and west of it, and stretching on for miles—all a dreary picture of misery and neglect ; and all, both town and country, managed by a wealthy corporation. Is it, therefore, to be wondered at that strangers coming here and seeing such a wretched condition of things, have painted and described them as a disgrace to humanity and a scandal to the Empire (cheers)? Whatever be said or done about expropriating landlords, can there be I ask, a second opinion that these learned divines and managers ought to be wholly relegated to their books and to their prayers? (Cheers and laughter.) Then look at the great Liberal renegade's Iveragh tenants—I humbly beg my noble friend's pardon—look at the great Marquis's Iveragh tenants, and see how at almost every decade or recurrence of a few years of sunshine, the poor terror-stricken serfs have been, I won't say pounced upon, let us say visited, with the inevitable four or five additional shillings in the pound. Then look at Roads and Coomnahinshy, at Ballydarrig and the Killurlys. Look at Upper Carham and Cannuge, look at Ardcost, at Fermoyle, and at Ballard—in fact, look all along from Cara Lake to Foilhammerum, and from Kilealan to Bolloghasheen, and what can you see or find throughout but wretched·

ness, and wild wastes, and desolation all round (applause). Let me ask why and wherefore all this? Iveragh contains thousands upon thousands of acres of reclaimable soil ; and haven't you seen year after year the life-blood of the country flowing off in a constant stream of emigration from Iveragh, leaving the population now consisting almost of poor old decrepid people, broken-hearted parents, aud helpless children? Why and wherefore all this? Haven't you also seen but a few months ago, as, alas, was often seen before, almost the whole of Iveragh on the very brink of destruction, victims of hunger, of misery, and want? Why and wherefore all this? Ah! my friends, the answer to these doleful, dreadful questions is easy to be found. It is on everyone's lips. It is within your hearts. Here it is in your own simple, truthful words :—' If we improve our lands the rents would be raised' (true for you, sir). This is the cry I have heard yesterday and the day before, and have been hearing nearly every day since I was born. Is it a cry of justice that has pierced the heavens ; may it pierce the hearts of our rulers and of the Empire. At the eleventh hour let justice—full justice—be done to the tenant farmers of Ireland. Let rack-rents disappear ; let the fruits of honest toil and honest labour be meted out and secured to you for evermore. And then, and not till then, may we hope to see peace in the Empire, peace and plenty in the land, our young men and young women staying at home or coming back to Erin, the wastes of Iveragh growing green, Cahirciveen flourishing, and Ireland, all Ireland, becoming what nature intended, and, please God, she yet will be—

> " Great, glorious, and free,
> First flower of the earth, and first gem of the sea."

" Rev. Father Garvey, C.C., Eyries, proposed the first resolution, as follows :—' That, as the poverty of the land in

this locality, and the high rents charged for them have so
reduced the tenantry of the district that a single bad harvest
brings them to the verge of famine, we deem it our duty to
declare that any rent higher than the Government valuation
is excessive, and should not be exacted.' They were
engaged there in a holy war, a sanctified crusade ; and they
were there to demand from their lords and masters their
rights (cheers). And if they were united, if they were determined, and if they persevered in their efforts, those efforts
would be ultimately crowned with complete success (cheers).
He had some knowledge of the condition of the tenant
farmers in the parish of Eyries, and he would tell those
present that it was only removed by a few degrees from
simple starvation."

Mr. Healy, who spoke at this meeting, said :
" He was informed by the Parish Priest of Adrigole that,
out of 2,000 people in his parish, every man, woman, and
child, except twenty, were on the relief list during the past
season. (A Voice—That is true.) . . . .
Some of Mr. Hutchins' tenants were fishermen, and any of
them who had seines, had to pay him extra ; or, as one poor
man told him, he taxed them for nine miles of the 'say.'
Well, they were all very sorry that Mr. Hutchins was shot at.
It was a very bad act, but he (Mr. Healy) did not wonder at
it ; for so long as the Government allowed these outrages to
be committed by the landlords, it was no wonder that some
slight corresponding attempt at rebellion should be made by
the tenants (hear, hear, and cheers). That locality of Berehaven was so poor that the Poor-rates were the highest in
Ireland. In a portion of the town they were 5s. 6d. in the
£1, and in another part of the Union 3s. 2d., while the
County Cess was 2s. Out of that locality the landlords
drew a rental of £30,000, and not one of them ever visited

the district, and they did not spend 30,000 farthings in it. (hear, hear.)

"The Rev. T. Lawler, P.P., Valencia, proposed the second resolution, which was as follows :—'Some farmers, having so tempted the cupidity of landlords, by offering extravagant rents and fines for other people's farms, owing to their insane competition for land—be it resolved that, for the purpose of self-defence, we pledge ourselves not to take a farm from which another has been unjustly evicted ; nor to purchase cattle or goods seized for non-payment of a rack rent.'

" Mr. M. J. O'Driscoll briefly seconded the resolution.

" Rev. Michael O'Reilly, P.P., Dromid, proposed the third resolution :—' As rack-rents have been the principal cause of bringing on us in this remote district a famine, from which we were only able to escape by the charity of the world, resolved—that a local committee be formed to receive evidence of the people's grievances, and seek redress by persistent appeals to a sound public opinion.'

Mr. Blennerhasset, M.P., spoke also :—

" The object of wise men was to bring about reform, not revolution, and to promote salutary changes, by the wholesome agency of public opinion and the legitimate use of the weapons of political power. Many minds were busy with the subject, and a great variety of proposals found advocates and adherents. One thing he especially desired was, that when the question came to be dealt with, it should be disposed of thoroughly and completely. A weak and inadequate measure would be a calamity to every class in the community, and, most of all, to the owners of land. Courage and resolution were wanted to go once for all, to the root of the matter. It was more than thirty years since Lord Devon's Commission reported that it had been shown that the master evil of Ireland—poverty—proceeded from the fact of occupiers of land withholding the investment of labour and capital from the ample and profitable field for it which lay within their reach on the farms they occupied, and that this hesitation was attributable to the reasonable disinclination to invest labour or capital on the property of others without a security that adequate remuneration shall be derived from the investment. Had these words been acted upon, and that security been afforded, who could doubt that, in thirty years, the face of the country would have been changed, and the population would be no longer in such a miserable condition that two or three bad harvests reduced them, as they well knew, to the depths of misery, and even to the verge of starvation. He would quote the testimony of an intelligent and impartial Englishman, who had lately visited Ireland on an errand of mercy:—'Perhaps,' said Mr. Tuke, in his excellent pamphlet, 'apart from the wretched condition of the people and their dwellings, the fact which most impresses itself upon the mind of the traveller is, that nothing is made the best of, that the resources of the country are never really developed.'

"A Cabinet Minister, in a debate of last Session, quoted from the pamphlet already referred to, a sad and touching story. The writer was visiting one of the poor cottier tenants in Donegal. He had neither cow nor calf, nor ewe nor lamb, nor beast that treads the earth ; but he had a loom, and was sitting upon it. He had neither warp nor woof in it, but he was mechanically moving the frame backwards and forwards. 'When I read that story,' said the minister, 'I could not help asking, is this a real story or an allegory?' Are we in the condition of this poor man? Are we moving backwards and forwards the framework of our laws for Ireland to no purpose and in vain? Are we for ever working an empty loom, and driving an empty shuttle? While the present system of land laws existed in Ireland, and the great bulk of the population remained without the stimulus to property, or the protection of a secure tenure, all the efforts of Government to improve the condition of the country would be idle and profitless, as the labour of that poor Donegal cottier."

At a Land Meeting at Castletown, Berehaven, in the County Cork, at which the Rev. Father Larkin, P.P., presided, he said :—

"People of Berehaven, I must commence my observations by congratulating you on this really magnificent gathering. Your coming here to-day in such numbers is a strong and sufficient proof that this meeting has your approval, as it has mine (hear, hear). Your coming here in such numbers proves that, even in this remote locality, you are at present fully alive to the importance of the cause which the Land League is now advocating throughout the length and breadth of the country (hear, hear). The cause that the Land League advocates is your own. It is a cause that affects each and every one of you. What is that cause, and what is the object they have in view? I will tell you. It is to put an end to evictions and to rack-renting (hear, hear); and to put an end altogether to landlord oppression (cheers). Their object, my dear friends, is that; or, in other words, to make the Irish tenant-farmer independent, and to put him in such a position that he will be enabled to live comfortably—to support his family, and to clothe them and educate them (cheers). Their object was to give the Irish tenant-farmer a strong and firm grip of his holding (cheers), to root him, as they say, in the soil of his fathers (cheers); to give the farmer security of tenure—to impose upon him a fair and just and reasonable rent, and to insure the farmer that whatever improvements he makes in his little holding by his own toil and industry shall be his own (cheers). If that were the case, in a short time, Ireland would be prosperous, she would cease to be the periodical beggar she had been hitherto, aud the children of Ireland would cease to crouch as slaves beneath the frown of the man in power (cheers). That was the object of the Land League. It can be preached in open day, and no one need be afraid to profess the principles they taught. I ask you, is it at all unreasonable to seek to put the tenant-farmers in the position I have said (no, no). The landlords will say, ' Oh, it is altogether un- ' reasonable and cannot be expected ;' but I tell you, my friends, and I emphatically say it, that it is a thing most reasonable, and a thing that ought to be, and I hope will soon be (cheers), and if that thing comes to pass, as I have said already, Ireland will be prosperous, and Ireland's children will enjoy peace, contentment, and the blessings of heaven (cheers).

MALACHY O'SULLIVAN.

CHAPTER VIII.

WHAT IRELAND DOES NOT WANT.

" Commercial restraints, by destroying every other business, caused the excessive competition for land, which has been the proximate cause of our worst troubles."—Letter from Mr. Bagwell, of Clonmel, to the Editor of the " Freeman's Journal."

RELAND does not want Communism or Idealism, or any other "ism" subversive of law and order. If the English people would consider the subject impartially, they would soon see this. And there are Irish landlords who see it, and know it, and have the courage to speak the truth.

Mr. Bagwell, a well-known Protestant landlord of the County Tipperary, has written a number of letters to the *Freeman's Journal* on this subject.

I believe too much weight cannot be laid on the statement which he has made in one of these letters, which I have printed above. But here is another authority on the same subject, and one whose word will have more weight. The Earl of Dunraven cannot be accused of

Socialism, Communism, Parnellism, or any special leaning to the interests of Irish tenants. He wrote. long and frequent letters in the American papers during the Famine. These were precisely the same kind as the landlord correspondence which has been going on in the *Times* for the last few months. A candid admission that the Irish people are in a state of chronic distress from no fault of their own—this comes out from an unconscious honesty. A bitter abuse of them because they do not do, what has been, perhaps on the very same page, unconsciously admitted that they cannot do. Such is the inevitable result of looking at a most serious question, not from that point of view which will be for the general good, but from a purely selfish one. This selfishness is, no doubt, unconscious, but it is, nevertheless mischievous. Few English gentlemen, however, will exhibit it as freely as Sir George Bowyer[1] has done. Indeed we must hope no other Englishman would be guilty of such a public exhibition of self-interest.

---

1 This person, who seems to court publicity by delivering lectures in the papers to everyone, from the Protestant Dean of Westminster to the Irish Priests, has actually written to Mr. Gladstone to beg he will put a stop to Irish agitation, because his "eminent solicitors" cannot

Lord Dunraven not being one of the miserable few who look on public affairs only from that point of view which concerns themselves, is capable of some justice. He says :—

"Practically speaking, there are no other industries in Ireland to which the people can turn their attention. Such was not always the case. Ireland at one time showed plenty of disposition to originate and develop manufacture. England crushed every effort for her own selfish interests."

What an admission, what a calm dispassionate statement, what an indictment against England, from the pen of an Anglo-Irish landlord! If a Land League agitator said what we have quoted from Lord Dunraven and Mr. Bagwell, he would be denounced as setting the people against the English Government and people.

We quoted in a previous chapter a very strong statement from the *Times*, about the desire of English people to know the worst of themselves ; would that they were all willing to know it as far as Ireland is concerned.

---

find tenants for his farms in England, on account of the Irish Land movement. What miserable exposures are made when men exhibit the true cause of their hatred of Ireland. This is indeed Communism, which takes all for itself, and would leave its neighbour destitute, which places personal interest as the one great object in life, and the general good last, if anywhere.

But Lord Dunraven, like all English writers about Ireland, having made a candid, and, perhaps, involuntary admission, which shows that he is well aware of one of the great causes of Irish discontent, runs off into the usual charges against us :—

"Very many years have passed since any restrictions have been placed upon the same industry, and the country ought long ago to have recovered from the depression caused by bad treatment, and might have done so if it had been at peace. If, when the people got absolute fair play, they had turned their face to the future and set vigorously to work, the trade would have been started again. But they have never been let alone. They have constantly been agitated about something or other. They have been encouraged to look back, to gloat over grievances of the past, instead of addressing themselves to active exertion in the present, and have been taught to attribute their backwardness in agriculture to their lack of industries and their poverty, as compared with the wealth of England, to every conceivable cause under the sun except the unalterable difficulties connected with the natural characteristics of the country, and to difficulties existing in their own selves, and which they themselves alone can remove. Land may possibly be deteriorating in value. If so, prices will find their level through natural causes. Any action interfering with natural causes must have evil consequences in the future. It is impossible to reduce the value of land by a strike of occupiers against owners."

As happily there are few English gentlemen who make the selling or letting of their own

farms their sole object in the consideration of
public affairs, I turn to the many who have
some public, some true patriotism, and ask
their consideration of the following remarks.
The whole subject has a most important bearing on the present agitation in Ireland, and
on the charges of Communism and Socialism.

First—It is admitted by English gentlemen
that Irish industries were purposely destroyed
by England. Thus it will be seen that on one
point Ireland has not been treated as an integral part of the British Empire. What would
be said of an English government which would
deliberately destroy the industries of Sheffield
or Manchester? The idea is too preposterous
for consideration, but let it be remembered that
this *was* done in Ireland. Irishmen are very
bitterly blamed by some English writers for not
loving England, for speaking of England as a
step-mother, for not making themselves one
with the English nation. But let honourable
Englishmen remember that England first, yes,
and from the first, treated Ireland—well, let us
not use harsh words—let us say that she did
not treat Ireland as she would have treated
Yorkshire and Lancashire. But Lord Dunraven says Ireland "ought long ago to have

recovered from the depression caused by such treatment.[1]

No doubt Ireland "ought" to have recovered. Let one remark suffice. In places in England where, from particular circumstances, trade has been destroyed, has it recovered? Do you know Spitalfields? I do. Have you ever visited the poor there? I have; and a more pitiful sight under God's heaven, could hardly be seen. A dead trade. Vast rooms where the rich poplin was manufactured, and if the toil was long and weary, the reward was good and sure. But, then—for I write of some years ago—a ghastly stillness. I saw a poor man there dying, and cursing God and man as he died. The sight will haunt me to my dying hour. He lay on a bed of hard sacking, with scarcely decent covering, at the end of a very long room, where eight or ten empty dust-covered looms showed what had been. The August sun glared in from hundreds of panes of glass—a necessity of the trade, when there was trade. He lay at the head of a steep and narrow flight of stairs, which came into the room, so

---

[1] In noting Lord Dunraven's letters so specially, I do so because I believe he represents ordinary English opinion about Ireland; and it is this opinion which needs information and explanation. He does not indulge in extremes of invective, or manifest contemptible selfishness.

that he might, if able, at the last hour, call a
neighbour's child, his only caretaker. I knew
then, I knew from many another empty room,
what a dead trade was. Certainly trade "ought"
to have been revived in Ireland, but it has not
been, and it is no fault of the Irish people; and
it ill becomes England to utter one word of
reproach on the subject.

But Lord Dunraven says, "the people get
absolute fair play." When? How? Where?
A people depending on land which the best
authorities, even those who are most eager to
exact the last penny of rent, admit cannot support them in decency or comfort, how were they
to get capital to restore a ruined trade again?
How were they to get the business habits so
long out of practice? How were they to get the
ear of merchants and traders in foreign lands?

Trade does not spring into existence like a
mushroom forced in a night. It is difficult enough
to keep it when secured; how were a people to
obtain it again when it had been wrenched from
them?

And where was the absolute fair play? What
of the Irish fisheries?[1] And then Lord Dun-

---

[1] We shall enter into this subject again; for the present we leave it
to avoid breaking the thread of our argument.

I

raven takes up the stock argument that "agitation" is the cause of all the evils of Ireland. Why cannot gentlemen of common intelligence distinguish between cause and effect where Ireland is concerned ?

Irish industries have been destroyed by England, capital has gone, land is admitted to be the only resource for commercial enterprise, and land is said to be unable to support the people, so that emigration is the only remedy, and yet the Irish are assured it is all their own fault they are not prosperous. Truly the force of inconsistency could go no further. We ask to have laws made which will secure us the only means of industry we are admitted to have. 'We agitate when the request is refused. In our fashion of agitating there may not be all the wisdom and deliberation of conscript fathers. Then we are told we are keeping capital out of Ireland by agitation. What capital ? It is easy to make assertions. Let them be proved. Let it be proved that any real, honest, mercantile or other industry has been offered to Ireland, and that she has refused it. If the last sentence but one quoted from this letter has any meaning, it implies that every thing should be let alone, and no effort ever made to remedy a national deficiency. The last sentence shows the hopeless ignorance of the writer. The object of the "strike of occupiers against owners" is to increase the value of the land.

The value of the land can only be increased by the industry of the cultivator. The cultivator will not give his labour unless he is allowed a fair return for it. Land is the only industrial resource which has been left by England to the Irish people; and most assuredly it is but the honest justice that the people should have every possible protection and help in that industry, that England should not crush every effort for the selfish interests of a few land owners.

CHAPTER IX.

WHY IRISH LAND INDUSTRY HAS FAILED.

"I fear the scheme of striking down the Established Church, and abandoning the theory of our territorial system, is so broad, so good, so complete, that Parliament would stand against it. I can conceive a condition of things in Ireland under which such a great change might be accomplished, if Ireland were united in demanding it, and were menacing Great Britain if it were refused."—JOHN BRIGHT.

WHEN a number of witnesses give conflicting testimony, the only way to decide on evidence is to test the veracity of the witnesses. And this may be done in two ways—by character, and by fairly presumed motive. It is, unhappily, true, that persons of the highest character are sometimes so influenced by sheer crass prejudice as to be utterly unreliable as witnesses. "I hate prejudice—I hate the French," is as wise as their views on some public affairs. The malign influence of this prejudice of centuries is, unhappily, the cause of not a little of the difficulty experienced in discerning the state of Ireland. Those who are so sure that they are right—that they think it quite impossible they can be wrong —are quite incapable of judging any question, and yet they are precisely the very persons who are most certain of their own individual infallibility. Yet, the very fact that there are differences of opinion, should surely induce us to think that there must be some ground for such differences.

Hence, it is the part of true wisdom, when there is a conflict, to hear both sides carefully, and to weigh the value of the evidence.

Now, it is worth noticing, that men who have visited Ireland, like Mr. Childers and Sir J. Campbell, invariably admit that there is need for Land Reform. If there is need for Land Reform, it is clear England has not been just to Ireland, and yet this very day I have received letters from English gentlemen, literary men, and others, written in a style which, if they had been penned by women, would be called hysterical. And those wild protestations declare that England has never done any wrong to Ireland, and that all that is wrong in Ireland is our own fault. When such a prejudice exists, what hope is there that truth will find a place or a hearing?

It is this kind of ignorance which leads to such wild talking as that indulged in by Sir

Harding Gifford at Lancaster, when he declared that "just now in Ireland there was every kind of outrages," and that "justice to Ireland would include justice to all alike ;" his context plainly showing that he meant injustice to those whose wrongs had led them to do acts of violence which could be very easily averted in the future by doing justice to the poor.

What does all this clamour about "vindicating law and order" mean ? One is weary of the cry. Is it not the demand of a class of men who know no other meaning for it except the continual enforcement of injustice to the many, and the support by force and bloodshed of the injustice perpetrated by the few on the million.

Again, whose evidence is most worthy of consideration ? that of persons who have actually made it their business to inquire into the actual state of the Irish tenants, or that of persons, who, when they denounce the Irish tenant and his agitation, in the very act of denouncing, make it a political question.

I am not writing for politicians. I am writing for thoughtful men and women, who desire simply to know facts, and to form their opinion on facts. And to such I would earnestly say : doubt all statements in which you find that political (party) motives are largely introduced.

Such witnesses are altogether unreliable. When men like Sir Harding Gifford bring forward and enlarge on the state of Ireland as a subject of reproach or taunt to their political opponents; when the Conservative throws the "fearful" state of Ireland in the face of the Liberal, there is an end of fair discussion. Let men who wish for truth look elsewhere. If Ireland was equally in the minds of Englishmen as much a part of the empire as Yorkshire, such speeches would never be heard. Again, let it be said that we are very bitterly blamed for not having a very cordial feeling of union with England, but how does England act towards us? Has she not shown the example first of treating Irish affairs as apart from the interests of the empire?

But let me offer some unimpeachable and independent evidence as to the normal condition of the Irish people before entering more fully on this subject?

And, first, I will cite the evidence of His Royal Highness the Duke of Edinburgh. At the Annual Dinner of the Royal Geographical Society, held in London, on June 2nd, 1880, he said, at the conclusion of some remarks on the Famine in Ireland, the result, be it remembered, of personal observation :—

"It is to be hoped, too, that other things may be done,

such as the undertaking of great works, and the encouragement of the Coast Fisheries of Ireland. I feel sure that the organizing of the fisheries on the coast, which at present are very much neglected, would give the population there a more secure means of existence. The land is really incapable of supporting the population from natural resources ; and I feel certain that, without the assistance of the fisheries, the same distress which has occurred will occur again.

"Excuse me for having alluded to this subject. It was not included in the programme for this evening, but as you have so kindly drunk my health, and the fact of my having been recently in Ireland has been so kindly alluded to, I have taken the liberty of placing before you the facts as I have found them." (Loud cheers.)

A writer in the *Graphic*, not long after, said :—

"But for the unworthy jealousy of English manufacturers, Ireland might, nearly a couple of centuries ago, have become an important industrial region."

The jealousy of English manufacturers certainly had nothing to do with the state of things to which His Royal Highness called attention and deplored, but Irish landlords had a great deal to do with it, as we shall show presently.

We give next a report of the *normal* state of the people of St. Johnstown, endorsed by the Marquis of Hamilton, and given in a Report of the Duchess of Marlborough's Relief Committee, from 1880.

The Rev. M. Martin, P.P., .says : " You may rest assured that those Catholics, whose normal state at best is miserable, and this year is considerably aggravated by the want of fuel, potatoes, credit, and employment, are proper objects for your charitable consideration." A letter strongly endorsing this statement, from the Marquis of Hamilton, was read.

The following are extracts from the reports of Dr. Sigerson, Mr. Fox, and others, to the Mansion House Relief Committee in June and July, 1880, and they show the state of the country apart from the effects of the famine :—

" Neither Camus nor Carraroe are islands ; they are portions of the mainland. Yet, such is the absence of roads here, they are only accessible by sea from Rosmuck. The distance by water to Carraroe South cannot be less than six or seven miles, through difficult channels. Midway we have to leave the boat and travel over an isthmus (at low tide) of stones, slippery with fuci, across which it was necessary for the men to drag the boat. Their being no pier, our course on landing lay again over a broad shore of shaggy rocks. If we refer particularly to such points as these, it is in order that you may realise the difficulties presented to the conveyance of the sick to hospital (some thirty miles away !). Consider also that these are obstacles to the visits of medical officer and clergymen. In rains and storms their course must be painful and dangerous ; whilst in winter, if overtaken by darkness or tossed by tempests, there is imminent risk of life. Hence we would urge that, in all such districts, the channels should be improved where necessary, and small boat-piers built, where so much required.

"Carroroe South is almost a repetition of Camus, with its grey granite walls ; but the cabins here are a shade better, and some employment has been furnished by the making of a small road, which cannot be completed (we are told) for want of funds. Carraroe North, however, is worse than even Camus. In some parts the laborious peasants have succeeded in forming fields and raising scanty crops, but over a wide range the eye beholds nothing save a dreary expanse of brown bog, broken at intervals by white reefs of granite rock. There have been nineteen cases of fever reported to the relieving officer in the Carraroes, Clynagh, and Kuranbeg since the 1st of April, but more have confessedly existed. It is our duty to add that (as in the instance of the Ballintadder fever families) notices of eviction had been obtained against the peasants of the Carraroes. Obviously, there could be no more efficacious way of disseminating infectious disease over the country than by compelling persons sick in fever, or just convalescent, to quit their isolated homes and wander about, seeking shelter from others, probably at a distance and not yet smitten. Whilst the disease is thus being spread the mortality must be increased.

"Hence it ought to be the first policy of the State in such cases to suspend the power of eviction until the risk of infection shall have disappeared. The conditions of such a suspension is not for us to suggest, but, as regards the vital importance of such a measure, no doubt can be possible.

"Rosmuck.—Remote, in one of the wildest parts of Connemara, lies the district of Rosmuck, composed of mountains, moors, granite rocks, long winding creeks, intricate straits, and many islands, occasionally inaccessible. Green patches of ripening crops, fenced by high walls of loose stones, and interspersed by erratic boulders and pyramids of great grey pebbles, gathered from the field, attest the incessant industry of the peasant, striving against innumerable obstacles. Large breadths of this district are utterly without roads, or even lanes. Seawrack for manure, turf for fuel, crops for market—all must be carried on the backs of men or horses to or from the shore or distant highway when necessary. Then, with a thrust of the hand, the stones fall from the loosely-built walls, and a gap is made for the passage of the burthen. To visit fever-stricken Camus, a portion of this district, we had to take a boat, and, after a long row up a sinuous creek, to traverse a slippery shore of rocks, covered with shaggy seawrack. Our way next lay over pathless bogs, fields, and through new-made gaps, to cabins whose reedy roofs rose but little above the grey walls that divided the fields. Some of the doors were only breast-high, and the interior was often correspondingly small. Smoke often filled the inside, for there was no lime with which to build a chimney, though in some cases an ingenious screen of interwoven reeds supplied its place. In one almost empty cabin we found a poor mother, Mary J——, lying on the ground, in fever, with none to tend her but a son. Her anxiety was all about him, lest he should catch the disease. The son stated that the relieving officer had first refused relief, saying he was able to support her (yet they are very poor) ; then informed him nothing could be given until he should see the medical officer, who lives on an island in the centre of his immense district. After her illness had lasted three weeks twopence worth of bread and some wine had been obtained. . . .

" Meanwhile there is unlimited scope for road-making in Mayo, for nowhere else, perhaps, are the public highways so dangerous to life and limb. Yet at best even these can scarcely be described as works of a reproductive character

or of permanent utility. Indeed, many of the baronial
works which I saw in operation in the shape of bog road
fences would scarcely withstand a sharp rainstorm, which
would speedily reduce them to their original element of peat
and mud. On the other hand, what might be done in the
way of reclaiming waste lands is often visible to the eye as
well as to the imagination. In many districts through which
I travelled I saw patches of meadow and smiling corn-
fields, where only a few years ago there was nothing but
savage bog and moorland. The great evil of the times in
Mayo is not the question of rent, but rather the circumstance that the holdings of the small farmers are deficient in
quantity as well as quality. This it is that necessitates the
annual flight to England, an evil in itself, to enable them to
eke out even a miserable existence on their return. If it
could be remedied without injury to the vested interests of
others, you might have a prosperous and contented peasantry, instead of one whose present condition is a scandal
to the empire."

The special correspondent of the *Daily Telegraph*, July, 1880, writes thus of Donegal : —

"All accounts agree that the soil is capable of feeding its
inhabitants for no more than three months in the year.
How, then, as to the wherewithal for the remaining nine?
It is provided, in the first place, by the labour of the male
population in Scotland and England. Every spring, as soon
as their farms are 'cropped,' the men tie up a little bundle,
swing it on the end of a stick, and take the road to Derry,
whence for a few shillings they cross to Glasgow, returning
after the Scotch harvest with six, eight, or ten pounds of
money saved for winter use. Meanwhile the younger people
of both sexes hire themselves out in the eastern districts, or

Why

work on the shore gathering kelp, while the women who stop at home add a little to the common stock by hand-knitting. Thus, in ordinary years, the poor people contrive to make both ends meet. It follows that the failure of a season's crop is a matter of comparatively small importance, and I am assured that had nothing but potatoes and oats been given out last year, we should not now be hearing much of distress in western Donegal. Unhappily, everything failed; the men went away to Scotland as usual, but could obtain no employment, and in numerous cases had to be helped home again. Such cattle and sheep as the country could send to market were sold at literally an 'alarming sacrifice;' while the agents who once gave three shillings and sixpence for a hundred weight of kelp, made a favour of purchasing the article at less than a third of the price. No people could stand an accumulation of troubles like this, and hence the present very serious condition of the Donegal sea-board. It is computed that the income of the district around Gweedore fell short of the average last year by £16,000, while a memorial just presented to the Lord Lieutenant from the adjacent parishes of Templecrone and Lettermaca-ward states that the falling off there amounted to no less than £22,000. No wonder that from all the region round about we are now hearing 'an exceeding great and bitter cry.' I sometimes see emigration recommended as preventive of such a state of things in future, but before a reasonable mind can accept this it must be distinctly understood that the resources of the country are to remain undeveloped. Were western Donegal exploited to the utmost, it would sustain not only the present population, but ten times their number. Unquestionably, if no more is to be done than has been accomplished hitherto, emigration is the only cure. But if man's great mission to replenish the earth and subdue it embraces this district, emigration means a wicked waste

of the life-blood of the country.   Here are thousands upon
thousands of acres lying idle, waiting now, as they have
waited from the beginning, for some one to do the work
achieved in Connemara by Mr. Mitchell Henry.

"Advocates of change in the Irish land system do not
forget to urge the existing condition of the drainage of the
country as a proof that the present owners have failed to do
what was expected of them, and are still incapable of placing the occupiers in a position to make the best of the land.
It is true that vast exertions were made at the period of the
famine ; and great improvements were then set on foot, with
a progress in some degree maintained in later years.   Under
loans from the Board of Public Works, from 1847 to 1878,
the quantity of land underdrained was 260,665 acres ; and
of this 2,472 acres were drained in 1877, at a cost of
£6 7s. 3d. per acre ; 2,617 acres the year before, and so
on : about 2,100 to 2,600 acres annually for a series of years
back.   In the year 1878 loans amounting to £158,300
were advanced for drainage, farm buildings, labourers' dwellings, fencing, planting, &c.   Under the Land Improvement
Acts, in 31 years, from 1847 to 1878, the loans amounted to
£2,844,700, or an average of £91,764 a year. .The works
were executed in all the counties of Ireland ; the largest
sums being expended in Antrim, Donegal, Tyrone, Galway,
Mayo, Roscommon, Meath, Queen's County, Limerick,
Tipperary, Kerry, and Cork.   Yet all this is a fleabite in
comparison with the work which ought to have been done.
For here is an island, complaining that its arable husbandry
is depressed by the dampness of the climate, yet leaving
millions of acres of its land still in need of drainage.   I
have seen a statement of a high authority that at least
6,000,000 acres in Ireland are open to this fundamental
improvement ; but, whether the acreage be so vast as this or
not, there can be no doubt that the drying of anything like

such a proportion as a fourth or a fifth of the total superficies of 20,820,000 acres would go far towards clearing away the excess of vapour in the atmosphere which too greatly attempers the summer heat and clouds the direct rays of the sun. It is reckoned that the work could be executed for £5 per acre, say, repayable by a rent-charge of 5s. per acre. Upon hundreds of thousands of acres of bog soil and of wet, cold clay, the increased value of the land might soon amount to 15s. or even £1 per acre. Supposing that 4,000,000 acres were improved in letting value to the extent of 10s. a year, we should have a profit of £2,000,000 a year; and at the higher estimate I have quoted the gain would be a million more. The figures may be too broad; but at least the mere fact that a sound, practical authority could make such a guess indicates the immensity of the default still remaining after all these years to be remedied in the draining of Ireland.

" There is no practical difficulty in the way. Labour and stones, or labour and tiles, are the instruments in the case; and labour, the greatest item, is ready and waiting for employment on the largest scale of operations which any body of employers, either landlords, agents, engineers, or public companies, can set afloat. Besides, this is work which the small tenantry and labourers, under good, well-organised supervision, can execute. If questions are put why the work has not been accomplished long ago, the answers are multiform, but all reflecting severely upon the conditions under which very much of the soil of the kingdom is held by persons whose interest or whose ability does not lead them to make such remunerative investment in their estates.

" In another description of permanent improvement—namely, planting —the proprietors again are to be blamed. Professor Baldwin says that, ' next to drainage, the necessity for which all persons admit, there is nothing which would pay, in many parts of Ireland, so well as planting. We have at least a million acres, now waste or nearly so, in which trees planted now would in the course of 20 years be worth £20 an acre, and thus pay a higher rent for the use of the land than could be made of it in any other way. Why do so few landowners plant for future profit as well as for present shelter, improving the value of elevated sheep pastures, and by plantations protecting against winds and cold the early and late depastured cattle on the lowlands? The soil and climate are favourable, for woods and forests flourished in primeval Erin and in the middle and later ages; but limited and encumbered proprietors lack both the means and the will to beautify the island with slow-returning investments in timber.

"The arterial drainages of Ireland have acquired a name, including the noted works on the Shannon and other of the noble waterways of the island. Under the Arterial Drainage Acts were expended £2,390,600, of which £2,249,500 were advanced as Government loans. But the costly system of executing river improvements by the Board of Works came to an end in 1861. Many important drainages have been carried on since that date under the powers of the Drainage Act of 1863. And any civil engineer in Ireland will tell you that, when you have excepted the few undertakings projected or warmly espoused by certain enterprising and large-minded noblemen and other owners, the bulk of the beneficial works of this nature which have been completed have been originated and carried through mainly by the teaching and the zeal of leading men in the profession, whose knowledge and faith enabled them to see what advantage would accrue and to persuade majorities of the persons interested into acquiescence with well-designed plans of improvement. The greatest obstacle to progress lay in the complicated nature of the landed proprietorship. By the Act of 1863, a majority in a proposed district for an arterial drainage work could bind the minority—that is to say, an undertaking required the assent of the owners of land whose valuation amounted to two thirds that of the whole district. But this course so frequently nullified initial proceedings in cases where the support of the most important owners had been secured that the Act was amended in 1878 so as to make necessary the assent of proprietors up to only half the value. However, the same Act provided that the dissent in writing of proprietors of one-third can bar proceedings. The consequence is that, when argument has convinced a majority of the proprietors who may be resident or accessible, when compromises and arrangements have settled ignorant or factious opposition, and a number of absentees have been left out of account as neutrals, a most important and valuable work can be stopped by a minority, composed of many sections, some disbelieving in the promise of benefit, some considering the proposal mischievous, but most part of them unwilling or unable to saddle their estates with any further expenses, no matter how the beneficial outlay might ultimately be. The great prohibiting causes operating against improvements have been the sham nature of ownership, the life interests, the estates held in trust, and other conditions which interfere with the ability or willingness of the nominal owners to do the best for the productiveness of their land. I am told, moreover, that one unfortunate effect of the Land Act of 1870 has been to deter landlords from proceeding with arterial drainage works for the advantage of estates on which they feel less chance of reaping profit in future increase of rent."

Exactly. This is the key-note to the whole disturbance cry. Landlords are afraid they will

K

get less rent, and to satisfy this miserable greed on the part of men who possess tens of thousands, the vast multitude of the Irish people are to remain in a state of semi-starvation, or to emigrate from their homes ; and are to be continuously taunted with every vice, while their patience shows that they possess no ordinary degree of virtue.

Because they ask for *legal* measures which shall prevent this miserable state of things, described, not by Irish agitators, but by grave English writers, they are taunted with communism and disaffection.

Some future Carlyle will, perhaps, write about all this, and will marvel that under such a state of things there was so much "rose water," and so little bloodshed.

Future generations will do justice to the Irish people, if a present generation refuses to do so.

The *Times* wrote the above account a few months ago. It commences a leader in November, thus :—

"It has been truly said that nothing is certain about Ireland, except that whatever statement be made about it is sure to be disputed. Many are ready to tell us all the facts we seek, but they contradict one another. The English travellers who have been wandering in the south and west

during the autumn come back to us with a wonderful diver-
sity of views. This is very perplexing for the patient men
who want to know what is the truth concerning the condition of the Irish people before considering what is to be
done for them. They are distracted by the different tales
that reach them."

But does not the *Times* believe itself? Are
all its statements given about a matter of doubt,
or are they facts? They were given as facts a
few months since, and they can scarcely have
ceased to be facts since then. Let us appeal
from Philip incapable of judging from libations
of prejudice, to Philip when his head is free
from the fumes of political or religious iutoxica-
tion, and truth will be easily ascertained.

English gentlemen pay themselves a bad
compliment when they express such difficulty
about understanding the state of Ireland. They
have facts before them. Let them judge from
facts, and the matter is accomplished.

CHAPTER X.

HOW IRISH LAND INDUSTRY HAS BEEN CRIPPLED.

"The importance and absolute necessity of *securing* to the occupying tenant in Ireland some distinct mode of remuneration for the judicious permanent improvements that he may effect upon his farm is sustained by *a greater weight of concurrent evidence than any other subject which* has been brought under the investigation of the Commissioners.' 'The want of some measure of remuneration for tenants' improvements has been variously stated as productive, directly or indirectly, of most of the social evils of the country.' '"—*Devon Commission.*

HAVE purposely refrained from quoting Mr. Tukes' work in the preceeding pages, because my object was rather to show from authorities, which are known to be altogether above suspicion, the unhappy state of the Irish people apart from their condition in the Famine. What needs to be already understood is, that though the Famine was the immediate occasion of fearful distress, yet, even so great a failure of the one crop on which Ireland depends for support, ought not to have resulted in such a calamity. If the condition of the people was not so miserable as it is, the failure of one crop could not have caused such overwhelming misery and distress. It is then, it should be, the object of government to

T. M. HEALY.

ascertain what is the cause of the permanent
state of poverty and trade depression in Ireland,
and having ascertained the cause, to remove or
find a remedy. English gentlemen pay themselves a very poor compliment when they write
and speak as if it were impossible to understand Ireland. It is only impossible to those
who do not choose to take facts as they are.

For example, there was very severe distress,
little short of actual famine, in parts of Cork,
and in nearly the whole of Kerry. Here is an
extract from a letter of the bishop, which gives
evidence of the utter indifference of Kerry
landlords.

The Most Rev. Dr. M'Carthy, Bishop of
Kerry, says, writing to a Liverpool priest :—

"The Palace, Killarney.

"MY DEAR FATHER O'KANE—In the name of my poor
people, I thank the gentlemen who laboured so earnestly in
getting up the Irish Relief concert in your parish. Your
offering is by no means late, for unfortunately the distress is
at its height in this month. We have been deluded with
relief works which were never opened. The money applied
for as loans will never leave the Treasury for the greater
part. In the same way baronial sessions have been held in
various districts, but the roads approved of will never be
made. The whole scheme is a mockery. Take this Killarney Union as an example. Except Lord Kenmare, I
know no other landlord who has expended this year £500
above the usual labour account. The Town Commissioners

applied for loans, but they have given so far no employment. The Guardians have not expended a shilling for drainage or other necessary sanitary works. Were it not for the liberal donations of our American brethren, the famine of '47 would have again revisited many lonely and beautiful glens in your native Kerry. God bless those who have helped us.

" I remain your much obliged and faithful servant,

"✠ D. M‘CARTHY."

It is a miserable thing to say, but it is true, that Irish landlords, with rare exceptions, took advantage of the famine to advance what they believed to be their own interests, instead of trying to help their unhappy tenantry. This I shall prove.

The Land Commission has been sitting in this district lately, and amongst those who were examined we find the Rev. Mr. M‘Mahon, P.P. His parish is in Cork, but it belongs to the diocese of Kerry. The report of his examination, and that of Mr. Barry, a very extensive tenant farmer, was published in the *Cork Examiner*, November 4, 1880. It shows plainly and clearly why the failure of the potato crop had such fearful consequences. It shows that the poverty of the people in consequence of excessive rents was so great, that a far less disaster would have crushed them :—

" Rev. Father M‘Mahon, P.P., Boherbee, was the first

witness examined. He spoke very strongly in favour of the reclamation of waste lands, and gave very striking instances of it in his own locality. In the year 1832, the Crown lands around Kingwilliamstown passed into the occupation of the Government, and at this time the place was only moor and swamp, and worth nothing as land. In the year 1854, the Government sold the Crown lands without making any provision for the tenantry, who, accordingly, became the helpless prey of the purchasers, and had their rents doubled. They also actually sold the schoolhouse, which cost £800 to build, and the people of the locality were deprived of the blessing of education until the year 1862, when a new National school was built. Mr. Dunscombe, who did appropriate the old, certainly contributed liberally to the erection of the new one But the Government both sold the people and consigned them to ignorance. In 1854, two townlands were sold to Mr. Vincent Scully for £6,800, who, four years later, parted with this property to Mr. Nicholas Dunscombe for the sum of £10,000. When the Government got the land originally some of the old tenants were allowed to remain in possession, and they paid a rent of £322. When Mr. Dunscombe made the purchase in 1854, he doubled the rent, making it £644; and after Mr. Dunscombe became the purchaser, the rent was further raised to £700. Mr. Dunscombe also became the purchaser of another townland for £1,400; the Government rent was £50 17s., and the present rent was £80. The late Dr. Twohill, in his day, purchased the townland of Carraganes for £1,600; the Government rent at the time of purchase was £84 16s., while it is now £139. The townland of Tweenglannahee was purchased by Sir James Mackey for £2,700; the Government rent was £147 13s., it is now £344. All these were striking instances of how waste lands could be improved and reclaimed if the landlords afforded to their

tenants the proper facilities for doing so. As a general
statement, Father M'Mahon gave it out that the improvements in his district were all made by the tenantry, for the
place he had spoken of was only moor and swamp within
living memory, and the labour of the tenants had brought it
into its present cultivable and valuable state. He mentioned
it as a case of hardship that the landlords refused to get
money from the Government for the purpose of draining and
reclaiming the farms of their tenants. ·Mr. Dunscombe refused to borrow money for this purpose, although the tenants
asked for it. The Earl of Cork had only done so on a
small scale, although it is badly wanted, and the people had
earned it. Mr. Longfield promised to get money for some
of his tenants, but he had not done so up to the present.
As a general rule the tenants in his (Father M'Mahon's)
parish were charged a rent of double the valuation, and in
some cases it even exceeded this. He stated most positively
and unreservedly that Griffith's valuation was a sufficient
rent for any land in his parish, in order to enable people to
live comfortably on their farms. The late depression had
shown already that the tenants could not hold on under the
old rents. They were in debt to the country shopkeepers,
and if the latter pressed the tenants for payment there was
not one of them would have house or home. The Cork
traders then, in turn, were indulgent to the shopkeepers, and
between the two the tenants were saved, although the traders
and shopkeepers ran the risk of ruining themselves."

Ex uno disce omnes is true of the state of
Ireland. Rents have been demanded which
the people could not pay and live in decency,
nor even procure the poorest necessaries of
life ; then, when these necessaries failed, there

was famine. And there was more. There was a partial, but also an *actual*, national bankruptcy.

At the best times, people were living from hand to mouth, were living on a most precarious credit, were deeply in debt to bankers, *gombeen men* (local money-lenders); shopkeepers, &c., &c., all because the inexorable rent must be paid ; it was paid at ruinous loss to the national credit. Is this a state of things that should be allowed or continued in this nineteenth century, in a civilized country ? If the " unspeakable Turk" was ruler of Ireland, what epithets of indignation and scorn would be heaped on his devoted head. But we are only governed by England, and we are considered very wicked and ungrateful if we express disapproval, or state our case. We have, indeed, been stating our case for a great many centuries, and we have been getting a little justice by instalments, but the instalments are small, and the process of reparation is slow.

Here is what Mr. Tuke, an English banker who visited Ireland in 1879-80, has to say on the state of the country. At present I only quote what will show that excessive, or rather usurious rents, were the principal cause of the late famine :—

" Mr. Pike is giving work to over 100 men on his estate,

who earn each from 1s. to 1s. 6d. per diem. I was much struck by the hearty, pleasant way in which, wherever we drove, the tenants met or received their landlord. He had a kindly greeting for each, whether man, woman, or child. His estate is 14,000 acres in extent, of which a little fringe, chiefly on the sea-coast, can only be said to be cultivated, giving three to five acres of arable ground each to the 400 little tenants, whose rents vary from £3 to £5. In addition to the cultivated land, each village has the right of stray over a large extent of mountain land for the cattle : for this they pay a small sum per head in addition to the rents mentioned above. As compared with the rents charged in many other places, these seem very moderate. Moderate as they are, the people holding land under these favourable conditions cannot live on the little holdings without some paid labour; and the whole able-bodied population of Achill, I was informed, migrate annually to Scotland for work. Last year, as in other districts, their earnings largely failed, and this and the failure of crops have brought them down to great poverty, and left them deeply in debt to the shopkeeper for the previous year's supplies. Hence the very large number I have mentioned who are receiving relief in the island. The usual rate of interest charged here by the 'gombeen' men is 20 to 50 per cent.

" I was driven over to the Protestant settlement, and told that the smaller farmers on that property were equally indigent and in equal need of assistance. In addition to the employment given by Mr. Pike, he and his family are doing much to relieve the distress. The benefit thus rendered by one resident family is inestimable, and I heard nothing on this estate of the bitter feeling and hostility to landlords, so common elsewhere.

" Leaving the island, and coming on the mainland again, to the estate of a non-resident landlord, where the people, in addition to being in great destitution, had no one to look up to for employment or help or guidance, I was once more painfully impressed with the grievous injury resulting from the non-resident system."

I am happy to say that I was able to send help to this district from my Relief Fund, and the letters of thanks which I received, both from the Catholic and Protestant clergymen, show that Mr. Pike certainly did not overstate the distress.

It will be noted also that religion had nothing to do with the case. Protestant tenants are quite as great sufferers as Catholics by excessive rents. If they are more contented, or more "loyal" in the North, it is because they are favoured by the English Government with Ulster tenant right, and *their* trade—the linen trade—has not been crushed.

Here is the cause of the fearful effects of the Famine near Westport—again excessive rents :—

"This estate is one which, I fear, is a sample of many small ones which have been sold by the Encumbered Estates Court. It was purchased some years ago by a mere speculator, who sent down a valuer for the purpose of raising the rents to the highest point. 'He doubled them,' it is said, but probably raised them from 50 to 80 per cent. This was done without any regard to the question of improvements or reclamations of the tenants. It was merely

looked at as a question of the letting-value of each little
farm, without considering the tenant at all. When done,
the estate, with its nominally largely-increased rental, was
again sold at a large profit, and the rack-rented tenants have
grown poorer and poorer, until the calamities of last year
have brought them to the utmost verge of poverty. No
rents having been paid, processes were served, or rather,
attempted to be served, a few weeks ago. Fifty or sixty
police constables were collected to protect the process-
server. The people hearing of it, assembled from all sides
by hundreds, and, by sheer force of numbers, kept the
police at bay, whilst the villagers closed up their doorways
with timber, or brushwood, or with the near-at-hand manure
heaps. The result was that the police had to retire without
effecting their object. I heard afterwards that some processes had been served by the bailiff, and a little rent paid.

"Many of the families were seven, eight, or ten in
number, and the small weekly allowance of two stones of
Indian meal per family was hardly enough to support life.
The children especially looked thin and wan. Poor as these
people are, their kindness one to another is always striking.
Of this we saw an instance in a very small hut in which a
poor 'daft' woman lived alone, supported chiefly by her
neighbours. The hut was not more than six or seven feet
square, and had recently been very neatly re-thatched by
two of her neighbours."

Here is Mr. Tukes's account of the late Lord
Leitrim's dealings with his tenantry. The present Lord Leitrim is a very different landlord.
But again, why are Irish tenants to be at the
mercy of the caprice, or the sanity, or the
morals of their landlords? Why are they not

to be protected by law, and why are they to be called rebels and traitors, when they ask simply for the protection of law? This protection the English Government was obliged to extend to India, as we shall show presently. Why not, then, extend it to Ireland also?—

"We visited a number of cabins, from some of which the inhabitants had been capriciously evicted by the late lord. The present Lord Leitrim has permitted the people to return, and it is felt to be an act of great kindness on his part by priest and people ; but to us it appeared of doubtful future benefit, to permit people to return to the cabins which had been unroofed and ruined by the late lord, and to lands which had fallen out of cultivation, and to give no help at the same time to restore either (except, we believe, the gift of a few fir poles for the roofs). The rents, too, are, it is said, to be higher than those paid before ; yet such is the extraordinary attachment of the people to their homesteads that they are returning and patching up their miserable dwellings as best they may. The cabins, reconstructed to their own taste by the people, were absolutely windowless and quite dark. One elderly woman, who had been in service at Carrickgart, had come back alone to her ruined homestead, and out of the stones had constructed herself a hovel, in which she was living. It was doorless and windowless, and the size of a pigsty. The distress is great among the people in this townland, and they are all receiving relief. Clothing is very deficient, bedding *nil.* Relief in this district began February 9th. This Union (Milford) has adopted the Seed Act, and notices of a very clear and practical character have been sent out on the subject.

"We heard a curious instance of the late Lord Leitrim's capricious, arbitrary treatment of his tenants : In passing by a tenant's holding Lord L. noticed that a good new cabin had been built, in place of the miserable hovel. He stopped and asked how it was that he had not been consulted, and at once ordered his bailiff to pull the chimney down and partly unroof it, and the man was compelled to leave it and live in the old hovel again."

What of the moral murders that are committed in Ireland, and for which landlords and land agents are accountable ? How many evicted tenants have died from want and hardship ? How many are even now cast out on the streets of great American cities to perish slowly there ?

Here is another evidence from Mr. Tuke's pamphlet of the fact that evictions are cruel, and that rents are perpetually raised beyond all power of paying them and living :—

" *Cavan, March 11th.*—In the coffee-room the all-absorbing question of the Tenure of Land was under discussion.

" A commercial traveller said that, owing to the depression in trade, not more than half the usual number of travellers were now engaged in the West of Ireland. He gave the experience of his own family as an illustration of the need for 'fixity of tenure,' or greater security for improvements effected by tenants. His father, who formerly resided in Ulster, had built a corn-mill on land belonging to one of the London companies. When the lease expired, the rent was raised, probably not very highly ; but again he built, adding this time a flax-mill. Unfortunately for him, the rent was again raised, and the property sold by the company. The purchaser also raised the rent. Aggravated by the sense of injury done him in having to pay so dearly for his own improvements, the landlords having done nothing, he, though considerably advanced in life, determined to give up his holding and emigrate to America. He accordingly advertised his tenant-right in the property for sale, for which he expected to obtain £600. The agent for the owner, in order to oblige a person whom he wished to favour as the future tenant, gave out at the sale that the rent would in future be raised very considerably, and thus he destroyed or lessened the value of the tenant-right to such an extent that the seller only realised a very small sum. This stung the old tenant to the quick, and, aggravated by the fact that, after all, the rent was not raised, he and his wife, like so many others, left their native land with the bitterest animosity in their minds."

"Although apart from the question of Peasant Proprietorship, I may, perhaps, be allowed to add (having spent many weeks in the ' scheduled districts ' of Ireland), that I regard the right settlement of the question involved in the ' Compensation for Disturbances Bill' as of the utmost consequence to the tranquillity of the West of Ireland. Without entering into details, I can hardly refrain from asking the opponents of the measure whether they really sufficiently take into account the entirely exceptional circumstances of the distressed districts, and the wholly different character of the relation of landlord and tenant which prevails in Ireland as compared with England?

" 1. As to the actual poverty existing. The returns of the Agricultural Produce in Ireland for 1879, prepared by the Registrar-General, show 'that the depreciation in the money value of the crops for that year amounts, at its lowest esti-

mate, to £10,014.788, as compared with 1878'—a sum
nearly equal to the annual rating value of the agricultural
land of Ireland. Of this large sum, nearly one-half,
£4,238,484, is the estimated loss on the potato crop alone,
as compared with 1878, the returns showing that the quantity of potatoes was only 22,000,000 cwt., as against
60,000,000 cwt., the average for ten years—a most alarming
decrease. In addition to this, very severe losses have been
sustained in cattle, not only from heavy casualties, but also
from a great depreciation in prices, owing in part to the
forced sales, and inability of those around to purchase. I
heard of sheep selling at 10s. or less, and small cows at £3
to £5. Nor must the heavy losses sustained by the tens of
thousands of men, who annually come for employment to
England or Scotland, and who, last year, returned home
without any wages, be overlooked. I believe the estimate
of a loss of a million sterling to be under the exact figures.
When to this is added the inability to obtain the usual
credit from the shopkeeper, whose debts for the previous
year were unpaid, I think the extreme poverty of the little
Western farmer cannot be doubted.

"2. As to the difference in the relations between landlord and tenant in the two countries. In the one we have
the *landlord* who has built the house and other buildings,
and let his land drained and fenced and cultivated. In the
other, the West of Ireland, we have the *tenant*, whose
families have lived on the same lands for generations, who
have reclaimed whatever land has been reclaimed, and cultivated whatever is cultivated, and built whatever is built of
home or out-buildings, and who, in consequence, feels that
he has a vested right in the soil, which, even out of Ulster,
he can in ordinary times sell to an incoming tenant.

"Is there not some claim, on the part of this tenant, for
consideration, if, under the very exceptional circumstances,

he is unable to pay his rent, and has, in consequence, notice to quit?

" Nor is it easy to prove a correct estimate in England of the extreme hardships of eviction in a country where the only resource for the evicted family is either the roadside or the workhouse—it may be twenty, or thirty, or forty miles distant. In my recent visit I came upon several villages where processes had either been served or attempted to be served, and heard of many others, some of which have a public notoriety from the conflicts which have taken place with the Constabulary, ending in serious injuries on both sides. In addition, it did not appear to be in any way concealed by many landlords that they intended to evict for non-payment of rent, and it was often reported that the number of summonses applied for was without precedent.

" The task which the Chief Secretary for Ireland is called upon to attempt, and to which he brings, in addition to his great abilities as a statesman, the highest sense of duty and the determination to act with justice to all, whether poor or rich, is one before which a less able man, or one less devoted to duty, might well quail ; and for him, there may well come times when he begins to shrink from the thankless task, in face of the determined opposition of his opponents, or the defection or cool support of his friends, and the worrying of a small body of determined men, who, under the guise of friends to Ireland, daily prove themselves her enemies.[1]

Is it any matter of surprise that Irish industries and manufactures fail, and are our people to bear all the blame, when we find discouragement in the present, and positive prohibition in the past?

[1] Mr. Tuke, in *Nineteenth Century* for August, 1880.

CHAPTER XI.

THE SOCIAL RELATIONS BETWEEN LANDLORDS
AND TENANTS.

"I am convinced that confusion and disaster will continue to mark the relation between the islands, till Englishmen confront the facts courageously, and with a determination to discover the springhead from which discord flows."—Gavan Duffy.

I AM convinced that if the unworthy devices resorted to by landlords and land agents were once known to the public as they are, that there would be a cry of indignation. But they are not known, and who is to proclaim the miserable story ? How men bearing the name of gentlemen can degrade themselves so low, is a mystery. There is no public opinion to bring them face to face with their miserable selfishness. Hence, they are probably blinded to it. They act as men would do in a foreign land with savage tribes, rather than as Christian gentlemen with Christian men. These acts of theirs which are so unworthy, are, indeed, noticed and exposed from time to time in local papers. But this concerns them little. Nothing is known in

England, where public opinion would soon see it at an end. Nor, possibly, are these acts so dishonourable as they appear. These gentlemen have the traditions of centuries to support them in treating the Irish people as outside the pale of English law. They have the traditions of centuries to support them in getting all they possibly can out of their dependants, and treating them as an inferior race, fit only to be used as serfs. What they would not do, probably, even if they dare do it, on their English estates, they do as a matter of course in Ireland. Yet Ireland is taunted with disloyalty, and with not being devoted to a Government which certainly has done little to give her common justice.

Sir Gavan Duffy, in his recent work on Ireland, says :—

"At present they [the English people] see with amazement and dismay a whole people who profess to have no confidence in their equity, who proclaim that they do not expect fair play from them, and who fall into ecstacies of triumph over some disaster abroad or embarrassment at home which endangers or humiliates the Empire ; and they will not take the obvious means of comprehending this phenomenon."

This is the unhappy truth. The great majority of the English people are so perfectly satisfied "they know all about Ireland," that they will not take the trouble of informing themselves. They do not know how completely they are led by preconceived opinions; still less have they even an idea how wrong their preconceived opinions are. English gentlemen send me over English papers with paragraphs strongly marked, but only such paragraphs are so noted as agree with their own preconceived opinions. To-day I have a *Times* sent me by an English gentleman, who I know in his own fashion wishes well to Ireland, but hapless prejudice has so blinded him as to render him actually incapable of reasoning fairly. He marks passages in English papers where we are told that capital is being driven out of Ireland by agitators, which, no doubt, he believes. But *what* capital has been driven out? or who is being driven out? Whenever there is an agitation in Ireland we are assured that some mysterious and beneficent individual has just been on the point of doing something very wonderful for Ireland, but all his good intentions are defeated by those dreadful agitators. We have lost, it is insinuated, what would for ever more have given peace and prosperity to Ireland, and it is all our own fault, and we do not deserve to have anything more done for us !

But somehow this mysterious benefactor, this wonderful merchant prince, always selects an unfortunate time for doing this wonderful good to Ireland. In peaceful intervals we never hear of him, and, yet strange to say, we are begging such persons to come always, or better still, we are asking permission to develop our industrial resources, to extend, for example, our fisheries, and yet we cannot get help. But there is always this mysterious capitalist who hovers in the misty skies of incipient "risings," and vanishes in our hours of peace. What marvel is it if Irishmen who know that he is a myth conjured up at a special time for a special purpose, have lost confidence in English justice and in English truth.

Then, there are " the best friends of Ireland" who are always driven out of Ireland (by the English press) at this particular time. We never hear who they are. One of our great complaints is that Irish landlords will not live in Ireland. We never get the name of any individual landlord compelled to flee the country. But, yes, I mistake, now and then an English paper is rash enough to name an injured and marked landlord. Lord Kenmare, for example, was shot at (in the English papers) but as his lordship denied the accusation promptly, generalities had to be resorted to again. Still, these writers have the courage of their opinions. If one landlord denies being shot at, or compelled to go into exile and leave a thankless people on whom he has lavished untold favours, there is always the resource of falling back on generalities, and that answers all the purpose with a public prepared to believe them. There is no one to contradict what is said of every one. But is *this* the way to make Ireland love England ? Nay, rather, is this the way to make Ireland respect England ?

We have already given so many specimens of this style of calumny, of this grave injury which the English people are doing to themselves, that more seems scarcely necessary. Yet, as the following speaks directly on the subject of the social relations between landlord and tenant, we append it here.

"Lord Lucan writes to the editor of the *Daily News :*—

"'SIR,—My attention has been called to your paper of Saturday last, the 30th October, in which your Special Commissioner, in a letter from Castlebar of Oct. 28th, alluding to me, states that 'The popular party gloat over the spectacle of an aged peer compelled to ride over his "amateur" Castlebar farm attended by a brace of constables to protect him from public vengeance.' I am happy to be able to state that you have never attempted to circulate a grosser untruth. I have never received, never required, and

most certainly never desired, any police protection whatever. During the forty years that I have been active in the
discharge of my public and private business—more fortunate
than many others in Mayo—I have never been offered by
anybody, in writing or otherwise, one word menacing or
offensive.' "

What is to be said of the hope of any justice
being done for Ireland by England when the
special of an English paper who is supposed to
have come to Ireland for the express purpose
of writing facts, writes to his paper, and for the
English public, what a nobleman characterises as
the "grossest untruth." And that this should
be done by the *Daily News*, is certainly a painful sign of the times. Society papers, which
write exclusively to please the upper classes,
may be pardoned for keeping up a delusion
which helps to support their existence, and they
do not send out special correspondents. But
the *Daily News*, which is supposed to be a
Liberal paper, might at least be expected to do
justice to the cause of an oppressed people.

Again, I ask sensible Englishmen, is it any
matter of surprise, not that there is discontent
in Ireland, but that there is so little hope of redress from England. If popular organs of English opinion persist in writing what is false, what
is, in truth, so outrageously false, about the relations between Irish landlords and their tenants,

what hope is there that the Irish people will obtain a fair hearing from England? And what an injustice all this is to England.

There is a remarkable similarity between the relationships of landlords and tenants as they were, till quite recently, in Bengal, and as they are now in Ireland.

The subject is one of immense importance, and it is one which demands the most careful consideration of the English people. We shall enter into this more fully in another chapter; but in connection with the present subject we may remark that it was obliged actually to be made *illegal* for an English landlord in Bengal to exact any excess above the legal rate of rent.

Now, let us see how Gladstone's Act is evaded in Ireland.

Mr. William Barry, of Carrigtwohill, County Cork, was examined before the present Land Commissioners. This gentleman farms 286 acres of land (statute measure). He was appointed by the Midleton Board of Guardians as a deputation along with General Roche. He said :—

"Lord Bessborough asked what Mr. Barry thought of the operation of the Land Act of 1870.

"Mr. Barry said he considered the Land Act one of the best measures ever introduced into Ireland if it had not been evaded. In every instance he knew in the granting of new leases the tenant was contracted out of the Act. This was especially the case as regards the county cess, which is now added on as an addition to the rent. He would suggest that all clauses and provisions in future leases, depriving the tenant of the benefit of the present or any future Land Act, should be declared void. Mr. Barry continued to say that improvements had been made by the tenant; and in some instances, by large landed proprietors, farmsteads had been erected and drainings carried out, but at the expense of the tenant, by reason of an addition to his rent. Mr. Barry proceeded to remark that it was deplorable to witness the ignorance which the great majority of the landed proprietors in Ireland, and of the agents also, displayed as to the productiveness of their properties. This, he believed, led to considerable misunderstandings between them and their tenants on the question of rent. A tenant complains of holding at an exhorbitant rent, and he has to apply for a revaluation to a man who has no practical knowledge of the value of the article he is about to put a price on. As a practical farmer he had been appealed to in many cases of late years to give his opinion, and he had been the means of settling many disputes between landlord and tenant. . This greatly strengthened his opinions as to the necessity of having a Board of impartial and practical men to adjust rents between landlord and tenant."

We, in Ireland, are called "lawless;" but who are the lawless class in Ireland? Might we not expect an example of respecting law from Irish landlords, and yet they are, as a class the most notorious—I will not say "law breakers"—but law evaders in Ireland.

The Devon Commission in its report, in 1847, said :—

"That the safety of the country and the respective interests of both classes call loudly for a cautious but *immediate* adjustment of the grave questions at issue. . . In every district of the country we find that a widely spread and daily increasing confusion exists ; and it is impossible to reject the conclusion that, unless they be distinctly defined and respected, much social disorder and national inconvenience must *inevitably be the consequence.*"

Mr. Bright wrote thus as late as 1868 :—

"ROCHDALE,
"*January 27th*, 1868.

"MY DEAR SIR,—I have read the 'proposals' over with great interest and care. They are wide, and embrace the whole Irish difficulty, and, if adopted, would at once apply a remedy to the two branches of the grand question. For twenty years I have always said that the only way to remedy the evils of Ireland is by legislation on the Church and the Land. But we are met still with this obstacle, even yet, I fear, insurmountable, that the legislation must come from and through a Parliament which is not Irish, and in which every principle essential for the regeneration of Ireland is repudiated. The knowledge of this makes me hesitate as to the wisdom of your 'proposals' in their present shape. I fear the scheme is so broad, and so good, and so complete, that Parliament would stand aghast at it. To strike down an Established Church, and to abandon the theory of our territorial system by one Act of Parliament would be too much for Parliament, and would destroy any Government that suggested it. I can conceive a condition

of things in Ireland under which such a great change might
be accomplished—if Ireland were united in demanding it,
and were menacing Great Britain if it should be refused;
but now, I suspect our rulers, though uncomfortable, are not
sufficiently alarmed to yield. The English people are in
complete ignorance of Irish wrongs, and know little or
nothing of the real condition of your country. This is a sad
picture, but it is not coloured too darkly."

In 1870 Ireland got a Land Act. Slow,
indeed, was the process by which the ignorance
of Ireland was removed, which made it at last
known that such an Act was necessary. ·No
doubt the Act was one of great benefit; but let
English people say what they think of Irish
landlords who evade the laws made for them in
England, and actually render the Act of no
avail to the very persons whom it was made to
protect.

What shall be said of the honour of these
gentlemen; and yet, "they are all honourable
men."

Let it be distinctly understood that evasion
of this Act, in one form or another, and often
in many forms, is the usual custom of Irish and
Anglo-Irish landlords in Ireland. Ireland is
governed by those gentlemen, and by their
arbitrary "estate rules," and not by English
law. Ireland asks to be governed by English
law; those gentlemen, naturally, prefer their

own code, which has many of the miseries of a feudal system without any of its mercies.   Will England tolerate this longer?   Are Englishmen to expend enormous sums in Ireland for military force and police officials, in order to enable certain gentlemen to carry out an arbitrary code of oppressive private regulations?

And all this is to be done for the doubtful benefit of a few gentlemen.   The *Freeman's Journal*, commenting on the recent visits of excited landlords to Dublin Castle, says :—

" Out of a population of 5,300,000, 4,300,000 are reckoned as the agricultural population of Ireland. These millions are in a vast majority of cases completely dependent upon the land for support, and it may be said *a priori* that if there is any country in the world in which it is desirable to have a large and widely distributed body of yeoman proprietors, that country is Ireland. Such proprietors, wherever they exist, are always found to be Conservative in the best sense of the word, deeply interested in public peace and order, self-denying and saving, prosperous and contented. But how can there be any sufficient number of such owners in Ireland when twelve men hold in the aggregate 1,297,888 acres, and it is possible for a hundred individuals to represent half the land?   Nor is it only that so large a portion of the soil is in the hands of a few. A large proportion of the great landowners of Ireland are absentees, spending nothing among their tenants and neighbours—taking everything out and putting nothing in. The total value of the rent of Ireland, as given in the return called for by Mr. Bright, is £10,180,000. Of this sum not less than £3,000,000 is paid annually out of Ireland to proprietors who never reside there—to the persons represented by the deputation of Thursday. In the course of their interview with the Lord Lieutenant, the spokesman of the landlords thought fit to say that they should in future keep away 'from the discharge of any public duties.' A curious conception of what is required of men in their position at a critical period of their country's history, but entirely in accordance with the traditions of Irish landlordism. The marvel is that landlords on this side of the Channel should be anxious to make common cause with individuals who are, as a body, as neglectful of their duty to their country as they are regardless of the just claims of the tillers of the soil. The English proprietor, though he takes much, gives not a little in return both to his country and his property; but what do the hundred representatives of 'half the property of Ireland' give to the one or the other?" [1]

Unquestionably it is time for the people of England to have a clear idea of the causes of Irish discontent. Excessive rent is, no doubt, one great cause, but the whole subject of landlord government of Ireland is a great cause; and not the least extraordinary part of the extra-

---

[1] Of the whole 20,327,764 acres which form the area of the island, nearly *one-half* is owned by 740 persons, apportioned thus: 4,152,142 by 110 persons, 2,607,719 by 193, and 3,071,471 by 440 others. Against this the last census shows that 5,250,000 persons own *not a rood*, and that 94,000 families (averaging from six to seven each, or, in all, nearly one-tenth of the whole population) inhabit one-roomed huts of about twelve feet square, while the absentee rents drawn from the country, and chiefly spent abroad, amount to nearly £9,000,000 a year.

ordinary social history of Ireland is the fact that
on occasions English writers, even in the press,
admit the whole case.

"In 1847, property in Ireland (said the *Times*) is ruled
with most savage and tyrannical sway. The landlords there
exercise their rights with a rod of iron, and neglect their
duties with a face of brass. And again, eleven years later,
when publishing the remarkable exposures of abuse made
by its special commissioner in 1858 : ‘For generations the
proprietors of the land in Ireland have been Spartans among
a helot peasantry, almost planters among negro slaves.’ In
1868 Mr. Butt bore witness : ‘Nearly the whole peasant
population of Ireland hold their farms as tenants at will.
Never in the worst days of the penal laws were the occupiers so much at the mercy of the proprietors. Imperfect
as the protection was which he formerly received, even that
little is now gone. . . . And this power is now wielded
mercilessly by the majority of Irish landlords. On some of
the estates tenants dare not. harbour in their houses a
stranger, a poor person, or even a poor relative not immediately belonging to the family. Nor can marriages be contracted without the sanction of the landlord or his agent.
Many of the landlords serve notices to quit regularly every
gale day after they have received their rents, in order to
keep eternally in their hands the power of immediate eviction. Can slavery be more completely established than
this ? Can industry make its way under such circumstances ?
Can enterprise do aught to lift these poor serfs ? Can
capital venture out in a community so unsettled, so oppressed, so unsafe ? Landed property in Ireland can show
us no title which requires us to tolerate such a terrible condition of society.’"

—

Even Mr. Froude is compelled to admit that :—

"The landlords of Ireland represent conquest and confiscation, and they have gone on with an indifference to the welfare of the people that would never have been tolerated in England or Scotland."

But more valuable than anything that precedes, is the testimony of Lord Dufferin—himself one of the best of Irish landlords—in his speech last year in the House of Lords :—

"What," he said, "is the spectacle presented to us by Ireland? It is that of millions of persons, whose only dependence and whose chief occupation is agriculture for the most part cultivating their lands, that is, sinking their past, their present, and their future upon yearly tenancies. But what is a yearly tenancy? Why, it is an impossible tenure—a tenure which, if its terms were to be literally interpreted, no Christain man would offer, and none but a madman would accept."

Yet such is the tenure under which more than 75 per cent. of the 600,000 tenant farmers of Ireland—who with their families number one-third of the whole population—now occupy their holdings. [1]

"To go back little more than a century and a half ago, Swift then testified as to the state of things in his day:

---

[1] *Irish Land Reform*, Fraser, March, 1880.

'Another cause of this [Irish] nation's misery is that Egyptian bondage of cruel, oppressive, covetous landlords, expecting all who live under them should make bricks without straw, who grieve and envy when they see a tenant of their own in a whole coat, or able to afford one comfortable meal in a month, by which the spirits of the people are broken and made fit for slavery—the farmers and cottagers being almost through the whole kingdom, to all intents and purposes, as real beggars as any of those to whom we give our charity in the streets.' "

Is it any matter of surprise that a people so used should rebel, and that they are so used the present Land Commission will prove past all possibility of dispute or denial.

CHAPTER XII.

(Continued.)

"Ten years ago, Bishop Nulty, having witnessed the heart-rending
scenes at an eviction, went home and wrote a pastoral, in which he said
that the sentence of an eviction on each of these tenants amounted to a
sentence of death."—*Cork Examiner,* November, 1880.

BUT grave as is this injustice to the Irish
tenants, by which his landlord, noble or
esquire, obliges him to sign a document
for the purpose of depriving him of the benefit
of the laws made by England for his protection,
there are other social injustices, may I not say
frauds.

And here let me answer one favourite objection of Irish landlords. It was made to myself
both by Lord Lansdowne and his agent, Mr.
Trench. Both said that some of the tenants on
Lord Lansdowne's estates had been offered
leases and had refused them. I know further
that many Irish landlords have used this same
plea of justification, a plea to prevent legislation, which they seem to dread as much as the

poor desire it.   If they are willing to give their tenants leases, why do they object to do so under legal regulations ?

But, it will be said, why do Irish tenants refuse leases? Simply because when they do get a lease, except in some rare cases, they are obliged to deprive themselves of their legal rights.   Because, in some cases now, they hope against hope that a fair and just land law may be given them by the English people ; because, alas ! they dread with a dread the fruit of centuries of injustice, that there will be some evasion to their disadvantage in any dealings with their landlords.

I must confess that I know the ignorance of the English people on the social state of Ireland so well, that I can scarcely expect to be believed..   And yet facts are not less facts because they are doubted.

That Mr. Gladstone's Act is perpetually evaded to the grievous loss of the tenant for whom it is intended, I have given proof past dispute.   I might multiply this proof, but to what avail ?

Let me now give proof of how this dread of overreaching on the part of landlords has acted in this very famine year, and show how painfully just the apprehensions of the people were. It was announced that in order to give employment in the Famine, Government would give loans to Irish lands, and Irish landlords were suspiciously willing to accept these loans. Irish landlords were held up as models of virtue for giving employment to their tenants. But the tenants were not grateful at first. I must admit that I feel indignant myself that those for whom I had laboured hard to provide actually necessary food—food required for bare existence—should be so shamelessly idle as to refuse employment. The landlord made a wonderful complaint, and, until we heard the other side, how just it seemed! Here was, indeed, an exemplification of Irish laziness and Irish ingratitude. The following paragraph from the *Kerry Sentinel* will explain the tenants' side of the question, and will show how, even in a time of dire distress, the first object of too many Irish landlords was to get their property improved at the expense of their tenants, and, it will hardly be credited, to make their tenants actually pay in perpetuity for it. Is it then any matter of surprise that Irish tenants are *not* devoted to landlords or land agents ?

"Some persons are disposed to look upon the present depression in Ireland as a harbinger of good to the farming classes. They suppose that it has opened the eyes of Irish landlords to the evil effects which must result from excessive rents and wholesale eviction of the peasantry. There could be no greater mistake. The landlords of Ireland are the only class of the community who will benefit by the Famine. The merchants, the traders, and the artizans of America, France, and Australia, are supporting their tenantry for them at present—helping them over the bad times—while not one penny goes out of the landlords' pockets for their relief; and when the present deeper gloom clears off, the oppressive rack-rent on the Irish farmers resumes its gradual crushing functions again. The landlords are wonderfully benefitting themselves by the trying exigencies of the occasion. Lately we had occasion to refer to the conduct of the M'Gillicuddy of the Reeks, who has got his tenants to sign an agreement to pay 8 per cent. for the money for which he pays 3½ per cent. for a certain number of years, but the principle is then discharged ; whereas there appears to be no hope that there will be a termination to the burden of 8 per cent. and 10 per cent. imposed on the tenants. But the M'Gillycuddy is not the only landlord who seems determined to benefit by the 'charity' which the Government seems to think it is extending towards Irish farmers. Will anyone believe that the most noble Marquis of Lansdowne is charging his tenants *five* per cent. on the money which he has borrowed on the terms we have before stated, and the 5 per cent. is put on as a *permanent* increase of rent. We have heard even Kerry landlords express their disgust at the course pursued by The M'Gillicuddy. Will the exalted position of the Marquis of Lansdowne save him from the odium which honest men are disposed to attach to such proceedings? But the Marquis is determined to benefit by the Government loans in another way. Hitherto, lime was given to the tenant farmers at Kenmare for 1s. per barrel to all who took 100 barrels of it. Now, with the increased facilities which Government gives to landlords, the tenants on the Marquis' property have to sign a written agreement that they will pay, in the form of an increase of rent, one penny per barrel for every barrel of lime which they take. This is percentage with a vengeance. We see a placard posted up in Tralee at present announcing that Mr. J. T. Trench, agent to the Marquis, is to deliver a Gospel Address in the Protestant Hall this evening. Now, it seems to us that Mr. Trench would be doing a great deal of Scriptural good if he gave the Marquis (and himself) a lecture on the Scriptural condemnation of usury, such as we have described."

But, lest it should be supposed that this peculiar style of giving charitable employment in the Famine was confined to Kerry, I add the following, which was published in the *Cork Examiner.* I had also a private communication from Mr. Irwin on the subject :—

"Strand House, Clonakilty,

"*August 24th*, 1880.

"Dear Sir,—A few days ago I was shown a printed document, the copy of which I annex, viz. :—

"'Land Improvement.—I hereby agree that I will pay Arthur H. Smith Barry Esq., interest at the rate of £3 8s. 6d. per cent. on any sum expended by him in drainage effected on my holding in——; such interest to be added to my rent from the 1st day of May, 1882, and to be recoverable as part of it, and in same manner and with same powers of recovery; and I also admit that I shall have no claim against said landlord or his successors in respect to the principal sum expended by him in such improvements, or any claim in respect to them under the Landlord and Tenant Act,

1870, simply undertaking to pay interest at the rate of
£3 8s. 6d. per cent. on the outlay.

    " ' Dated this——day of————18 .
    " ' Signed,   ——————.
    " ' Witness,   ——————.
    " ' The interest to be payable for thirty-five years, from
1st May, 1882.'

    "Leaving you, sir, to comment on the above precious
document,

                " I beg to remain,

                    " Your very obedient servant,

                        "T. W. IRWIN."

It was proved in evidence before the present
Land Commission, that the Earl of Cork inserts
a clause in his leases depriving his tenants of
compensation under the Land Bill.   But there
is a lower depth.

If men like Mr. Smith Barry and Lord Cork,
and Lord Lansdowne, and The M'Gillicuddy,
deprive their tenants—"the mere Irish,"—of
the benefit of English law, they do not require
" duty work " and other " straws " which add so
heavily to the burthen of the unhappy and
much maligned Irish tenant.

Again, I quote from undisputed and public
documents.

The following letter was published in the
Cork Examiner, in September, (1880) :—

"THE BAWNMORE EVICTION.

"TO THE EDITOR OF THE CORK EXAMINER.

" DEAR SIR,—There are so..e facts in connection with the above case of eviction that have not yet been brought to light, and as they may not come under the notice of the Land Commission, I ask you to permit me to place them before the public through the medium of your columns. I do so, thinking that there are many cases as hard and cruel which will never be known to any Commission, or to the community at large, but which, on this very account, have intensified the hostility of the farming classes to its present point against the system under which they have suffered so patiently and so long.

"The holding in question is nine acres in extent, and is situated in the Townland of Bawnmore, which is the highest and hardest soil in the Parish of Kanturk. Cussen, the elder, father of the evicted tenant, came into possession of the farm forty-eight years ago, paying at that time £17 fine, and a rent of 30s. an acre, exactly 50 per cent. over Griffith's valuation. In addition to this, he was obliged to supply once every two years one cwt. of pork or bacon to the landlord, Mr. Tom Leader, and to deposit, carriage free, the said supply at the landlord's residence, some fifty miles away from the hill of Bawnmore. This continued to be exacted till the old landlord's death, and with such strictness was the flesh insisted on, that an equivalent in money would not be received in its stead. Master and tenant passed to their rest, and the evicted man, young Cussen, came into possession and struggled hard for many years to pay his rent and support his aged mother on the holding. The past severe seasons crushed them. They could make nothing, beyond a miserable existence, from the land, and though the present proprietor made the very magnificent reduction of five per

cent. on his property last winter, Cussen was exempted from
the provisions of this gracious act, inasmuch as he was in
arrears as to rent. A month or six weeks ago the law was put
in force against him, and this was done in a very unusi a
form. The room where the old mother had lived for hail
a century was levelled, and she and her son were obliged
to rest in a dilapidated barn, the roof of which is almost
swept away by the storms that rage round that elevated and
highly-rented region. The force of public opinion has now
left the land without a tenant, and in that condition it is
likely to remain till some consideration is shown to the
family who occupied it for fifty years, and on whose labours
and bacon the proprietors so long lived and fattened.

"I remain, yours faithfully,

"SPECTATOR."

As the name of Mr. Hussey has been much
before the public as a land agent, and as he has
obtained a ready hearing in the *Times*, I append
a short article from the *Freeman's Journal*,
which will show that his cause is not always as
just as he would wish to make it appear :—

"The causes which have led up the present crisis in the
country are well illustrated in a case which came before the
County Court Judge of West Cork on Tuesday last. The
case was one of those to which allusion was made by Mr.
Healy in his speech at Bantry, for which he has been prosecuted. The parties to it were two farmers named Tobin
and Hennegan, the plaintiffs, and the Earl of Kenmare, the
defendant. The facts of the case were briefly these—that
Tobin took a farm from the Earl of Kenmare as far back as

1848, at £36 a year. The farm was subsequently divided with a man named Sullivan, each party paying half the rent. The Earl of Kenmare some time ago offered a lease of the farm for a fine of £90, and Tobin sent in a cheque for the amount. Meanwhile, however, a change had taken place in the agency. Mr. Hussey was appointed to the office, and he induced Tobin to take back his money and sign a release. When this was done Tobin was asked to pay an increased rent, and, failing to do so, was evicted. The other tenant, Sullivan, did not sign the release, and was therefore able to hold possession. Hennegan's share in the transaction was not very clear. The defence was that the farm was originally underlet, and that Tobin would have been permitted to sell his interest if he had agreed to give back a sum which it was said he had borrowed from Sullivan to pay the fine asked in consideration of the lease. After Tobin was evicted the farm was let at £30 a year, and a fine of £250 paid. This shows how eager was the competition for land at the time. The judge did not see any justification for the course pursued towards Tobin in these circumstances. It was plainly a case of capricious eviction, and he regretted that he could not, under the Act, award a larger amount of compensation than he did. He gave a decree for the maximum amount under the scale—five years'—less a year's rent due at the time of the ejectment."

It would be well if those who are now struggling so fiercely for a retention of the present Land Law on the statute books would ponder over these facts. Let them remember that the state of things now revealed is going on over hundreds of estates all over Ireland, and they can hardly wonder that the Land

Question has at last reached a dangerous crisis.[1]

If I go into this subject at some length, it is because I am convinced it is one of the greatest importance.

There is too general an impression that the whole cause of Irish discontent is Irish laziness. That even if rents are a little high, that they could be paid by excessive industry and thrift. But the English people have yet to learn that rents are more than excessive, that they are too often ruinous; and they have to learn what I have stated above, that there is a system of deliberately taking advantage of the tenant at every turn, of putting every burthen on him, and of even depriving him of his absolute legal rights.

Here is another evidence of this evil and miserable system, on high and important authority.

Mr. H. C. Marmion, of Skibbereen, is a land agent, a landlord, and a tenant farmer; hence, he is in a position peculiarly competent to form an opinion on these vexed questions. I ask a

---

[1] The Rev. P. Hill, P. P., Skibbereen, giving evidence before the Land Commission in Cork, said: "Judges were disposed to take a landlord's view in the administration of the land laws.—November, (1880).

very careful consideration of his evidence, given
before the Land Commission, at Skibbereen,
in November (1880.

" He handed in the following statement in evidence:—I
hereby declare that the tenant farmers never will be happy,
prosperous, and contented until they are secured in their
farms at fair rents, and protected from capricious evictions.
I am confirmed in this opinion by my own experience,
having given on the Castletownsend estate 300 leases in
the year 1869; the term of each farming lease being 61
years, and the building leases 300 years. Those leases were
given at an average of about 15 per cent. over the Poor Law
Valuation. During the following five years I believe more
improvements were made than for a half century previously,
and I felt no difficulty in collecting the rental. I believe,
also, that so far from those leases damaging the landlord's
interest, that the result has been exactly the contrary. I
take the Castletownsend estate as my model, having had for
several years unlimited control in its management, for which
I received the warm acknowledgments of the then owner.
When I contrast the state of the tenantry on this estate with
others where rents have been repeatedly raised, and the
tenants charged for their own improvements, the consequences are apparent—the people are poorer, discontented,
and cease to be industrious. Another fruitful source of
discontent is the utter want of sympathy which the landlord
class, as a body, entertain towards their tenantry, particularly during the last three disastrous years. With very few
exceptions, the landlord is scarcely ever seen upon the lands,
and, save when the tenant is called upon to pay his rent, he
is only known to the landlord by name, and is never the
recipient of any mark of consideration at his landlord's

hands. This estrangement produces a feeling of degradation and disgust, and leaves the tenant to conclude (oft' too
truly) that his landlord favours more his domestic animals.
Another source of discontent is what is called the 'rule of
the estate.' That rule is necessarily arbitrary, often capricious, and frequently unjust. I know of two brothers named
Sullivan (Cumba) who purchased from a needy neighbour
his holding, for £30. They would not be recognised as
tenants, though perfectly solvent and exceedingly industrious,
and they lost their money. On the same estate, some
farms, when they get into the landlord's hands, are let by
auction for grazing plots annually. This is a very mischievous practice, and breeds discontent. To show you the
extent to which rack-renting is carried upon some estates,
and the excessive and cruel means adopted to enforce it, I
will give an instance or two. I hand you a lease called
'Richard J. Campion's compound form.' Notwithstanding
the sounding name, the rent is anything but agreeable to
the poor, struggling tenant. The rent is £23, the Poor-law
valuation, £9 10s. I know another holding, held under
the same agent's (R. J. Campion's) management, where the
rent was £16 16s. Mr. Campion sent the tenant a lease to
execute, raising the rent to £30. The tenant refused and
protested, and what was Mr. Campion's written reply?
That, if the lease was not executed before ten o'clock next
day, the rent would be raised to £40. I respectfully invite
your perusal of some of the clauses of this lease. I know
other estates where the rent is double the valuation;
without compulsory powers for valuation, I do not see a
remedy for this state of things. I am of opinion that fair
rents and fixity of tenure, with free right of sale to a solvent
successor, would make the Irish tenantry loyal, industrious,
peaceable and happy. I have raised in the local banks
upwards of £100,000 for tenants, and I have had but three

defaulters, one of whom is a magistrate for the county. There are little or no improvements made where the tenant holds from year to year. Emigration has drained the country of its best blood. While condemning bad landlords, I am happy to say I know several good ones. Drainage and improving the breeds of cattle should be encouraged. Conciliation, not coercion, should be the order of the day."

There is one feature noted in this very clear statement on the social relations between landlord and tenant which has, I think, it may safely be said, received no consideration; and it is one bearing seriously on the whole state of Ireland. Mr. Marriner says, " A fruitful source of discontent is the utter want of sympathy which the landlord class as a body entertain towards the tenantry." The whole of this paragraph given above demands a very thoughtful consideration.

There is a common, and not unnatural, idea in England, that if a man is evicted for non-payment of rent, the eviction must be a just one. In Mr. Russell's letters to the *Daily Telegraph* he further mentions a case of eviction under circumstances of singular oppression ; and yet in the very next issue of that paper his statement was attacked on the ground that an eviction for rent *must* be a thing of the past.

It is this terrible ignorance about Irish affairs

which leads English people so seriously astray. Not unnaturally, they consider "that a man," as they say, "ought to pay his rent." Certainly, he ought—if he could. The non-payment of rent is looked upon naturally as the repudiation of, or failure to meet, any ordinary debt would be. But the circumstances are wholly different in Ireland. We have said—it has been said by far higher authority than ours—that there is no freedom of contract in Ireland.

I think it may be said, with little exaggeration, that the freedom of contract between landlord and tenant in Ireland is like the freedom of contract between a highwayman and his victim; the only difference being the elevated social rank of the landlord, and the public protection and approbation which his threatening demands receive.

The highwayman demands your money or your life. There is a choice, certainly, but the choice is not very desirable. In Ireland, too often, the landlord demands of his victim his money—his all—or his life, also. For, if a man has no choice left him except eviction, or a rent which will not enable him to live in common decency, he must sacrifice what is dearer than life.

That such is the case in Ireland is but too

well known, for it is simply an every-day occurrence. In England, unhappily, it will not be believed that noblemen and gentlemen would act thus. But the fact is none the less true, because it is not credited. At the same sitting of the Commission, from which we quoted evidence above :—

"Mr. Tarr was examined, and gave evidence with respect to his own eviction from a large farm held under Lord Middleton. The farm contained 417 acres, but a large quantity of it was under timber, and of no use to him. The rent when he took the farm was £350, but when the lease lapsed it was raised to £475, the valuation being £405. He felt the farm would not pay such a rent. Then, why did you take the farm? I had a young family, and I did not wish to be disturbed, so I agreed to the terms. I complained at the time, but I thought if the times were good, I might be able to pay the rent. The seasons having proved the reverse, I was not able to pay a year and a-half's rent; I was also made a bankrupt of, in consequence of a statement made to the bank that my creditors were to look for compensation; the landlord made a counter claim against them for dilapidation."

Here is a plain indisputable case. Mr. Tarr had the traveller's choice from the highwayman. No doubt, those Irish tenants who hold land, or rather who try to keep their homes on such conditions, are to be blamed. But who shall apportion the blame between the tempter and the tempted?

And it is obvious that this system of perpetually raising rent must cause general bankruptcy, misery, and distress.

. No; what is needed in Ireland is not coercion laws for these unhappy tenants at will, but rather protection laws both for them and for their landlords, for in truth these same landlords need the protection of common law, since they will not use the protection of common sense, to win them from the inevitable evils of their own avarice. And let it be remembered that it is not themselves or Ireland alone which is injured by this unhappy system; England will and must inevitably suffer bitterly for it in the end.

Here are the words of an Irish gentleman, a magistrate and a Protestant, words which English gentlemen would do well to consider very seriously. Writing to the *Freeman's Journal,* Nov. 10th, 1880, he says :—

"I beg to tell the *Express* that the class of Irishmen to which I belong is the class who seek to stay the evictor's hand, to prevent the sad and heart-rending scenes of extermination and depopulation. Witnessing the ruthless expulsion not of tens, but of hundreds, of families turned out of house and home, no house or farm to get, and no trade or profession to turn to whereby to earn a livelihood for their families, no prospect but the poorhouse—it was witnessing those scenes that led me to raise my voice against eviction. I sat on the bedside of an exterminator half an hour after his back was plough ed up by the slugs of the assassin. There was no Land League then. I said to him, " The law ought not leave you the power of endangering your own life.' He said the land was his own ; could he not dig it into the sea if he liked ? That is the doctrine of the class, I won't say of Irishmen, but of men holding land in Ireland represented by the *Express.* I never belonged to them. I belong to a class who grieve to see their countrymen in a state of chronic starvation, who grieve to see the hat going round the world to save them from starvation, who grieve to see a peasantry living on the most fertile lands, their existence depending on the absence of an extra summer shower or autumn flood, without one accumulated meal to fall back upon.

" I have had opportunities of knowing this fact in this, the Athlone Union, of which I have the honour of being vice-chairman. On one day in February last I allocated charitable funds to feed eight thousand four hundred and twenty people. If allying myself with a party who endeavour to have the laws that we believe have brought the peasantry to that miserable condition changed, the statute laws of eviction done away with, thereby fixing the tenant while paying a fair rent in the land, makes me unworthy of the class the *Express* represents, I am quite content, but I must repudiate the charge of being a deserter from the ranks in which I never served, and never shall, while they maintain the right of any man to exterminate and depopulate the country.

" As to the last charge of being unworthy of the creed I profess. That creed is Protestant Christianity. That creed teaches me to do good, even on the Sabbath ; and I believe to raise my voice on the Sabbath against the extermination of the Almighty's people is as much, if not more, in conformity with His wishes as to pull my ox or my ass out of the ditch on His holy day. Now, repudiating the charge of

Communism, and apologising for trespassing on your
columns, I will only say I think my taking the chair was of
use to our cause, and notwithstanding the severe castigation
of the *Express*, I shall be prepared to fill the same position
if required so long as it is legal to do so.—Dear sir, truly
yours,

"JOHN TALBOT D'ARCY, Major."

Some one has said with equal wit and truth
that the *Times* holds a brief for Irish landlords.   If this is so, it explains why the letters
of Mr. Charles Russell, Q.C., were refused insertion in that paper at the last moment, and
why no letters are admitted in that paper except such as defend the peculiar views of
government and political economy held by these
gentlemen.   If it is true that Mr. Russell's
calm, moderate statements, made from careful
and patient personal investigation, were refused
a place in that paper, which is supposed to represent English opinion, how lamentable for the
future of England.

Men who do not wish to have the truth told
are either fools or knaves.   Men who will not
hear the truth are incapable of governing, and
proclaim to the world their own incapacity.

But Major D'Arcy is not the only Protestant
Irish landlord who has spoken out boldly for
truth and justice.   The name of Mr. Villiers

Stuart, M. P., is too well known for high integrity to need recommendation here, and he is
no Land Leaguer or Home Ruler. This is his
opinion, given before the Land Commission, of
the needs and wrongs of Ireland :—

"Is there much land still waste which is capable of profitable reclamation? Yes; thousands of acres on my estate
and in my neighbourhood ; but much of this is on entailed
properties, and tenants for life will not spend their money in
reclamation unless the money could be borrowed at a low
rate of interest, and charged on the estate. The Board of
Works rate is too high—five per cent. for life ; three per
cent. interest and one per cent. sinking fund, with two years'
grace, before collection of interest and principal began,
would induce many proprietors to reclaim who are now
deterred from doing so. My experience in the reclamation
of mountain land is that, on an average, it may be reclaimed
and put into cultivation for £15 per acre, and when reclaimed it will be worth ten or twelve shillings an acre, per
annum, *i.e.*, that will be the letting value, but not the entire
gain to the nation, because to the letting value must be
added the profit of the tenant and the addition to the food
producing powers of the country and the general development of its resources.

"I consider a Land Board (armed with ample power to
regulate all matters relating to land tenure, to decide disputed valuations, and to serve as a Court of Appeal, also
to carry out any provisions that may be enacted against rack-
renting, either by landlords or middlemen), to be a very
necessary institution,. I consider the suppression of rack-
renting to be one of the most vital points in the problem of
land tenure reform. The argument that neither occupying

proprietorship, under the Bright Clauses, nor limited leases at rents liable to be raised have hitherto been found to promote improvements by tenants to the extent expected, does not apply to experiments upon fairer conditions.

"The disappointment, in the first place, has been caused by the tenant being unduly hampered by too onerous conditions; in the second by the fear of improvements, leading ultimately to a raising of the rent. Leases practically perpetual, at fixed and fair rents and on easy conditions, which shall not cripple the tenant by absorbing the capital that ought to go to the improvement and development of his farm, and make him the slave of banks and money-lenders, by compelling him to borrow at high interest—such leases have never yet been tried, and, if tried, I feel convinced the results will not disappoint our expectations, but will lead to contentment and an indisposition for change, and to an important development of the industrial resources of Ireland."

The English public have heard a great deal of Captain Boycott; they have sympathized deeply with him; they have pictured him to themselves as a perhaps strict but just man, only desiring to get his master's rents. But have they heard, or do they care to hear, the other side! The *Times* of Nov 1880 tells it, and for once copies from the *Freeman's Journal* the true tale of a most miserable case.

"A special correspondent of the *Freeman* gives the popular version of the case of Captain Boycott and the causes of the enmity against him. He states that Captain Boycott is brave to a fault and is also eccentric. He says his rules in his dealings with the labourers were punctilious to a harsh and Quixotic degree. The labourers state that, instead of summoning them, he used to fine them himself one penny a fowl for every hen that trespassed on his grass farm; that a man was fined if he left a spade or shovel in the wrong place; fined if he left a gate open; fined if he took a short cut across a field; fined if he was two minutes behind the ring of the bell, with the result that a man employed at nine shillings a week sometimes found himself only entitled to seven shillings after his week's labour. His dogmatic and domineering tone with the people appears to have been another prolific cause of enmity against him. 'He treated his cattle better than he did us,' said one of the tenants; 'he never had anything but a curse for us.' A certain amount of gratuitous 'duty work,' was done upon his farm by the tenants for some time after his appointment as agent. His unpopularity led to a refusal to continue the duty work any longer. The tenants suspect (and, of course, it can be only suspicion) that this had something to do with what they conceive to be his steady hostility to their interests with the landlord. Lord Erne has an excellent reputation as a land lord. These lands are let, for the most part, little above the Poor Law Valuation, and, unless in years of grievous pressure, nobody grumbled about paying their rents; but, since the old Earl has, as they conceive, given up the control to his son, Viscount Crichton and his agent, they state that they have been subjected to a series of petty deprivations and humiliations, which appear to have maddened them without enriching the landlord. For example, prizes were formerly offered by the landlords for the best crops and the tidiest houses. These have been discontinued; but the chief immediate motive of the present attitude of the tenants is resentment against Captain Boycott, for having, in September last, attempted to serve eighteen processes of ejectment

against tenants who, according to their allegation, owed but
six months' rent with the hanging gale. The tenants had
accepted the ten per cent. abatement offered last year, and
had paid their rents, but they refused to pay this year's half
gale without an abatement of twenty-five per cent. The
gale was no sooner due they say, than a process-server was
sent round. He was surrounded, with his police escort, by
a dangerous crowd, and was forced to fly for his life after
serving three of the processes. Decrees were duly obtained
against the three persons who were served. A memorial
signed by all the tenants, who number only thirty-eight, was
thereupon presented to Lord Erne, reciting their grievances
against Captain Boycott, appealing to the old traditions of
the Erne family for considerate landlordism, and intimating
in plain terms that, while they were perfectly willing to
pay their rents, with any abatement decided upon by
Lord Erne, they had come to the conclusion never again
to work for or hold communication with his present
agent. The answer was a firm refusal from Lord Erne
to change his agent at their dictation. The tenants
forwarded a reply in which they reminded his lordship that
dire necessity alone could compel Irish tenants to set themselves against the agent of a non-resident landlord, to whose
tender mercies they were left. They repeated firmly their
determination to hold no further relations with Captain
Boycott, and their readiness to pay their rents to any other
person his lordship might appoint. At the same time they
respectfully appealed to him to shield them from the expense
of the policemen with which the neighbourhood was flooded,
reminding him that he had a remedy in his own hands
which would restore good feeling and peace to the estate.
Lord Erne ended the correspondence by a curt note stating
that he had no intention whatever of changing his agent,
and that if they would not pay their rents to Captain Boycott

they might take the consequences. The policy of isolation was then entered upon. It is evident from the above statement that there has been some ill-adviser behind the scene, and that there is more of obstinate pride and personal pique than of any real grievance at the root of the unfortunate quarrel."

I may mention here an amusing instance of the land agent style of government. A land agent who was exceedingly fond of bicycling, ventured one day into the middle of an unfortunate flock of geese on a remote country road. In England if any legal action had been taken for such a trifling matter he would probably have been fined for furious driving ; but as it was in Ireland, and as he was both land agent and justice of the peace, he fined the geese, or at least their owners.

No doubt there are a few persons in England, who either from political opinions or from sheer prejudice, are unwilling to believe the truth where Ireland is concerned. But I will not do the readers of this work the injustice to suppose that they belong to this class. It would be an injustice to their intellect, and would suppose them incapable of reasoning ; it would be an injustice to their moral sense, and suppose them incapable of discerning between truth and falsehood.

I would ask, then, a careful consideration of

the above paragraph copied from the *Times*. Elsewhere I had something to say of the action of land agents as magistrates. I do not know whether Captain Boycott is or is not a magistrate, but let it be observed that he takes the law into his own hands. Again let me implore English people to consider the grave injustice to themselves which results from all this. Ireland is supposed to be governed by English law. It cannot be repeated too often that on the very matters which most closely and intimately concern the welfare of the people, Ireland is NOT governed by English law. It is governed by the caprice—alas! too often by the greed and the cruelty—of a class of men " who treat their cattle better than their tenants."

And this is utterly unknown in England. If it were once known, if it were once realised, there would be, as I have said, a cry of indignation from end to end of the land, and such barbarity would be no longer tolerated.

No, it is not excessive and usurious rents alone which have caused all this misery in Ireland. It is little acts of tyranny; some might call them great. It is the burdens added to burdens already too oppressive. It is this " duty work," often demanded at the very moment that the unhappy tenant should be raising his own crops to pay the oppressive rent of the very landlord who, in addition to the rent, demands the sweat of the brow of his unhappy dependents, who require what even Pharaoh's task-master might have blushed to demand.

I conclude with the account of the special correspondent of the *Daily Telegraph*, November 14, 1880 :—

"The cabins of the peasantry seemed to be about the very worst dwellings for human beings I had ever viewed. There was scarcely a living creature about as the car sped on, the horse being urged forward with a continual storm of blows and remonstrances. I noted that many of the cottages I passed boasted no windows, that they all had mud floors, and most of them mud walls; that many were insufficiently thatched, nearly all were shared by the family pig, as well as by the family children; that in the majority of cases a very slough of mud faced the door, and that the utmost misery of appearance characterised every dwelling. I have been in many lands, and have seen many so-called oppressed people at home, but I declare that neither in the Russian steppes, nor in the most neglected Bulgarian villages, still less in the very poorest Hindoo hamlets, have I ever seen such squalid kraals as the farmers of this part of Mayo inhabit. Here they are not hidden away from public view, but front the high road, a dreadful testimony to mismanagement and uncleanliness, such as can be met with nowhere else. An officer of one of her Majesty's regiments, who lately served with honour in Zululand, declared to me that not even in the worst parts of Cetewayo's dominions did he come across anything so bad as here, and I am inclined to believe that he was not exaggerating in the slightest."

CHAPTER XIII.

THE DIFFERENT RELATIONS BETWEEN ENGLISH AND IRISH LANDLORDS AND TENANTS.

"I attribute the discontent amongst the farmers to the want of sympathy towards them on the part of the landlords, want of interest in their welfare, and to insecurity of tenure."—Evidence given by the Rev. P. Hill, Skibbereen, before present Land Commission.

THE difference between the social relations of English and Irish landlords and their tenants, is a subject which has received but little attention, and it is one of great moment to the well-being of both countries.

An Irish landlord, Lord Belper, I think, writing to the *Times*, lately made it a special landlord grievance that Irish tenants would not leave the fixing of their rents to the landlord or land agent. Would this gentleman like to allow his wine merchant to fix the cost of his wines, if his lordship was obliged either to deal with him exclusively, or to do without wine?

Probably, in the whole history of the world, there never was a class of men so utterly destitute of the most common consideration for their

T. SEXTON, M.P.

tenants as the large and noisy class of Irish
gentlemen who are now calling out for coercion.

For coercion! that England may compel the
Irish people by bullets and buckshot, by the
habeas corpus or by state prosecutions or legal
disabilities, to submit to the exorbitant rents
which they cannot pay and live! Coercion!
that these gentlemen may be allowed to continue a system, which will in the end be as
ruinous to them as to the unhappy serfs over
whom they wish to tyrannize, to whom they
would deny the rights of freemen. Coercion!
that those English lords may be allowed to continue to break English laws unmolested, that
they may be allowed to break through the Land
Laws which were so reluctantly framed by England for the protection of the poor. And these
same poor, who are evicted because they cannot
pay impossible rents, are to have the burden of
supporting military and police; and those scarcely
less poor are to pay large sums of money for
their support, in order that these Anglo-Irish
landlords may be allowed to continue breaking
the laws which England has made.

Do not say that I am exaggerating, that I am
making a case, that all this is fiction. Look at
the extracts which I have already given from

the evidence, the unimpeachable evidence, given
before the present Land Commission, and by
English gentlemen, and you will see that I state
a simple truth.   Mr. Gladstone's Land Act is
" evaded ;" to use plain English, it is broken by
these landlords habitually and persistently.

Even the *Daily Telegraph* says, speaking of
Mr. Adair, " he may have made an inequitable,
and even cruel, use of his landlord rights," and
describes Captain Boycott's district thus :—

"The district was miserably poor, and the dwellings
thereon something like cruel parodies of the neat homesteads that gladden the eye of the traveller as he passes
through England."

We have already written on the important
subject of rules of estates—a law, not only
within the law, but actually a law which breaks
the law of the land, to the terrible cost of the
unhappy tenant.

One remarkable and painful instance of this
is mentioned in Mr. Russell's letters to the
Times.   He says—writing of the Trinity College estates at Cahirciveen—where the distress,
or rather the Famine, was most severe in
1879-80 :—

" In a good many instances I found that the tenants had
reclaimed land from bog, and in some they had in recent

years rebuilt their houses. One gentleman in the neighbourhood informed us he believed that within the last forty years at least one-third of the land now in tillage had been reclaimed and made arable without allowance from the landlord. He added that the land was of such a nature that it would, if neglected, speedily relapse into wildness. A tenant some seven years ago built his house and got £40 7s. from the college towards the cost, of which, however, £35 only was given to him in cash, the difference being (£5 7s.) charged for a piece of timber. The tenant produced the stringent agreement under which this advance was made, of which I had a copy taken, by which he bound himself to repay the advance by forty half-yearly instalments of £1 1s. each, with the proviso that, if he failed in payment of any one instalment, the whole should forthwith be recoverable. This hardly sounds very liberal treatment on the part of a great corporation. The man assured me that his house had cost him £120, and he added with some bitterness, ' I wish I had my money clear out of the place, and I would leave it to them altogether." He complained that he had been promised the money as a gift towards building the house, but faith had not been kept with him. This was probably a misunderstanding. Another man who had been tenant for thirty years, and whose father-in-law, through whom he got the land, had been tenant for sixty years, told me that the rent had been raised in his time from £8 to £26 10s. One of these rises was in 1864, when some kind of general valuation was made by valuers from Dublin, Messrs. Brassington & Gale, who in some cases reduced, but in the much greater number considerably increased, the rents. It is significant of the relations between landlord and tenant in Ireland how these rises take place. It throws a strong light upon that cherished principle "freedom of contract."

"Later on I shall have one or two striking examples to quote on another estate. But the mode is simple; the tenants are informed that for the future their rent shall be so much. Indeed, instances were quoted to us in which the increase of rent was retrospective. So much for freedom of contract between the Irish landlord and his tenant! Another of the tenants of the college told me that, having laid out some money in drainage, and having a wish to lay out more, he applied to Captain Needham, the agent, for an allowance, and, finally in October, 1879, memorialised the Board. The following is the answer of the Board :— 'The Bursar of Trinity College has received A. B.'s memorial of the 23rd inst., respecting the advance from the Board of Trinity College, for the improvements of his farm. If A. B. will place in Captain Needham's hands the written agreement consenting to pay the increased rent at the rate of 1s. 7d. in the £ for any advance of money which he may require, the Bursar will lay his application before the Board.' Thus, not only would the tenant have to pay nearly 8 per cent. yearly for the money expended in the improvement of landlords' property, but, according to the existing law, expose himself to have his rent increased by his then or subsequent landlord, and increased upon the basis of the improvements which he himself had made, and for which he himself had dearly paid! This is no fancy sketch, for be it borne in mind that when an increase of rent takes place, even where the form of a valuation is gone through, no account is taken how far the improved value may have been created by the labour and the capital of the tenant. It was so in the case of the valuation of Messrs. Brassington & Gale. I was anxious to have some authentic information as to the more remote portions of this property, which I did not myself visit, including that at Port Magee; and a gentleman—a member of the English

Bar—who knows the locality well, writing to me generally,
of the condition of the estate, uses this emphatic language:
'As to the College Estate, it is simply a disgrace to the
country. It would be impossible to describe the filth or
misery of the dwellings. I could not find out that the agent
had ever taken any trouble about them. I was told everywhere that he had never been inside the houses.'"

But the Trinity College Estates are by no
means the only examples of this style of government. Anglo-Irish landlords are quite as cruel
offenders as any corporation or middle class
landlord.

Mr. Russell writes thus of the Lansdowne
Estates and their management :—

"The management of these large estates is in the hands
of Mr. Townsend Trench, son of the late Mr. W. Stuart
Trench, to whom he succeeded. It is difficult to say how
far the judgment of the community over whom their powers
as land agents were and are exercised is just or reliable.
Unquestionably, father and son were spoken of almost
universally with fear and dislike—to use no stronger language.
It was painful to notice the mortal dread of agent and
bailiff in which many of these tenants live. I noticed
nothing like it elsewhere in Kerry. Their conduct may be
misjudged, but assuredly no kindly recollection of the late
Mr. Trench seems to survive, and no kindly feeling towards
his son, the present agent, exists. Lord Lansdowne, although he resides a portion of the year at Derreen, near
Kenmare, does not seem to be generally known to his
tenants. Those on the Iveragh portion of his property have
never seen him since his visit there, on the occasion of his

attaining his majority. More than once when—some harsh
case being cited to me—I suggested to the tenants to appeal
to Lord Lansdowne, the answer was always the same: "Oh,
he leaves it all to the agent ;" or, "It's no use—It all rests
with Trench."

But again, let me call attention to the serious
evils of this government of Ireland, which is not
according to English law, but which is according to those " rules of the estate," this landlord
code, which is the cause, as I believe, far more
than excessive rents, of the disturbed state of
Ireland.

   Mr. Russell says :—

" One extraordinary institution prevails on this estate, not
only on the Kenmare, but also on the Cahirciveen portion
of it—namely, what is called the hanging two gales or hanging year's rent. At first I supposed that this merely meant
that instead of the hanging gale, or half year, which is
common on Irish estates, carelessness or liberality had recently suffered this to be increased to two hanging half-
years. But I found this was not so. I found it dated back
to the pre-famine years, and that while treated as non-exist-
ing, so long as the tenant continued to pay the accruing
gales, the hanging year was used as an engine of terrific
power in the hands of the agent where the tenant fell in
arrear. It is difficult to understand this, and I was slow to
believe it; but over and over again, and in all directions
upon the estate, I was informed that this outlying year
counted for nothing, and dated back to a time older than
many of the inhabitants. They added that, although it

counted for nothing, so long as the accruing rent was punctually paid, it did count for much if the rent was half-a-year in arrear; for that then, and then only, was the dormant year brought forward as the basis on which an ejectment was founded, and by which (it is not too harsh a word to use) the screw was applied to the tardy-paying tenant. More than one instance was cited to us of cases where an ejected tenant, whom the agent did not desire to continue on the estate, was not allowed to redeem, except upon payment of this stale demand; whilst if the tenant were not obnoxious to the agent no such demand was made. I confess I was incredulous for a long time, until I was informed by the Rev. Mr. M'Cutcheon, Protestant Rector of Kenmare (himself a sturdy Northern), that when he succeeded to the incumbency of Kenmare, upon paying his first gale of rent, he looked at his receipt and, to his surprise, found that it was dated a year back. So that he was made to appear not only to be owing a year's rent, but to be paying for a period when in effect he was not in occupation. He complained of this, and received for his comfort the assurance of Mr. Trench that it was a mere matter of form, that it was the custom of the office. I mentioned the circumstance, first to Lord Kenmare's sub-agent, and afterwards to Mr. Hussey, and each of them laughed. The story was obviously not new to them, and Mr. Hussey significantly added that, in his opinion, it gave to Mr. Trench more power over the tenants than any law could give him. On this estate, as on all others to which I have adverted, there lies in all directions land apparently capable of reclamation in the hands of those who had the will and the interest to reclaim. I was not without skilled advice on this matter; I am not speaking merely from my own rude notions of the subject."

Here is again another instance of the misery

caused by what is certainly little short of
tyranny :—

"Bitter complaint was made that, even in cases within
the jurisdiction of the county courts, writs of ejectment are
issued from the superior courts—what the tenants call
'Dublin Writs.' These not alone necessitate the employment of a Dublin solicitor, either directly or through some
local solicitor, but suggest to the minds of the tenants a
fearful unknown field of expensive litigation Even the
initial costs often are, in proportion to the rent demanded,
enormous; but yet the screw is so powerful that the effort
will be made to pay, even if the payer is to denude his farm
of the greater part of his stock, and himself of the means of
turning his holding to account. I find that from Sept. 1,
1879, to Sept. 1880, sixty superior court writs of summons
in ejectment, exclusive of Quarter Sessions processes, were
issued. Of these, forty were issued about September, 1879,
and twenty were issued in May of the present year. I have
the list before me. The former comprised rent due up to
May 1 (but by the custom of the office collected in July),
and the latter twenty comprised rent up to May 1, 1880.
Excepting one case, the greatest amount of rent due was
two years' rent, or, excluding the stale or fictitious outlying
year, one year's rent. In the great majority of instances,
three half years' rent only were due, or, excluding the fictitious year, one half year's rent was due."

It is no wonder that noblemen who are
anxious to continue this system of oppression
and terrorism, should leave no effort unused to
prevent the public from knowing the truth.

Such gentlemen acted with perfect consistency in voting against the " Disturbance Bill."

Would any English landlord act thus towards his tenants; and, if he could do so, dare he do it. A case in point was put before the Land Co.nmission at Clonmel, and Baron Dowse's remark should be printed in every paper in the United Kingdom : " Is it possible," he said, " such a thing could be done in any civilized country ?"

Here is the case, and the culprit is again a nobleman—one of that class who clamour so loudly for their own " rights," and for " coercion " for the unfortunate people who object to such practices :—

"Amongst those who appeared for examination, was the Rev. Father Finn, P.P., Newcastle, Tipperary, when the following startling facts were brought to light with regard to two properties in his neighbourhood—the Perry and Ashtown Estates.

" Baron Dowse—Are you conversant with land ? Do you know its working and value ?

" Rev. Father Finn—I am the son of a tenant farmer, and have been always living where I could see farming work done, and know perfectly well the value of land. I will first refer to Mr. William Perry's property, Newcastle. He became owner of the estate by succession in the year 1851. The rule on the estate was to give short leases.

" Baron Dowse—What is the property worth ?

" Nearly £3,000 a year, and a great part of that property

is reclaimed land. In proof of the short leases I will lay before your lordship five leases granted since 1853 to one man, and he only represents the other tenants on the property.

"Baron Dowse—Is it possible such a thing could be done in any civilized country?

"The Rev. Father Finn then handed in the five leases in question, and said that a tenant on the property had to take out in the seventeen years four leases, and each time a lease was taken, an increase of rent was put on. This rule applied to all the tenants. He thought it was a great hardship that a man with 18 acres should be obliged to pay £4 for every lease during the last seventeen years. There was one clause in the lease which he would wish to draw the Commissioners' attention to. First, that no tenant on his (Mr. Perry's) property could harbour a stranger for two consecutive nights without the landlord's written permission. The hardship that resulted from this clause was such that he (the Rev. Father Finn) was often obliged to relieve an old man, nearly eighty years of age, at his door, and his daughter, a tenant on the property, able and willing to take him in, but she dared not, owing to the clause he referred to in the lease. A great deal of the property was situated on the mountain side, and it would be the greatest advantage to the tenantry to be able sometimes to use a little artificial manure. They dared not, because there was a clause in the lease forbidding them to use anything but farm-yard manure. A drain, or ditch, or house, dared not be built without the written permission of the landlord. He knew a tenant on the property whose family were dwelling in a house, the roof of which had fallen down, and they had to face the inclemency of an entire winter because the landlord would not give the written permission.

"Baron Dowse—What would you recommend?

"Rev. Father Finn—You have property in the Incumbered Estates Court, and I myself saw within the last three months four properties put up for sale, and were withdrawn for the want of a purchaser. Could not these be bought up and portioned out?

"Baron Dowse—Where is the money to come from?

"Witness—Let the Government give the money, as they are doing under the Board of Works, and have a lien in the land, and thereby take the first step towards a peasant proprietary. The money would be paid to the Government as promptly as in the case of those two men who purchased the glebe lands.

"Baron Dowse—Do you believe by creating a peasant proprietary it would make the people more attached to the Crown?

"Rev. Father Finn—I believe it would. I never knew yet a well-to-do man to be rebellious.

"LORD ASHTOWN'S PROPERTY.

"The Rev. Father Finn then proceeded to give evidence with regard to Lord Ashtown's property. He said that about five years ago, Lord Ashtown purchased the Glenbury property from Lord Stradbroke, who was an absentee landlord, living only a week each year on his property. He (Lord Stradbroke) kept on the estate an agent, Abraham Coates, who certainly knew how to put a heavy rent upon the tenantry. The property changed hands about five years ago, and, as he had mentioned, was purchased by the late Lord Ashtown at a time when every tenant on the property was almost out of lease. The agent, Mr. Uniack Townsend, proposed new leases to the tenantry, but they, discovering that a great increase of rent would be put on if they accepted the new leases, refused. They subsequently took the new leases.

"Baron Dowse—Why did they take those new leases out? Were they not acting as free agents in signing the contract?

"Rev. Father Finn replied he did not consider them at all free agents, because they were compelled to take the new leases under threat of eviction, and if they did not take them out they had two alternatives before them—either to enter a workhouse, or go into an emigrant ship at Queenstown.

"Baron Dowse—Do you know of your own knowledge they were under threat of eviction?

"Witness—Certainly; a number of men will come before you to prove that such was the case.

"The Rev. Father Finn then mentioned the following cases, to show the effect the taking out of the new leases had on the tenants on the property:—Thomas Butler, of Deerpark, owned about 36 acres of arable land. He got a new lease about four years ago, by which the rent was raised from £51 8s. to £58 10s., Griffith's valuation of the man's holding being £29 5s. Michael Tobin, Crouchnagree, under threat of eviction, took a new lease about the same time. He held about 30 acres of arable land, chiefly reclaimed by his father and himself from the mountain side. The rent was raised from £42 to £47 under the new lease, and Griffith's valuation was £25. Patrick Flynn, of Crouchateskin, got a new lease about four years ago, under threat of eviction. He was deprived, in getting the new lease, of 15 acres of land, and still his rent was raised. Under the old lease his rent was £92, under the new, £98, Griffith's valuation being £41 10s. John Walsh, Bawnfaun, got a new lease in 1872 from Lord Stradbroke. Under the old lease the rent was £134 12s.; under the new lease the rent was raised to £165, while Griffith's valuation was only £79. There was a clause in the lease depriving the tenants from getting compensation for any improvements they might have made on their holdings. In the case of Patrick Mulcahy, Ballydonoch, he got a new lease in 1869. His old rent was £2 2s. per acre, and in getting the new lease the rent was raised to £2 10s. per acre. He built a dwelling-house and out-offices fit for any man, and there was a clause in the lease, that if he were put out to-morrow, he would not be able to recover one halfpenny. His holding was on the banks of the River Suir. He was paying for about 7½ acres of a river, and he would not be allowed to cast a line on it to catch a salmon. The present agent offered to let the river for £10 to another gentleman. The farm of John Mara, Crouchateskin, was entirely reclaimed by himself and his father. His rent was raised under the lease got from Lord Ashtown's agent. He paid at present £50 for that farm, although Griffith's valuation was only £10. These were, the Rev. Father Finn added, only instances of how the rest were treated in the same way."

" Baron Dowse.—Have you any other evidence of land grievance to lay before us?

" Rev. Father Finn.—Yes ; I have a tenant-farmer in my parish who wishes to make a statement to you.

"John Nugent was then called in, and, in reply to Baron Dowse, said he lived at Boulahalla; that Mrs. Stephen Murphy was his landlady, and that she lived at Banard. He had sixteen acres of land reclaimed from the mountain. His rent was £21 a year. Griffith's valuation was about £12.

"Baron Dowse.—Do you refuse to pay that rent now?

" Witness.—No; but my landlady, to whom I have offered it on two gale days, refused to take it from me, unless I would pay an increased rent of £30 a year.

"Baron Dowse.—Did you pay her the increased rent?

"Witness.—No ; because if I did I would be soon in the poorhouse.

"Baron Dowse.—And what did you do with what you call the honest rent to this woman?

"Witness.—By the advice of my parish priest, the Rev. Father Finn, I put my two rents into the bank, and there it will remain until she accepts it.

"Baron Dowse.—Will you pay her any day what you say is your honest rent?

"Witness.—I will, to the farthing.

"About eighteen of Lord Ashtown's tenantry then appeared before the Commissioners, and gave evidence corroborative of the Rev. Father Finn's statement."

Such evidence needs no comment; but as a great deal has been said about the action of Irish priests in the present crisis, a few words may not be unnecessary.

It has been made a reproach to Irish priests even recently, in the English papers, that they do not come from the upper or fashionable class of English Catholics. There are some who might think that the reproach might be reversed, and that the upper or fashionable class of Catholics might be reproached with giving so few of their sons to God's service. They, at least, should treat with singular respect that great spiritual army of Irish priests, so many of whom fill the places which, perhaps, some of their own children ought to occupy. Unhappily, however, this class in England are quite as ignorant of the true state of Ireland as any English Protestant, and with far less excuse.

The word politics has unfortunately been taken of late years as synonymous with party, and as such it has led a most important subject into disrepute. What are politics ? or rather what idea ought the word to represent ? Politics are the regulation of the public action of states; but since there can be no multiple without a unit, no multitude without distinct individualities, politics concern each individual in a state—above all, when the particular subject refers to national politics.

In Ireland the very existence of the people is a question of politics. Are they to be decimated periodically by famine ? or is Ireland to be depopulated by emigration ? These are political subjects ; but they are also most important social and personal subjects. Those who form their opinions on such points without taking sufficient care to obtain correct information are unworthy of their manhood ; yet that such is the case we know but too well.

Mr. Bright's argument is irresistible. He says :

" They [the young] have no ambition to go wrong (politically) ; they are not subject to the temptations which beset monarchs and statesmen ; they err from mistake or ignorance, and it is because we wish them not to err that we ask young men everywhere to make themselves thoroughly acquainted with the political interests of their country. I spoke of those great crimes of those great leaders of mankind, of the calamities they had brought upon us, or upon some of us, and not always upon us. I take a glance for a moment to a country which is our next neighbour—France. Look at what France has suffered for the last hundred years—how much of war, how much of insurrection, how much of anarchy, how much of expenditure and of needless taxation. Some of you recollect—it was only a few years before my life began—when the French Revolution broke out, and when there was an explosion and catastrophe which shook the whole of Europe, and which impoverished in the course of its career many nations, which sacrificed hundreds of thousands of lives, and which for very many years unsettled the relations and systems which had been existing on the Continent of Europe; but now, when we can look back, dissect, and examine, it is not very difficult to tell how these things came about. If there had been no Louis XIV. with his wars, no Louis XV. with his odious profligacy, and no Louis XVI. with his feebleness, and if there had not been the exactions of the nobility of France, and the terrible corruptions of the Church of France, the catastrophe which followed could not have taken place. The population of France were little advanced—almost not at all advanced—in freedom. They had no political clubs in those days; their young men were taught nothing of politics; their population were subject absolutely to the central authority of the country; and that central authority, and the powerful classes that surrounded it, led the country to the disasters to which I referred. Now, if you cross the Atlantic, and come to a transaction of our own times—I refer to the United States—if all the people in the Northern States, who held no slaves—confining my observation to them—if they had been instructed on that question, if they had been unanimous in the condemnation of slavery, it is almost certain, I believe it thoroughly, that that great crime against human nature might have been removed long before, and removed without the sacrifice of more than a thousand million sterling in money and more lives (cheers). Well, now, if these tremendous events come upon countries, and curse their population by reason mainly of the ignorance of the people and their unacquaintance with political principles and the true path of political success, is it not commendable that there should be clubs, if clubs be an adequate and good mode of spreading political information amongst the people? And, stepping a little farther, and leaving France and America (with its great civil war and grand results), we come to our own country, and we behold Ireland, not an insignificant portion of the three kingdoms, which should form a united kingdom, suffering, not from anything that the existing Government or Legislature has done, not from anything which has been done even from the reign of the present monarch, but suffering from things which had been done in any time during the last two centuries, and which, if our forefathers had understood these questions even as well as we now understand them, these evils could never have been inflicted upon the Irish people. It had been said that the soil of Ireland had been confiscated, that there had been planted in that country great proprietors who went over from Scotland and England, and who were settled there as an English garrison in a conquered country, that there never was any attempt made to win the conquered people over, and that there was no attempt to make them feel that the English power, even though it was dominant, yet that it was still just and merciful in the treatment of the Irish people."

If we have given this extract at such length,

it is because of the importance of the subject. We are told, we hope, that the English nation will cease to treat Ireland as a dependency, to be kept under by a *quasi*-martial law, and that enactments will be made which will secure her people ordinary prosperity in their native land. But all depends on the class who have authority in their hands to make such laws. If they remain in ignorance, Ireland will remain in misery, and a golden opportunity of doing justice—a long deferred justice—will have passed away.

The lamentable ignorance and prejudice of the upper classes of Irish and Anglo-Irish lords may work deadly evil. But, as Mr. Bright has well said, younger men have not the same temptations. Let them save England, for though, for a time, England may not suffer by continuing to refuse justice to Ireland, neither countries nor individuals can prosper when they practice injustice.

It is certainly exceedingly painful to read the persistent misstatements of Anglo-Irish noblemen in the *Times.* Lord Dunsany writes that the "surplus population" of Connaught is to be provided for by quartering the people on Leinster landlords. No doubt thousands will believe him. Then he rushes into the usual platitudes about the government recommending agitation ; never does he express one word of commiseration for the starved people of Connaught, never does he say one manly statesman-like word of consideration of, or calm discussion of why the agitation has been caused. There is no calm asking of what will be for the general good of the whole nation. Only cries of anger and reproach and fear for supposed personal interests. Then he says :—

"The Land League is by far the best cry yet adopted for Irish agitation, for it appeals forcibly to the greed of men not over scrupulous by nature. Yet, were it known in Ireland that the government were honestly determined to stand by their own law of 1870, we should soon hear as little of the Land League as we do of Repeal.

But who are the men who are not over "scrupulous by nature?" Alas! are they not those who should show the best example to their dependents. Is it unscrupulous to object to pay a rack rent, or is it unscrupulous to put it on? Is it unscrupulous to ask Irish land agents to stand by the law of 1870, or are they not rather unscrupulous who habitually insist on their tenants signing agreements that they will not ask the protection of that law?

One complaint of the Irish people at the present day is that the landlords "will not stand by their own law of 1870."

CHAPTER XIV.

THE IRISH PRIESTS AND THE LAND AGITATION.

"I am not ashamed to be called an agitator; but I scorn to be called an assassin."—REV. P. O'CONNOR, P.P.

IN Mr. Bright's speech, from which we have quoted so largely in the previous chapter, we find a strong and manly condemnation of the English government of Ireland for the last two centuries, and he attributes that misgovernment plainly to ignorance.

Mr. Bright especially alludes to the penal laws, and includes them, in a marked manner, in the category of ills which knowledge has banished.

I think that no one who considers the public pronouncements on the present agitation in Ireland, can fail to be deeply struck by the absence of polemical abuse. Whenever Irish landlords have alluded to Irish priests in their letters to English papers, they have done so courteously.

· No doubt if the Church could be got to use her influence against the people it would be attempted. But beyond very marked approval of any person or expression which could be construed as against the present demand for legal protection for Irish tenants, there has been a marked and happy absence of all religious recrimination. This is the result of more knowledge. Ignorance of Catholic faith and practices led to the enactment of penal laws. When men came to know better they acted more wisely ; and, probably, the descendants of these gentlemen, who are now so ignorantly denouncing the demands of the Irish people for legal rights, will write as men write to-day about the ignorance which caused the English misgovernment of Ireland in past ages.

In Lord Dunsany's letter to the *Daily Telegraph* he says :

"There are three powers which influence emigration in Ireland—the landlord, the professional agitator, and the priest. The landlord in over-peopled districts promotes emigration ; the professional agitator opposes it, as it ruins his trade ; the priest opposes it not only because it deprives him of his income, but also because it strips him of an influence which he justly prizes."

Lord Lifford, writing to the *Times*, says :—

"The Bright clauses of the Act of 1870 I have always liked ; but what are called the "three F's"—viz., fixity of

tenure, free sale, and fair rents, as propounded by the Roman
Catholic bishops and clergy of Cork and Cloyne, contain
within their lines the material of a not altogether unsatisfactory Land Act, always supposing that ordinary law and
political economy are abandoned in Ireland."

The paragraphs above quoted are a remarkable example of the course of public opinion.
Public opinion has, slowly indeed, but nevertheless surely, informed itself as to the character
and motives of the Irish priest. There is no
longer gross invective or gross misrepresentation. And yet, it is well to remember that there
was a time when both prevailed. Ignorance
and prejudice are the parents of innumerable
evils, and it would be wisdom if we learned what
absurdities have been believed and defended
from pure ignorance and prejudice, and took
care now that we are not guided by their false
and lurid lights, as we so frequently were.

Lord Dunsany says the priest opposes emigration because it deprives him of his income.   If
Lord Dunsany knew the Irish priests as, let us
hope, his descendants will know them, he will
know that the Irish priests' income is a matter
of very little moment to him, and that the only
influence he desires is to keep his people from
the eternal ruin, which is too often the sure end
of wholesale emigration.

Lord Lifford writes not unkindly of the plans propounded by the Catholic bishops and clergy of Cork and Cloyne.

But why, it will be asked, do the Catholic priests of Ireland take such a decided part in the present discussion? Let me answer first in their own words.

We give first the published letters of the Irish bishops, which speak for themselves :—

The following letters were read at the Ballinasloe meeting :—

"Loughrea, Nov. 15, 1879.

" My dear Father M'Keigue—In reply to your communication, I cordially approve of your meeting as a means of indicating to the Government that their primary duty is to utilise the resources of the country to save the lives of the people. A dereliction of this obligation may lead to calamitous results in the present critical emergency. With the memories of the last great famine fresh in my mind, I shudder to think of the consequences that may ensue if the people are left again to the operation of the Poor-law system, which implies the abandonment of home—the witnessing the ploughshare uprooting the old rooftrees, hallowed by so many endearing associations, and entering by one door those fatal workhouses to be carried out at another in a few weeks for burial in shroudless, coffinless grave-pits ; or, on the other hand, to see money squandered, and thousands of lives sacrificed in useless and often noxious public works. The people need not ask eleemosynary aid from private or public sources. They are able and willing to earn the wages of

P

honest work, and there are abundant sources on every side
for their profitable employment.

"The Government have now a grand opportunity of
renovating the face of the country by inaugurating a system
of reproductive operations that will not cost the State one
penny, whilst at the same time they will profit the owners
and occupiers of land and increase the revenues of the Exchequer. Now is the hour for bold and wise statesmanship.
Will the present Government grasp the opportunity of laying
the foundation of solid industry in this country, and thus dry
up the resources of agrarian discontent?

"Why those cycles of famine in Ireland? There are
millions of waste but reclaimable lands. Why not reclaim
them, and settle upon them an industrious peasant proprietary? Why not by the arterial drainage dry up the soil
and sweeten the herbage for innocuous pasturage, the want
of which is causing such havoc in stock through the country?
Why not aid in developing our utterly inadequate railway
system? Why not give facilities to the tenants to thorough
drain and improve their holdings and habitations? In England the owners of land do all this. In the present state of
the law fully 90 per cent. of the tenants are excluded from
borrowing from the Board of Works. None can borrow but
landlords and tenants with a lease of forty years unexpired,
and no less a sum than £100 can be obtained on loan.
Why not give tenants with restrictions as to amount borrowed,
and protection for mutual rights, facilities for making, as in
England, the improvements which owners have not made
and are not making in this country? Why not improve the
harbours about the coasts?

"Your resolutions are moderate in tone and well considered. There is a stern inflexibility of resolve in the men
of Ballinasloe and its vicinity which will, I am confident,
urge them to press those considerations upon our Govern-

ment with respectful but determined energy. To prevent the recurrence of these periodical famines the land system requires a radical change. Hence the tenants must be rooted in the soil as the prelude of a large increase in the number of peasant proprietors. All these beneficial reforms can be attained by peaceable agitation within the lines of the Constitution. By energetic action on the part of our representatives much has been already gained ; and more, including Home Rule, will be attained if the constituencies are true to their own grave responsibilities. The policy of inaction has been weighed in the balance and found wanting.

"I am, faithfully yours,

"✠ PATRICK DUGGAN.

"Rev. John M'Keigue, C.C., Secretary."

"St. Jarlath's, Tuam, Nov. 19, 1879.

"REV. DEAR SIR—The public and patriotic action of the clergy and people of Ballinasloe has never been backward in steadily urging on the alien rulers of our country their manifest duty with respect to the seasonable relief of our suffering people in years of general distress like the present.

"In pressing our claims to relief we must not be considered mendicants, prostrate at the feet of our haughty neighbours ; neither should we be called upon to display our gratitude before a single favour is conferred upon us. Rather let us be looked upon as a nation justly claiming a portion of the taxes of our own country which, by a process of financial jugglery unknown to honest men, are annually transferred to the British Exchequer instead of having them employed for national purposes at home, such as, at the

present moment, the relief of impending want, the reclamation of waste land, arterial drainage, and the construction of
railroads in remote districts. When those benefits are bestowed upon us, their acknowledgment on our part will be
proportionate to such favours.

" Had Ireland her own domestic Parliament, legislating
for the common weal, and dispensing relief with paternal
solicitude in the hour of need, those ever-recurring years of
distress and famine would be unheard of in this country, as
in all civilised nations where the well-being of the people is
the patriotic object generously sought for by their representatives in their own Parliament, unlike socially wretched and
down-trodden Ireland, whose fate, in modern times, has been
divided by Saxon gentlemen confessedly ignorant of our
wants, or, what is still worse, heedless of our very necessities, especially whenever the real or pretended welfare of
their own country is concerned.

"By all means let the people be rooted in the soil of
their native land ; let their pecuniary relations with their
landlords be divided by periodical valuation ; let those and
similar well-digested projects be demanded with vigour and
earnestness by means of a constitutional and healthy organisation of the political power of the people. With the view
of realising those social blessings let energy, activity, and
the old principles, so unjustly censured by dishonest and
crafty politicians, of independent opposition to all British
parties by Irish members of Parliament be vigorously required of them as a condition to senatorial honours by their
constituents at the approaching general election, and the
disorganisation recently witnessed with pain, of what should
be a compact body, will no longer dishonour our country in
a foreign legislature.

"At the same time Irishmen at home and abroad must
never forget that without their own independent Parliament

legislating not for a class, but for the welfare of Irishmen regardless of all British interests, the people of this land must ever remain the slaves of their powerful neighbours, and can never ascend to the intellectual and social heights to which they are entitled to ascend by the genius and virtues of their race.—I remain, rev. dear sir, your faithful servant,

"✤ John, Archbishop of Tuam."

"Sligo, Nov. 16, 1879.

"Rev. Dear Sir,—In reply to your favour of the 13th inst., relative to the public meeting to be held at Ballinasloe on Sunday next, I am happy to express my approval of the resolutions to be proposed at that meeting, and of which you have kindly sent me a printed copy. In substance, and almost in terms, your four first resolutions coincide with those which were lately adopted by the bishops of Ireland, and presented to the Irish Government by a deputation of which I had the honour to be a member. I need not say, then, that I heartily desire the realisation of the views expressed in those resolutions; and I beg to assure your meeting, including those of my own flock who will attend it, that my best efforts shall be unceasingly directed, in accordance with those views, to the relief and welfare of our people.

"It is simply our duty to guide and assist our flocks to obtain by every legitimate means, not only the repeal of the oppressive laws, by which they have been so long impoverished and degraded, but the enjoyment of perfect civil and social liberty with their fellow-subjects, without which there can be neither contentment nor prosperity in our country. History attests, and our own experience proves, that if the mass of the people, especially the cultivators of the soil, are not treated with justice and humanity by the upper classes, if their rights are not acknowledged and protected by the Legislature, the result may be, sooner or later, discontent and hatred, ending in social disruption and misery. It is, therefore, the interest as well as the duty of all classes, without distinction of creed, to bring speedily about a peaceful constitutional change in our laws, and especially our land laws, which will give full security to the occupier and tiller of the soil, and allow him to bestow on it his toil and capital, so as to derive from it an adequate support.

"That change can be effected in one of two ways—both of them already familiar to the public—either by allowing and helping the tenant to become the owner of the land he occupies, or by securing him in its tenancy at an equitable rent. That such a change depends entirely on the will of Parliament is admitted by all ; and it is my conviction that if it were earnestly and perseveringly demanded by the people and their united representatives it would be soon granted by Parliament.

"Hoping that the speakers at your meeting will sustain the just and temperate character of the resolutions to be proposed, and thus promote the great objects for which the meeting is to be held, I remain, rev. and dear sir, your faithful servant,

"✠ L. GILLOOLEY."

In acknowledging the receipt of a grant made by the Liverpool Committee for the Relief of

Distress in Ireland the Bishop of Clonfert
writes :—

"Loughrea, Co. Galway, May 25th, 1880.

"My Dear Sir,—On the part of our local committee
and the poor of the parish, I tender to you and the committee in Liverpool our united thanks for cheque for £20.   I
really look forward to the crucial months thut must intervene
before the harvest with anxious alarm.   Want is widespread
and intense, and if the coming harvest be another failure I
shudder to look into the future.   An organic change in our
land system is needed to prevent the recurrence of those
famines which, unfortunately, have become normal in our
social condition.   The poor creatures are willing and anxious
to work.   We have by deputations of bishops, M.P.'s, and
otherwise, solicited the attention of the Executive to the necessity of devising public works of utility.   Opportunities
lie scattered around us on every side that would give employment profitable to the occupier, the landlord, and the
public exchequer.   But no use.   Hence, no wonder that
discontent, as well as destitution, prevails amongst the
masses of the Irish people.   Be assured that misery arising
from the culpable indifference with which our great natural
industrial resources are neglected is the root of the discontent around on every side.   God grant that the eyes of our
rulers be opened before evils, future but not distant, come
upon our country.   If, during the coming hard months, the
resources at the disposal of your benevolent committee put
it in your power to aid us, I am sure we will not be forgotten.
—Yours, &c.,

"✠ Patrick Duggan, Bishop of Clonfert.

"J. Hand, Esq."

"A meeting was held in St. Mary's Hall, Belfast, on the 17th November, to protest against the action of the Government, to declare sympathy with Mr. Parnell and the members of the Land League, and to organise a defence fund. The hall was crowded. The Chair was occupied by the Rev. M. H. Cahill, C.C. Mr. Miskelly, Honorary Secretary of the meeting, read the following letter from the most Rev. Dr. Dorrian, Bishop of Down and Connor:—

"In reply to your circular, I beg to say that the traversers have a right to at least a fair trial. They are engaged in what they say is a legal and constitutional effort within the moral laws to remedy a great social evil, rescue from misery and starvation thousands of our people, and elevate our country from hunger, mockery, and contempt, to its proper rank in civilisation amongst the nations of the world. This is surely worthy of approval. The Government, therefore, might have done better to have begun by removing the cause of our wretchedness and discontent, and formulating the law to give to every tiller of the soil a motive to improve and protect his holding; but, as I have fully explained my views on this question, according to our religious teaching, in my last letter and address, I shall not further trouble you than to enclose £5 to the Parnell Defence Fund, and shall be glad to see the case fully ventilated—misrepresentations as well as misunderstandings removed."

At the Clonmel meeting, where Mr. P. J. Smyth, M.P., presided, the following letter from the Archbishop of Cashel was read :—

"MY DEAR FATHER RYAN,—It is well, I think, to let the hereditary legislators of England know what we in Ireland ·

think of their lordships' latest manifesto of hostility against us. It is well, also it is fit and proper, that Tipperary should take the initiative in the matter, sounding the first note of defiance and denunciation, and by further more proclaiming to the peers of the realm their determination to live in the land in which they were born, and to be fed together with their families out of the produce of fields which they alone have tilled and toiled upon and rendered fertile. 'The husbandman that labours,' says St. Paul, 2 Tim. ii. 6, ' must first partake of the fruits of the soil.' 'No,' says the English House of Lords; 'St. Paul is wrong in that, and was obviously socialistic in his teachings; for the rent must be our fruit, however ill it may fare with the husbandman, and, as certain dangerous theories are being propounded nowadays by irreligious men, we wish, by this our overwhelming vote, to have it made known to them and to the empire that even for an hour we will not part with any chartered privileges of our class, and that, consequently, our wretched Irish dependants may now, as ever, be mercilessly flung out by us on the roadside, because they cannot possibly manage at one and the same time to pay us our rent and prevent their families from perishing.' There is, besides, a grave constitutional question now at stake. That question, will, no doubt, be dealt with at the proper time in the proper place. The great statesman, now happily convalescent, who stands at the head of her Majesty's ministers, and whose goodwill to Ireland has been abundantly made manifest, will see in due course that the voice of the people's representatives shall not be trifled with or set aside. For the rest, feel assured, that the men of Tipperary will state their views at Wednesday's meeting plainly and fairly, without bluster or exaggeration, or the senseless parading of any fanciful theories, and, above all, they will give no pledge or promise which they are not prepared at all hazards manfully to redeem.—I am, my dear Father Ryan, your very faithful servant,

"✠ T. W. CROKE, Archbishop of Cashel.

"To the Rev. John Ryan, New Inn."

This letter was the subject of no little comment and correspondence in the English papers. The landlords were terrified. They knew well that if priests and people united in their demand for legal justice to Ireland, that legal justice would be done. Hitherto they had the Irish people at a tremendous disadvantage. The priests would not countenance a secret society, they denounced oath-bound associations; and the people not having the support of their clergy, in fact being opposed by them, were powerless. No wonder that those who could at one sweep of their autocratic power add £10,000 to the value of an estate, at the cost of a starving people, should look in amazement at the bold statement that men had a right to live first, and to pay rent afterwards.[1]

We have already given the letter of the Right Rev. Dr. Duggan, addressed to the sec-

---

[1] Mr. Russell, in his letters to the *Daily Telegraph*, states, that Lord Lansdowne's agent boasted how he had in one day added £10,000 to the value of his master's property by raising the rent.

retary of the land meeting at Loughrea; still
we give one short extract from it here again,
since it contains in few words, the only and
simple demand of the people of Ireland :—

"LOUGHREA, *October* 30th.

"SIR,—My earnest desire has been and still is, to witness
a settlement of the land question on principles that will
secure to the owners and occupiers those rights that have
their sanction in the laws of justice. Less than this neither
should accept. More than this neither should claim."

We might occupy the present volume with
the letters of priests on the state of Ireland. A
few such must suffice.

The following letter was addressed to and
published in the *Freeman's Journal* in February, 1880 :—

"*February* 19th.

"SIR,—In the midst of cries of distress around me, in
the Cavan portion of my parish—while Protestant and
Catholics here, as elsewhere, are struggling to keep together
the soul and body of the victims of this year's visitation—I
was hurried off to the Meath portion, no less distressed, to
witness a scene—the first in my life—a heartless eviction of
six whole families, thirty souls in all, of ages ranging from
eighty-three to two years. When has this taken place? and
why? must be asked, and must be answered. Am I to be
silent and yet to witness such a scene in my parish this day?
Surely not. And I claim, respectfully, a space in the public
journal, the *Freeman*.

"At twelve o'clock to-day, in the midst of a drizzling rain, when every man's lips are busy discussing how relief can be carried to this home and that, an imposing spectacle presented itself through a quiet part of the parish of Kings-court. A carriage contained Mr. Hussey, jun., son of the agent of the estate of Lord Gormanstown. Behind and before the carriage came about a dozen of outside cars, with a resident magistrate, an inspector of police, about forty of her Majesty's force, the sheriff, and some dozen of as rapacious looking drivers and grippers as ever I laid my eyes upon.

"There is dead silence at the halt before the first doomed door. That silence was broken by myself addressing the agent, craving to let the poor people in again after the vindication of the law, when, to my disgust, but not to my dismay, one of the crowd is observed by me taking notes.

"The sheriff formally asks—'Have you the rent?' The trembling answer is—'My God! how could I have the whole rent; and such a rent, on such a soil, and in such a year as this?' 'Out, out,' is the word; and right heartily the grippers go to work. On the dung pit is flung the scanty furniture, bed and bedding; a search is made for pig or goat, and forthwith they share the fate of the evicted master, the door is nailed, and the imposing army marches on to the next holding, till every house has been visited and every soul sent forth.

"At this moment there is a downpour of rain on that miserable furniture—on that poor bed and bedding—and an old man, whose generations have passed their simple lives in that house, is sitting on a stone outside, with his head buried in his hands, thinking of the eighty-three years gone by. And are those tenants to blame? No; it is on the records of this parish that they were about the most simple-minded, hardworking, honest, and virtuous. Their only guilt is this, that an 'agreement' with my Lord Gormanston, some five years ago, disfranchising them of any claim under the Land Act and involving an intolerable rise of rent, together with the common misfortunes of the country these few years past, and this in particular has left them entirely unable to pay the entire rent of this year. Yes, entire rent—the half, the ninth-tenths, of the rent would not be accepted. Priests joined the poor tenantry in petitioning again and again. No answer was given, but 'Have you the whole rent? Have you law expenses? If not, out you go.'

"'Deliberately I say it—this work may invite Russian Nihilism in Ireland; and deliberately, I ask the government, whom are they to blame for this visitation? They may smile at the distant visitor being threatened upon us; but there is a rapidity of thought abroad to which men were not accustomed twelve months ago.

"JOSEPH FLOOD, P.P."

Many of the English people are ardent admirers of *Victor Hugo*. The *Freeman's Journal* gave, at some length, a report of an interview which their special correspondent had with this gentleman and with M. Louis Blanc on the Irish question. Here is M. Hugo's reply to one question :—

"The custom which is prevalent over in Ireland I understand to be that by which eight or nine hundred persons own the entire soil. That system means this—there are in Ireland eight or nine hundred lords and somewhat over five million slaves (esclaves). A miserably small fraction tyrannise—the rest, *i.e.*, the vast majority are the automatons that move at the beck of the fraction. That land system is, I have no hesitation in affirming, a glaringly unjust and absurd one. It is unjust, inasmuch as it pampers and enriches the minority of a people at the expense of the majority, and is, consequently, an outrage upon justice. It is absurd, for it contains an anomaly, and must have the effect of impoverishing the country. I say, and I hold, that a people who live under such a system are willingly, and with eyes open, advancing on the high road to political, if not personal, suicide. You know we broke partnership with that land system at the era of our great Revolution. Before that Revolution the French were accursed with the same system which at present afflicts you Irish."

Now, it is precisely because the Irish hierarchy and clergy wish to save Ireland from any sanguinary method of demanding justice that they support one which they believe demands it legally. And England owes them a debt of gratitude for their beneficent action. It is their love of peace which makes them desire a peaceful settlement of a burning question. It is their supreme duty to do all in their power to promote peace, and until the poor in Ireland are protected by law as well as the rich there cannot be peace. Even the peaceful " Friend" has joined issue on this point, and no one has written more strongly than Mr. Tuke on the whole subject. He says :

" Mayo was one of the proclaimed districts, and has been the centre of the great wave of anti-rent agitation which last

autumn swept across the country, and which has been productive of so much evil fruit. The districts around Claremorris and Swinford seem especially disturbed, and it may
be noted that there is hardly a resident landlord in these
districts, and that therefore the people are more left to
themselves than is the case where a good resident landlord
exists. Here, too, the misery of the population has been
very marked, and the absence of men of independent position or judgment is most seriously felt in the administration
of the Poor Law. The difference in the disaffected state of
the people in North and South Mayo further illustrates this.
In South Mayo, from Westport eastward, the chief landlords
are nearly all non-residents—five or more—whose total
rentals taken out of the county cannot be less than eighty
thousand a year.[1] Captain Knox, at Ballinrobe, is an
honourable exception to this, and he, as chairman of the
union, and also of the relief committees, is working hard in
that district. It is in South Mayo that the great seat of
disturbance exists, and where, as I have noticed, the largest
body of police is quartered, and where there are many men
who dare not stir out of their houses without their escort.
In North Mayo a less hostile spirit, as a rule, exists. Many
of the landlords are resident, and exercise a beneficial influence over their poorer neighbours and tenants. Sir C.
K. Gore, Colonel Knox, and others, are instances of this.
Nor must it be overlooked, in reference to the disaffected

---

[1] In Connaught, 427 owners of 1,111,000 acres, the annual value of
which is £283,000, are non-resident ; whilst 925 proprietors, with
1,750,000 acres, of an annual value of £632,000, are resident, or partly
resident, in the province. In Ulster, 517 owners of 1,400,000 acres of
land, with an annual value of £778,000, are absentees ; whilst 1259,
having 2,100,000 acres, and an annual value of 1,355,000 are resident.

condition of Mayo, that it was in this county that the greatest number of evictions occurred in 1846-50 ; thousands were thus turned out of house and home, and the records of the Famine year have left a tale of suffering and sorrow which will not be soon forgotten." [1]

A recent number of the *Graphic* has a picture of an Irish landlord bidding a pathetic farewell to his friends before he goes on his round of rent gathering or evicting his tenants ; but who shall picture the bitter agony and anguish of the farewell of millions of people, driven from their homes by the irresponsible fiat of the same land-lords.   If we are all descendants of the brute creation, one animal, no doubt, does no moral wrong when he desolates the homes of hun-dreds ; but, if we are all Christians, one Chris-tian man's feelings and his rights are sacred as those of his fellow-Christians.

I am unwilling to burden the reader with further documentary evidence; but as Irish papers are rarely read in England, and as Eng-

---

[1] The Census (in round numbers) of the population of Connaught shows the following remarkable figures :—

			Inhabited Houses.			Population.
1841	..	.	243,000	..	..	1,418,000
1851	..	..	169,000	..	..	1,100,000
1861	..	..	163,000	..	..	913,000
1871	..	..	153,000	..	..	846,000

Tuke's Report, 1880, p. 81.

lish. papers give only one side of the question, I
would do an injustice if I did not place such
matters before them fully. I will, therefore, give
a few documents to elucidate this point.

At a recent meeting of the Land League a
letter was read from the Rev. Daniel Monahan,
P.P., Drumcondra, Meath, in reference to
threatened evictions in that county. The rev.
gentleman states :—

" This quiet and peaceful district was excited and disturbed by the apprehension of the threatened evictions. In
Cloughnea there are 84 tenants ; 24 of these have been
relieved weekly by our committee here the last month. The
remaining tenants, with a few exceptions, by reason of the
depression of the times and the unjust agreement of 1874,
which nearly doubled their rents, are at present in very poor
circumstances. I was suddeny called, upon the eve of St.
Patrick's Day, to witness the sad and painful scene of the
eviction of four families from their homes. The resident
magistrate, sub-sheriff, inspector, with a number of her
Majesty's force, grippers, &c., were in attendance to carry
out the arbitrary wish of one individual. But, happily for
those poor tenants, who are good, honest, and industrious,
the evictions did not take place. In the case of Thomas
Farrell, his rent was paid by his friends up to the 25th of
March ; in the case of Bryan Nulty, by his sister; in the
other cases of Andrew Lalor and John M'Cartney, I paid
part and gave security for the remainder. There are other
evictions impending on this property, so that some are
voluntarily leaving who find it impossible to pay such high

Q

rents. For instance, on one holding the old rent, which was £60, was raised to £81, the valuation being only £52.*

The following letter shows too painfully the utter indifference of Irish landlords to the distress of their tenants in the Famine :—

"TO THE CHAIRMAN OF THE LAND LEAGUE.

" 10th November, 1880.

" SIR—Will you please accept the enclosed £1 note, my subscription to the funds of the Land League, and enrol my name as a member. I am slow to take an active part in any political movement; but, to my mind, the time has come for action, even in the timid and retiring. I owe the Land League a debt of gratitude for their prompt and generous contributions to our relief committee, by which many of my flock were rescued from starvation and death during the last awful season. In the face of famine itself the rents were paid up to some twelve landlords who hold property in my parish, and yet only one was found to contribute a single shilling to save the lives of the people, and the proprietor of Grenanstown estate was that one. I have painful recollections of the ever-memorable famine of 1847, and I know what Irish landlords can do. Day and night, and night and day, I had to administer the sacred rites of religion to the victims of their rapacity. With an unpitying eye and hard hearts they beheld the people famishing, the manhood of the country flying with their lives to a foreign land, and the helpless poor falling down to die like flies under their feet. The people then had no heart, no centre of action ; nobody like the League to lean on ; no leader like Mr. Parnell, who had the courage of his convictions, to teach them the secret of success. We are all very quiet here. If not 'peace and plenty,' at all events peace and poverty rule supreme. And yet, a local landlord and an extensive land agent was prominently present at the Castle of Dublin among the "105" maligners of the people. Another gentleman—a land agent, too, in the midst of "law and order"—surrounds himself with policemen, doing a friendly turn to his friend, and bringing a bad repute on a peaceful district. Notices to quit have been served, and already one of my parishoners is an outcast on the world. The sheriff has quenched the fire and locked the door of James Guilfoyle, of Cappa. He offered his landlord £13 out of the rack-rent of £16 10s. and all to no purpose. This poor man clings to the "old sod" with a life and death grip. He cooks his scanty meal by the side of a ditch, he rolls his cart under shelter and sleeps in it, "like a warrior taking his rest." Though he is persecuted by summons after summons to the petty sessions, still he fondly clings to the hope of being restored to the shelter of the old rooftree. No matter what the Government do to prosecute the Land League, on the cause must go, until justice is done the people. 'Salus populi suprema lex.'—I am, yours, &c.,

"EDMUND O'LEARY,

"Toomevara, County Tipperary."

The Rev. Dr. Rice, P.P., of Charleville, Co. Cork, at a public meeting, said :—

"He had for years regarded rack-renting and eviction as one of the greatest curses and scourges in Ireland. He said one of the greatest scourges because there were others. He regarded the destruction of their manufactures as a great grievance and loss. He regarded the ruin of most of their trades, and the hastening ruin of others by Englishmen, as another scourge, and he regarded the denial to the Irish people of the advantages of education afforded to a rich minority as another great and intolerable grievance."

At a meeting in the Queen's County, the Very Rev. Dr. Magee, P.P., Stradbally, proposed the following resolution :—

" 'That, in the opinion of this club, Ireland can never be a contented and prosperous nation so long as the present system of land feudalism is maintained.'

"The Rev. Dr. Magee said, without dwelling on the several tortures and cruelties of land feudalism, a subject now threadbare and exhausted by discussion, he would call their attention at once to the crisis in which these evils have resulted ; a crisis that now fills all classes with alarm ; and that, above all, threatens three millions of Irish tenantry with utter ruin and extermination if something be not done, and speedily and effectively done, to save them (applause). Never in the history of tenant disasters had Ireland presented a more ghastly spectacle. The last cruelty of landlord absolutism is extermination—when the tenant is ruined by excessive rents and stripped of everything, then to turn him adrift on the world, bankrupt and beggared, and this seems the present aim of landlordism (hear, hear). From north to south, from Wicklow to Connemara, nothing is now heard of but evictions, decrees, processes, notices to quit, fights for the harvest, constabulary rows, the wailing of widows and orphans, violence, outrage, and murder. What a sight for the stranger who visits our shores. Meantime the question arises, where is this all to end, or is there any constitutional remedy by which the calamity may be averted?

In his own parish there were at this moment twenty-five
unfortunate tenants of the rack-rented class under decrees
of eviction, execution stayed till the ides of January next ;
but when the ides of January come what will become of
them, for the present poor harvest can't save them (applause). What has given rise to this state of things ?
Landlords tell us 'tis all the result and curse of land agitation, and that if these horrible agitators were banished all
would be well. His simple answer was, land feudalism,
and above all the rack-renting power of the system, has led
to all, and has been ever at the root of all the disasters,
beggary, and murders of Ireland ; and he would go further,
so long as this power is maintained Ireland can never be
happy or prosperous (applause). For the last thirty years,
to go back no farther, we have witnessed the ravages and
excesses of this deadly power, nowhere, perhaps, more
fearfully carried out than in the Queen's County itself. On
lands of the most wretched character—cold, perished bogs,
and arid, barren hills—lands valued at from 9s. to 14s. and
15s. the acre, he himself had known rents to have been
twice and thrice, within eighteen years, squeezed up, under
terror of eviction, to an amount no mortal industry, or process of starvation, or sparing could meet. Twenty-five,
50, 80, and in some instances even 200 per cent. in excess
of the valuation, was added to the rent, and no alternative
given to the tenant that resisted (cheers and murmurs).
Landlords and agents sometimes give out platitudes, and
say rents must be a free contract ; no law or valuation
must meddle with it. Meantime the freedom given to unfortunate tenants themselves is somewhat like that given
by the highwayman to his victim—'Your money or your
life.' So with the tenant—the increased rent, or what is
equivalent to life, his home, his land, his all (applause).
For the last thirty years this cruel process had gone on ;

the rental of Ireland had been screwed up to the incredible and enormous sum of fifteen or sixteen millions yearly, and only that providence, as if to put a stop to the iniquity, had, within the last three years, brought famine and sterlity on the land, no man could tell where this process would end. An end, however, has come, and with it a new crisis and new peril to the tenantry. 'Tis now extermination—wide-spread extermination. The rack-rents can't by any human possibility be any longer paid unless stones and earth be turned into corn to pay them. The tenants may be exterminated, but these rents cannot be paid. The last three years of sterility and depression have settled the question, and no industry, no starvation, no sparing, even though the tenantry, in place of luxuriating, as Lord Cloncurry says, ' on poteen and potatoes,' lived on potatoes alone or Indian buck, can meet these rack-rents. Just let any generous and high-minded landlord look at the condition of the Irish tenantry at the present moment and say can such rent be met. In all Europe they are the most beggared, starved, and ruined race ; their stock diminished, their capital gone, trying to pay these rack-rents ; dipped in every bank, sunk in arrears, beggars before Europe, Government lending them the very seed of the land ; and meantime, what have the Irish landlords being doing during all this distress ? Ask any of the types of the exterminating class (applause). In the ancient Justinian Code, if sterility or famine came the landlord could exact but half the rent ; he shared the calamity with the tenant. How many landlords in Ireland, or of the Queen's County, have adopted this rule, or even reduced the rack-rent, or blotted out its arrears, during the last three years of distress ? Meantime the burning question arises, Where is all this to end, or how are the tenantry of Ireland to Le saved ?"

The following letter is an important evidence of the extraordinary difficulties our poor people have in obtaining justice; and it must be remembered that these are not exceptional cases. How can Ireland be other than disturbed and discontented when legal redress is rendered almost unobtainable? If our poor people satisfied the exorbitant demands of their landlords by weary and exceptional toil in England, year after year, surely in a year of famine a little mercy might have been shown them. And certainly they do not deserve the reproach of unwillingness to pay their rents or of laziness:—

"Dunmore, March 19.

"DEAR SIR,—Owing to the great distress of the year, I am obliged to appeal to the charitable public on behalf of the Cloondargan tenants. To those not familiar with the history of the case a few words of explanation may be necessary. The Cloondargan estate was bought by Mr. Revington, of Limerick, in 1868, the rental at the time being £215 18s 1d. One of his first acts was to raise it to £366 os od ! in some individual cases doubling, in others trebling, the former rents. These enormous rents the poor serfs, for the luxury of a home in Ireland, continued to pay till November last, when the failure of their crops, the depression in the price of stock, and, for them, worst of all, the dulness of trade in England, rendered the payment of these rents utterly and entirely impossible. Their land is very probably the worst in all Ireland; it never yielded an equivalent for the rent, which they always earned in England, and out of 51 tenants on the entire estate, only TWO could make the rent off the land.   Ejectment processes were served ; to which the tenants, after some fruitless efforts at an arrangement, entered defences.   Till about this time it was thought that a tenant disturbed for non-payment of rent had no redress, but a clause seemingly hidden away in the Land Act was discovered, under which tenants who consider their rents exorbitant have claims for disturbance, even though evicted for non-payment of such rents.   Under this clause Thomas Rice Henn, Esq., Q.C., Recorder of Galway, granted a stay of the execution of the decrees in cases of all the tenants who would have filed claims for compensation on or before the 9th of February last.   Thirty-eight claims, the first to be tried under the clause, were filed, and it is to enable the poor people to successfully maintain these claims I make this appeal to the public.   Every claim must be tried on its individual merits.   It is estimated that the purely legal expenses, not to speak of many incidental expenses, will amount to at least £50, towards which the people themselves are not able to subscribe even a single penny.   Forty-one of them are on the relief list, and every single tenant on the estate, except four, would require relief if we had it to give.   There are three families, with eight or nine members in each, who have nothing to subsist on from one Tuesday to another except the small pittance of Indian meal doled out to them by the committee.

"I, therefore, am reluctantly obliged to entreat the public to come to the assistance of these poor people.   They are abjectly poor; no words could convey any idea of their poverty.   Their cases will be tried on the 19th of April, just a month from the present time.   On the issue of these cases their very existence depends.   If they are beaten, nothing remains for them but the workhouse.   They will not be able to emigrate, and beaten they must be without the necessary funds. The importance to the tenants of Ireland generally of the principle involved cannot be exaggerated. To contribute something is a great work of charity—the smallest contribution will be gratefully and thankfully received, and as the time is so short it is particularly true that he who gives quickly gives twice. My apology for this appeal is, that owing to the prevailing distress an appeal to the people of the parish only would be a cruel mockery. All contributions will be received and thankfully acknowledged by, yours very sincerely,

"PATRICK LEVINGSTONE, C.C."

The following letter from the Right Rev. Dr. Power, Bishop of Waterford, was read at the Clonmel meeting, when Count Moore, M.P., presided :—

"WATERFORD, 22nd October, 1880.

"DEAR SIR,—In reply to your letter of the 18th instant, requesting, on behalf of the Committee of Management, that I would express approval of the objects for the attainment of which a land meeting is to be held in Clonmel on the 24th instant, I beg to assure you and the committee that every constitutional effort having for its aim the satisfactory settlement of the land question shall command my warmest sympathies and earnest co-operation. Every true Irishman must deplore the sad and sickening sight of witnessing the bone and sinew of our population forced to fly from our shores in hundreds of thousands as houseless outcasts, the victims of inhuman land laws. Scenes such as these can be arrested only by the enactment of such wise and stern laws as will wrest from the landlords the despotic power given them by anti-Irish Governments in order to up-hold them, as an alien garrison, to assist in crushing the legitimate aspirations of a down-trodden nation. An earnest and vigorously sustained agitation such as that now extending throughout the land, kept strictly within constitu-tional bounds and excluding all secret and illegal organisa-tions, must command the attention of statesmen, and sound the death-knell of landlord injustice and tyranny. Hence the usual faction cry for coercion, when the people demand the redress of their grievances, has been raised, and a friendly Administration is daily goaded by its astute and designing opponents to suppress a constitutional, though widespread agitation by suspending the safeguards of free and open dis-cussion. But I trust that the enlightened statesmen who rule the destinies of the empire may not be so pliant as to play into the hands of their unmasked enemies, and forfeit the confidence of the Irish people. In order to remove all pretence for the enactment of coercive measures, and to sustain the government in resisting the frantic demands for the suspension of the guarantees of free discussion, it behoves the leaders of the existing agitation to be moderate and guarded in language, and above all, should any cry savouring of bloodthirsty retaliation or injury of property be raised by mischievous individuals skulking in the crowd, the rule of action carried out by the immortal Liberator in similar circumstances should be adopted by calling on the well-disposed to hand them over to the police. Hoping that all such precautions shall be taken, and wishing a favourable issue to your proceedings, I am, dear sir, yours faithfully,

"✠ JOHN POWER."

I may add here a condensed report of some

remarks made at Naas in October (1880) by
the Right Rev. Dr. Lynch, as they bear strongly
on the question of emigration—the great landlord panacea for the distress they have too often
caused themselves—

"Dr. Lynch said he would rather see his people suffer a
little want here upon earth for a short time, and then enjoy
the happiness of heaven for all eternity, than have a little
more enjoyment and then suffer eternal misery. He knew
well, he went on to say, the dreadful dangers that beset the
paths of the Irish once they left their own shores, and he
was convinced that there was no place on this earth where
man or woman could so safely and surely save their souls as in
Ireland. He also said he had it on the authority of a priest
who had spent years on the American mission that nearly
seven out of ten who emigrated to America neglected their
religious duties. It is not surprising after all this that the
bishop strongly advised his people to stay at home as long
as they could."[1]

At a meeting, the date of which I have mis-
laid, Canon O'Keefe moved the following resolution :—

"'That we regard the present land system of this country
as the most odious, degrading, and disastrous result of the
foreign government of Ireland, and that we shall never cease
to contend, by every means in our power, until the tenant
farmers of Ireland shall be made the owners of the soil they

---

[1] Reported in *Nation* of same date.

cultivate.' They were taking the proper means of redressing their grievances by that constitutional agitation, which was spread like a wave over the surface of the land. They had against them the landlords of Ireland and all their minions and slaves. There was the Bar of Ireland, which if not against them would do nothing for them. At one time it was adorned by such men as Grattan and Flood, but to-day every spark of patriotism was extinguished from the profession. Another element against them was the venemous feeling of the late Administration. But they would carry this great question. He relied on the Irish party and the chief who ruled it (cheers for Mr. Parnell). Their enemies might ask what they wanted. His reply was that they wanted the land of Ireland for the people of Ireland. But did they want to rob the landlords ? His principle was —and it was the principle of the eternal law—that no man should take the property of another to the amount of a penny, unless he paid for it (cheers). If then the land were taken from the owner let him be paid the full value of it."

At a meeting near Ballinasloe [Oct. 1880] the Rev. Mr. Flanagan, speaking for the Bishop, said :—

" A crisis had now come which made it imperative on the Legislature to maturely consider the demands of the tenant-farmers of Ireland, and rendered a settlement of the land question inevitable. Of course, it should be admitted that in the settlement of this all important question grave difficulties would arise, and various opinions as to the best mode to be adopted would be formed, but he hoped that the bringing of tranquillity, peace, and prosperity to this country would be the outcome of the solution of the land problem.

In the agitation for land reform he would also observe that the priests, as they always were, would be with the people so long as they acted peaceably, orderly, and constitutionally. Heretofore the people followed the priests in all the great movements for the advancement of true nationality, and now in the present movement to show their great love for their flocks the priests were ready to follow the people to the contemplated land meeting at Kilreecle. His lordship accorded his warm approval, and expressed his most earnest wishes for its success (applause)."

Now, in the face of all the reiterated declarations of Irish bishops and priests, it is not the way to promote peace to charge them with encouraging lawlessness, and accuse them of encouraging crime. I must admit, indeed, that violent accusations of this kind have not been confined to the Orange faction in the North of Ireland; in a marked and scarcely less expressive form they have been reiterated by English Catholic papers. One gentleman, writing to the *Tablet*, gives the fact of his "having been previously a beneficed clergyman of the Church of England and ex-editor of a High Church periodical," as a reason why he is "constrained" to denounce Irish priests for joining with their people in asking justice from England. Some people might think it a reason why he should have abstained from such criticism.

The following letter has been addressed by

the Archbishop of Cashel to the editor of the
Freeman's Journal:—

"ROME, *November 17th.*

"MY DEAR SIR,—Under the heading 'Rome and Ireland,'
Saturday's *Freeman* contains the following paragraph, said
to have been conveyed to you from Rome by ' Reuter's and
Ordinary Telegraph':—

It is well-known in diplomatic circles accredited to the Holy See that
the Pope is much embarrassed to know how to deal with the Irish difficulty. He fully understands that it is not a question between Protestants and Catholics, but between the friends of order and anarchists.
He openly disapproves the agrarian movement, and entertains a sincere
desire to assist the English Government, were it possible. The great
difficulty is, that, were he to speak, it might be looked on as an improper
interference. Moreover, he is well aware that he is hearing only one
side of the case. What are the merits of the other, or the exact facts,
he has no means of learning, and he feels that, were he to break the
silence, he might, in seeking to do good, produce, through imperfect
knowledge, a contrary result. The Irish bishops have, in social conversation in Rome, not been reticent in describing Mr. Parnell as a great
benefactor to Ireland.

"Your readers will, I am sure, be pleased to learn, on my
authority, that, with the exception of what is set forth in the
last sentence, each and every statement in the above paragraph is utterly, absolutely, and notoriously untrue. Another
portion of the telegram ascribes words to me, when replying
to the Holy Father, which those who know me will hardly
believe that I used.

"I am, my dear sir, your faithful servant,

"✠ T. W. CROKE,

" Archbishop of Cashel."

CHAPTER XV.

*" The people are made slaves of, and then they are called slaves."—
A. Barrel.*

ISTORY, as we are told by philosophers, repeats itself. Unhappily in Ireland the repetition is somewhat monotonous. The Conservative party in England, and nearly all the landlords in Ireland (there are honourable exceptions), are calling out for " coercion" —they speak, they write, as if it was an hitherto unused and undiscovered panacea for all the ills of Ireland—and they taunt the leaders of the Liberal party with not administering their sulphuric nostrum.

They suggest the suspension of the Habeas Corpus and a little gunpowder, and all would be well. But I have forgotten. I am told that a London society paper, which patronises even royalty, has suggested seriously the deprivation of the franchise for the whole of Ireland. And this is in an age when the liberty of the

subject is supposed to be the great object of
philosophers, statesmen, and the public generally.

Let me say again : *Quem Deus vult perdere
prius dementat.* One is tempted to think that,
great as are the evils which have been committed by Irish landlords, by their violation of
English laws, they must surely have done even
more than is apparent to their greatest enemies,
or they could never have been given up to such
hopeless insanity.

Why, coercion has been the normal rule of
Irish government, if one may judge from its
perpetual re-enactment. Certainly it cannot be
asked for as a new experiment; we are long
since lost to all sense of novelty in that respect. But what a poor and pityful policy all
this is. One generation after another passes
away, and the cry of coercion is handed down
from father to son as the rallying cry for Irish
government. Might it not be well to try some
change, even as an experiment ?

Mr. Froude has happily lucid moments, and
in a lucid moment he wrote the following. It
is true he refers to the past, but what he has
said his children will apply to the present :

" Of all the fatal gifts," says Mr. Froude, " which we bestowed on our unhappy possession was the English system

of owning land. Land, properly speaking, cannot be owned
by any man—it belongs to all the human race. Laws have
to be made to secure the profits of their industry to those
who cultivate it; but the private property of this or that
person, which he is entitled to deal with as he pleases, land
never ought to be, and never strictly is. In Ireland, as in
all primitive civilizations, the soil was divided among the
tribes. Each tribe collectively owned. its own district.
Under the feudal system the proprietor was the Crown, as
representing the nation ; while the subordinate tenures were
held with duties attached to them, and were liable on non-
fulfilment to forfeiture. In England, the burden of defence
was on the land. Every gentleman, according to his estate,
was bound to bring so many men into the field, properly
armed and accoutred. When a standing army was substi-
tuted for the old levies, the country squires served as unpaid
magistrates on the commission of the peace. The country
squire system was, in fact, a development of the feudal
system, and, as we gave the feudal system to Ireland, so we
tried long and earnestly to give them our landowners. The
intention, doubtless, was as good as possible in both cases,
but we had taken no trouble to understand Ireland, and we
failed as completely as before. The duties attached. to
landed property died away, or were forgotten—the ownership only remained. The people, retaining their tribal
traditions, believed that they had rights upon the land on
which they lived. The owner believed that there were no
rights but his own. In England, the rights of landlords
have similarly survived their duties, but they have been
modified by custom or public opinion. In Ireland, the
proprietor was an alien, with the fortunes of the residents
upon his estate in his hands, and at his mercy. He was
divided from them in creed and language ; he despised
them, as of an inferior race, and he acknowledged no in-

R

terest in common with them.   Had he been allowed to
trample on them and make them his slaves, he would have
cared for them, perhaps, as he cared for his horses.   But
their persons were free, while their farms and houses were
his ; and thus his only object was to wring out of them the
last penny which they could pay, leaving them and their
children to a life scarcely raised above the level of their
own pigs."[1]

Here is what an Irish priest has to say of the
present state of Ireland, and let it be noted
clearly he speaks of facts :—

"The Rev. D. Ryan, D.D., president of the Cashel branch,
came forward. He said that the eloquent address of their
patriotic representative saved him the trouble of speaking
to them on the very important topic of organisation.   He
would not, however, allow the opportunity to pass without
offering a few remarks on the Irish land system and its
results.   The system was iniquitous and unjust, and was
opposed to the laws of God and nature.   There was no law
more solemnly enjoined by the Almighty than that which
defines the duty of the parent.   Well, that man was false to
that law who, through paying an unjust rent, allowed his
children to starve before his eyes, and permitted them to
grow up in rags and without education.   He was aware
that there were more inmates in the Cashel workhouse than
there were people attending the parish Mass of Roesgreen
on a Sunday or holiday (cries of ' Shame'), and he stated on
his experience as a priest that the average peasant and the

---

[1] " Romanism and the Irish Race," p. 36.

average peasant's children were worse housed, worse clothed, and worse fed than the pauper inmates of the workhouse (cheers). This disgraceful state of things could last no longer in a civilised country. For the past generation, since the years of the memorable famine, we had lost three millions of our people; and our population was daily dwindling, verifying the words of the great O'Connell that Ireland was a country blessed by God but cursed by man (cheers). There was no evil without a remedy, and a means was at length discovered to rid Ireland of the accursed system of landlordism. He advised the people to be constitutional, but to be determined at the same time; and told them that from this agitation they would get prosperity, and with prosperity would come in the immediate future that happy time when the green flag would float proudly over a free people, and a native Parliament would make its own laws in old College-green (great cheering)."

Such is the present state of things in Ireland; and let it be noted this is said of Tipperary, one of the (supposed) most fertile parts of Ireland. Yet we see that coercion is the only remedy for all this. Yes; coercion is needed, but it should be applied to those whose greed and selfishness have caused so much of this misery to their serfs. Coercion has been tried ever since the Union on the Irish tenant, it is only fair that the Irish landlord should have his turn. Good landlords will not object to legal restraint. The sooner the usurious and absentee landlord is made to feel its wholesome fetters the better. Coercion Acts have been passed again and again through Parliament with unusual rapidity and unanimity. Mr. O'Brien says :—

"On the 9th of July, an Arms Bill, which the Earl of Radnor denounced as 'vexatious and oppressive,' was, on the motion of the Duke of Wellington, read a second time in the Lords. It had a more fortunate fate than the Waste Lands Bill. Nothing is more melancholy in the history of English legislation for Ireland than the rapidity with which Coercion Acts have been passed, as compared with the apathy and neglect of Parliament in dealing with remedial measures. I once heard Sir Wilfred Lawson say, *à propos* of the late Zulu war, 'that the Zulus were a very fine people, and capable of being greatly improved and civilised;' but, he added, 'it seems to me that the only efforts which we have taken up to the present to civilise and improve them have been to shoot them.' England has left herself open to the charge that, for many years, her chief efforts to improve the Irish people were to imprison or to hang them. 'The gallows,' says Mr. Bright, 'has been the great preserver in Ireland.'"[1]

In Mr. O'Brien's admirable work he shows that Ireland, since the Union, has scarcely been left for even a year or two without some Coercion Act.

---

[1] "O'Brien's *Land Question*, p. 39. I earnestly recommend this work to the reader. It is not expensive. The publishers are Sampson, Low and Co., 188 Fleet Street, London.

But, we are told now, even by those who are anxious to do some little act of justice to Ireland, that we must have coercion first, and justice after. Was there ever such infatuation? Because an admitted wrong has been done to a whole nation, they must be first punished for saying so before the wrong is redressed. Is this English honour, of which we hear so much?

But it is said that Ireland has done illegal acts which must be punished. And have the English people no patience? Have they no high sense of justice? Have they no self-respect? They have done Ireland grievous wrong; and if Ireland, in complaining of the wrong, does not act quite wisely, is it the part of him who has inflicted the wrong to inflict punishment before he redresses it?

Is this how England has been governed? Are we still and ever to have one law for England and another for Ireland? Is England to govern Ireland, or is it to be governed by Irish landlords? If England cannot make Irish landlords amenable to English law; if they will not allow the same laws to be enacted for their dealings with their Irish tenants as those to which they are obliged to submit in their deal-

ings with their English tenants, then let us
have Repeal of the Union.[1]

I am convinced, indeed I need not express it
as an opinion, it is a matter of fact, that English
noblemen and gentlemen are by no means so
unwilling to do justice to Ireland. A few Conservatives who oppose it on political, shall I say
principle or principles, are the great exception.

When Lord Stanley, in June, 1845, intro-

---

[1] "It is well known that in England and in Scotland, before a landlord offers a farm for letting, he finds it necessary to provide a suitable
farm-house, with necessary farm-buildings, for the proper management
of the farm. He puts the gates and fences into good order, and he takes
upon himself a great part of the burden of keeping the buildings in
repair during the term; and the rent is fixed with reference to this state
of things. Such, at least, is generally the case, although special contracts may occasionally be made, varying the arrangement between landlord and tenant. In Ireland the case is wholly different. . . . In most
cases [there] whatever is done in the way of building or fencing is done
by the tenant; and, in the ordinary language of the country, dwelling-
houses, farm-buildings, and even the making of fences, are described
by the general word 'improvements,' which is thus employed to denote
the necessary adjuncts, without which, in England or in Scotland, no
tenant would be found to rent it."—"Report of the Devon Commission
Digest," vol. ii., pp. 1122-1123.

Mr. O'Connor Morris (the *Times'* Special Commissioner), writing in
1868-9, observes upon the law as to improvement :—" In Ireland, where
in most cases what is done in the way of improving the soil is done by
the tenant, not by the landlord, and where the tenant in the majority of
instances has not risen to the *status* of a free contractor, the law is in
the highest degree unfair; it refuses to protect what really is the property of a tenant, added to the holding, and exposes it to unredressed
confiscation."—"Letters to the *Times,*" p. 148.

duced a Bill for "the purpose of providing compensation to tenants in Ireland, in certain cases,
on being dispossessed of their holdings, for such
improvements as they may have made during
their tenancy," it was opposed by Irish landlords, and a solemn protest against it was signed
by Lords Monteagle and Brandon, Gosford,
Campbell, Chaworth (Meath), Crofton, Charle-
mount, Lismore, Somerhill (Clanricarde), Kinard
and Rosse, Carew, Clanbrassil (Roden), Lucan,
Charleville, Stradbroke, Massarene, Sandwich,
Rosse, Lorton, Egmont, Kingston, Londonderry.

On the 23rd July, 1849, Mr. Horsman moved:

"That an humble address be presented to her Majesty,
praying her to take into her consideration the condition of
Ireland."

"What have we done for Ireland?" said Mr. Horsman.
"Ireland has been truly described as one adjourned debate.
We found her prostrate in February; have we raised her in
July? Ireland is now entering on the fourth year of famine;
sixty per cent. of her population are receiving relief. What
are the causes which have produced such results? Bad
legislation, careless legislation, criminal legislation, has been
the cause of all the disasters we are now deploring."

Mr. Horsman's resolution led to an animated
debate—but to nothing else.

Mr. O'Brien says:—

"Seven years had now elapsed since the report of the

Devon Commission was placed before Parliament. That
report had recommended the enactment of legislative
measures to protect the fruits of the tenants' industry in
Ireland. The recommendation was not carried out. No
Bill was passed by the Imperial Parliament in the interests
of the tenants. But to use the words of Mr. Finlayson, the
able editor of Reeve's ' History of English Law,' ' An Act
was passed for the relief of the *landlords.* This was the
Incumbered Estates Act.[1]

This Act was well intended by England, but
it has caused not a little of the present distress.
Lord John Russell spoke thus, at the Devon
Commission :—

"However ignorant many of us may be of the state of
Ireland, we have here (in the Devon Commission) the best
evidence that can be procured —the evidence of persons
best acquainted with that country, of magistrates of many
years' standing, of farmers, of those who have been employed
by the Crown ; and all tell you that the possession of land
is that which makes the difference between existing and
starving amongst the peasantry, and that, therefore, ejections
out of their holdings are the cause of violence and crime in
Ireland.   In fact, it is no other than the cause which the
great master of human nature describes, when he makes a
tempter suggest it as a reason to violate the law : ' Famine
is in thy cheeks, need and oppression starveth in thine eyes,
upon thy back hangs ragged misery.   The world is not thy

_____

" Irish Land Question," p. 109.

friend, nor the world's law; the world affords no law to make thee rich. Then be not poor, but break it.'"[1]

. No wonder that the present Land Commis sion has been viewed with indifference or con tempt. We have had a great many Land Com- missions, and a great many Coercion Acts, to keep us quiet, until the English Government had time to do us justice; but we are still wait- ing for the justice.

In 1844, Lord Normanby said in the House of Lords :—

" In Ireland the landlord has a monopoly of the means of existence, and has a power for enforcing his bargains, which does not exist elsewhere—the power of starvation."

Land Commissions and Coercion Acts not- withstanding—this is as true in 1880 as in 1844.

. We hear a great deal about the sacred rights of property; but what of the sacred right to live? Did England meet the riotous demands of the English populace with Coercion Acts, when, from time to time, they have rebelled against injustice. No. A man who rages in fever does not cut off his hand while he is wait-

---

[1] Lord John Russell, "Hansard," 3rd series, vol. xcvii. p. 507.

ing for his disease to be cured. England will
not give a stone to her people when they ask for
bread. Can she blame Ireland, if Ireland
objects to be treated as a slave colony.
I quote below from a recent article in the
Freeman's Journal on this subject :—

"Lord Sidmouth passed his infamous "Six Acts" in 1819.
These Acts forbade the people to be armed and drilled, forbade public assemblies, gave constables the right of searching
for arms, and muzzled the Press. It was then, after this
repressive legislation, that the real English monster meeting
and rioting set in. Then came the Cato Street conspiracy
for the murder of the whole Cabinet, and in every one of the
great towns of England, Scotland, and Wales, there were
enormous mass meetings of people. The people marched
in drill bands, under flags bearing for inscriptions, 'No
Corn Laws,' 'Annual Parliaments,' 'Universal Suffrage,'
'Equal Representation or Death,' 'God Armeth the
Patriot,' &c., &c. One flag, which we believe floated at Mr.
Gladstone's town, Leeds, bore the picture of a yeoman
cutting down a woman, with the motto, 'Vengeance.' The
meetings everywhere denounced the Government measures,
and the riotings and burnings were terrible. Nottingham
was reduced to ashes, a good part of Bristol was in flames,
and the Duke of Wellington declared that Birmingham in
1839 was in a worse plight than any city he had ever sacked.
In 1843 the riots broke out again in various parts of England and Scotland, and were followed by the Rebecca Riots
in South Wales, which were as furious as the previous Lud-
dite Riots in the same place. There were also the alarming
'Radical' Riots in London, and later there came the Chartist
and anti-Corn Law monster masses, which counted their

numbers by millions. It was during the last named excitement that the late Sir R. Peel's private secretary, Mr. Drummond, was assassinated in London by mistake for Peel himself. The Reform mass assemblages all through England in 1866 and the Hyde Park Riot we all remember, and we remember, too, that it was these masses and riots that coerced or enabled Mr. Disraeli to take his ' leap in the dark.' This is a sketch of popular agitation in England, and we shall be glad if Mr. H. Gladstone will inform us what extra-coercive measure, and what suspension of the Constitution, was adopted by the Crown against all these demonstrations in England, since the time of Lord Sidmouth's tyrannical and abortive Acts?

And here let us call special attention to our subject; for it is of great importance. The poorest men and women in Ireland take an active interest in politics, which can scarcely be understood in England. To bribe a whole county of voters, as has been done lately in England, would be impossible in Ireland. I put aside the question of conscience. Every moment of the life of an Irish peasant brings him face to face with circumstances which affect his right to live. He has the keen sense, at least, of personal interest in every political vote and in every political question. Hence it is that politics are of such interest to him; hence it is that he takes such an interest in every public affair.

Is it not a question of the highest moment to
any man how he is to feed, and clothe, and
educate his young family ?   Is it not a question
of the highest moment to him, whether he is to
spend his life in exile from a country to which
he is passionately attached, or whether he is to
remain in that humble home which, though it
has few charms for others, has every charm for
him ?

It is not long since I saw a pathetic appeal
in some paper from Irish landlords, who pictured
in graphic and glowing words their love for
their "homes," and their fear that they should
be obliged to leave them if the land agitation
continued. Their homes ! The place where
so many of them only come for a few weeks, at
most, every year, or once in two or three years,
to see that their rents are duly paid and duly
received.   It would be fitter to call these places
their lodgings.   Their children are not born in
them ; they are not reared in them ; certainly
they are not taught to love them. These nobles
and gentlemen, who talk thus pathetically of
their possible well-paid dismissal from the offices
of rent-receivers in Ireland, find it their pleasure to reside for half the year in France, or
Germany, or England—perhaps much further.

But the Irish exile utters his lament if he

must leave his humble cot. To the last hour of his life, however prosperous he may be in foreign lands, he pines for home, and he cannot forget the cause of his compulsory and terrible exile; nor does he forget his home, as his abundant help "to pay the rint" and to get some trifling necessary for the old father or mother amply prove.

It is one of the most anomalous and disgraceful facts in all the world that Irish landlords should be supported, not merely by the labour and toil of their hard-working tenants, but by the labour and capital of the sons and daughters of their tenants in a foreign land. This is no matter of fiction, or sentiment, or romance. There are items—official facts and figures—to prove it.[1]

And yet we are told that the Irish are lazy. Lazy! Why, if the Irish were not the most industrious people on the face of the earth, they would long since have been swept off it; and those who now reap the fruit of their labour would have wept tears of self-interested sorrow for their loss.

---

[1] Between 1848 and 1864 the Irish emigrants had sent back to Ireland upwards of £13,000,000. Lord Dufferin's "*Irish Emigration and Tenure of Land in Ireland,*" p. 2.

Every public subject in Ireland is then a political subject, because every such subject touches in some way on that one great right— the right to live.

I have before me now a remarkable document. It is entitled :—

A FULL REPORT

[of the trials of]

Gerald O'Connor, Rev. Andrew O'Sullivan, Jeremiah O'Connor, and William M'Carthy,

At the last KERRY ASSIZES,

Held at TRALEE, on the 18th October,

For conspiring to resist the payment of Tithes, and exciting the people to that effect.

Containing the SPEECH of Mr. O'CONNELL, in defence of the Traversers.

DUBLIN.

1832.

History does, indeed, repeat itself; and we have here in this tithe trial one remarkably similar to the trial of the gentlemen belonging to the Land League for conspiracy at the present day. The comparison is so close I am publishing the whole case in the Appendix to the present work. The Counsel for the Prosecution spoke as the Attorney-General will probably speak in opening the case against the Land League traversers:— "The people were misled, the country was in danger, the spirit of insubordination was abroad in the land." "What!" he cries, "are the laws, the liberties, and the lives of the subjects to be held in subservience to these lawless agitators?" Could more be said of the land agitation to-day? Hence, the old story, always old and always new. Yesterday, the charge was for "preventing the levying of tithes;" to-day, the charge is for preventing the payment of rents believed to be in excess of the value of the land. Always the same; a people struggling against oppression in the only way left to them—by a guerilla warfare—attracting attention to their undoubted wrongs by actions which, if they are in themselves reprehensible, must be credited in some manner to those who inflict the wrong, or who refuse to redress it.

Again, there is the imputation that the agitators were not sincere when they repudiated violence; and men were to be judged, not by what they said, but by what their adversaries chose to think they said. If this was not a manufacture of constructive treason, it was certainly a manufacture of constructive conspiracy.

And by an infelicitous admission, the prosecuting counsel declares that the people may as well complain of rents as tithes.

The manner in which the accused carried out their anti-tithe crusade corresponds exactly with the agitation of to-day. The grand point was to send any man to a social coventry who paid tithes, and to refuse to purchase any animal or any kind of goods seized for tithes. There was the usual sergeant of police, who took notes, and, unhappily for himself, was relegated to the tender mercies of Mr. O'Connell for cross-examination. Mr. O'Connell made him remember a great many things which he had forgotten, and made him admit several matters which were certainly damaging to the prosecution.

For example, he was evidently instructed by the magistrates, to tell all he could against the accused, and to be silent on any point in their favour. To-day we have young girls taken, contrary to all legal right, and detained in Dublin, in order that they may be ready to give such evidence as it is supposed will be useful to a prosecution which may yet have to be abandoned for want of reliable evidence.

O'Connell's masterly defence will be found in the Appendix. O'Connell's speeches are not

for the day they were uttered, they are for all
time—for all time as masterpieces of eloquent
persuasive ability; but let us hope a time will
come in the history of Ireland when they will
be no longer quoted as appropriate to the
present moment.

There are a few lines so memorable that I
repeat them here :—

" The Government appear to be under the influence of
two antagonistic principles, one of good, and the other of
evil. They have revived the system of the Manicheans,
who worship their god of justice and of injustice."

Alas ! this has been the one uniform method
of governing Ireland. There always are, let us
hope there always will be, members of the
English Government who see plainly the injustice which causes agitation in Ireland; but
they let—

" I dare not wait upon I will."

They find Ireland is not a subject of sufficient
interest or importance to make a sacrifice of
political power or friends for it—they fluctuate
between coercion and justice. They would
willingly be just if they dared. They coerce
because they must. Coercion may silence the
cries of a long suffering people for the moment ;
they will only break out yet more cruelly in

s

time. Justice, and justice alone, will still their
cries for ever.

Again, Mr. O'Connell brings forward the
very remarkable and most significant case of
the printer who published Swift's pamphlet, recommending the people of Ireland to use Irish
manufacture exclusively. Those who taunt the
Irish to-day with laziness, and indifference, and
want of business habits and action, do not read
history, or they are seriously unjust. The
pamphlet was pronounced "factious and seditious," and the printer was prosecuted for publishing it. Swift says that great pains were
taken to pack the jury, and that they *were*
packed carefully and well, yet they acquitted the
printer. But the judge was not so easily bul-
lied. He knew his masters too well. He sent
the much-enduring jury back nine times, and
kept them in eleven hours ; and at last they
were forced to leave the matter to him by a
special verdict.

The verdict of the tithe trial may be anticipated. The Rev. Mr. O'Sullivan was acquitted ; there was not a particle of evidence
against him that could be even tortured into
criminality. The other traversers were both
fined and imprisoned.

There is a priest in Kerry to-day, the Rev.

Father O'Connor, P.P., of Ballybunnion, and he tells us that he was but a little lad of some six years old, when he saw his father carried off to gaol for this offence—for taking part in a peaceful agitation, in which it was proved that he especially recommended that there should be no violence.

It is sometimes conveniently forgotten that there are men who remember such times and such scenes, and who can scarcely be expected to be very devoted to a form of government which caused so much suffering.

CHAPTER XVI.

THE IRISH LAND AGENT.

" We must gird our loins to encounter the Nemesis of seven centuries of misgovernment. To the end of time 100,000,000 of people, spread over the largest habitable area in the world, and confronting us everywhere, by sea and land, will remember that their forefathers paid tithes to the Protestant clergy, rent to absentee landlords, and a forced obedience to the laws which these had made."—The *Times*, May 3, 1860.

HE Irish land agent is a being *sui generis*. He is an anomaly and an anachronism. To do his work, not always clean, he must combine something of the steel-heartedness of a Southern slave-driver and the tyranny of an eastern despot. You will say I exaggerate. Pardon. I shall give you facts, and facts are stubborn things.

I suppose the Irish land agent is the most absolute autocrat on earth. Laws are made in England for the protection of the Irish tenant; he smiles at them. The king's writ does not run his way. Who is to know in the wilds of Donegal or Kerry what the land agent does? Even when the land agent is not naturally in-

THOMAS BRENNAN.

clined to act the despot, his master's interests must be his first consideration.

The prestent agitation has had the advantage of throwing no little light on this subject. Lord Cork, an absentee southern landlord, is not considered a hard master. His agent, Mr. Leahy, is considered, and I believe justly, an honourable man. But the present agitation has brought out the remarkable fact that Lord Cork's tenants are obliged to contract themselves out of the benefit of the Land Act, made by England for their special benefit. This matter having been strongly commented on in the press, Mr. Leahy published the following letter in the *Cork Examiner* :—

"SHANAKIEL HOUSE, *Nov. 19th*, 1880.

"DEAR SIR,—As the Rev. Father M'Mahon, in a letter which appeared in your journal of this morning, alludes to the lease granted to tenants on the Earl of Cork's estate, will you kindly allow me a small space to explain matters.

"The Land Act of 1870 was so loosely framed that immediately after it became law solicitors in this country who had the dra⁹·ng of a lease took advantage of its vagueness and whether *legally or not*, inserted clauses in their clients tenants' leases endeavouring to set at naught some of the provisions of the Act. Lord Cork's solicitor was no exception, and in the leases there was inserted a clause in which the tenant bound himself to forego any claim hereafter under the Land Act.

" I candidly say I would much rather that this clause had

never been introduced, and further, I am perfectly certain that had any one noticed it at the time, or remonstrated, it would have been omitted. I am very glad to see that Father M'Mahon says he believes I never intended by permitting the introduction of the clause anything to the detriment of the tenants. In this he is right.

"I now wish to mention one fact in connection with this 'objectionable clause.' I was examined, at the special request of the commissioners, on the Tuesday of the week they sat in Cork, and the Rev. Father M'Mahon was examined on the day following. I had not the remotest idea that he was about to be examined, or of his intention as to evidence when examined. I took one of the estate leases with me and handed it in to the chairman purposely to *point out this very clause*. Why? To prove the looseness of the Act of 1870, and call upon the commission to have the new Bill so framed as to prevent landlord, agent, or tenant wriggling out of its provisions. Father M'Mahon was examined the following day and brought forward the subject again. On this I determined in my own mind (which I must confess was never very happy about it) to lay the matter before the Earl of Cork, and request him to cancel the clause. He at once consented, and gave me instructions to obliterate it from his leases. This decision I intended to announce when on the estate next week, but I am glad Father M'Mahon has now given me an opportunity of doing so.—I remain, dear sir, faithfully yours,

"D. F. LEAHY."

Now, here is a most curious instance of the fashion in which Ireland is governed. We have the land agent of an extensive property declaring that he did not know how the leases had been drawn. But, was it not his duty to know? And we find the curious and instructive statement that Irish solicitors are in the habit of depriving Irish tenants of legal rights.

There is, however, one noteworthy feature in all such cases. Land agents here have never let anything slip into their leases, or agreements with tenants, which is to the disadvantage of the landlord. No doubt this is their duty; but have they not also a most sacred duty towards those who are utterly and helplessly dependent on them? The *Times* said lately :—

"The Irish landlords themselves cannot fail to see that their own interests require change, it may be a great change, in the Irish land laws."

It is to be feared they will not see it, so long as it is possible for them to protect themselves on every side, and to have their tenants at their mercy.

A recent writer in the *Tablet* complains of the difficulty of hearing the truth about Ireland. He cites the famous, or infamous, Boycott case as an example. Lord Erne has declared that he heard nothing of the grievances of his tenants until after they became notorious. Now, if the writer had known anything about Irish land agents he would have understood the matter very easily. The Irish landlord's method of dealing with his tenantry is very simple. He never sees them, or, if he does see any of his tenants, he only sees those who live in the immediate vicinity of the place which he visits for a few weeks in the year. There are, I am convinced, millions of Irish tenants who have never seen their landlords. If any complaint is made it is always referred to the agent. Hence, for the most part, the people have ceased to complain. The agent makes very short work of the matter. His business, or at least his object is, to save himself as much trouble as possible.

I know that English gentlemen have not even the least idea of the autocratic rule of an Irish land agent. I am certain that they could not imagine it, unless they lived for some time in an Irish country district and knew the people and their surroundings intimately. But do not take my word for this. My object in writing the present work is to give information on reliable authority. Would any English gentleman believe that lunacy would be considered a special qualification for a land agent or a landlord? Yet the special correspondent of the *Daily Telegraph* describes one thus :—

" One of the difficulties under which landlords labour in Ireland undoubtedly arises from the smallness of their number. They cannot cope single-handed with the crowd around them, unless they are very determined and clever men. Occasionally such a gentleman does, however, turn up, and I heard of one of them yesterday. The man in question has been proved, by a court of his fellow-countrymen, to have been mad, at any rate during a portion of his life, and is regarded, rightly or wrongly, as something more than eccentric now. The bold peasantry, amongst whom he lives in Galway, are, in fact, afraid of him. He is known to be always armed, and as a "lunatic"—for such he would be considered, were he to shoot anyone—he would never be punished, were he to fire at another man in a moment of rage, while he is powerful and vigorous in frame and noted as a 'dead shot.' It is reasonable, then, that he should not be greatly admired by the people, who like 'soft' landlords to deal with. An attempt to 'Boycott' him, as the process of starving out is called, failed ignominiously, no shopkeeper having the hardihood to refuse him goods. One threatening letter received by him made him, so it is said, behave so wildly that no one dreams of favouring him with another."

The land agent in any Belgravian drawingroom and the land agent or landlord who acts as his own agent in the wilds of Connemara or Kerry are very different persons. Mr. Charles Russell, M.P., in his letters to the *Daily Telegraph*, mentions instances of this fearful terrorism in Kerry. He says :—

" I found the greatest dread prevailing amongst the tenants of having their names disclosed. At first I had difficulty in even getting them to converse, until they became assured that our feelings were friendly towards them, but even then, with hardly an exception, they spoke protesting that it would be ruin to them if it was known that they had communicated any facts to us. I do not doubt that this dread was to some extent uncalled-for, but it was assuredly real. Nothing impressed me more than the state of terror in which, speaking as a rule, they seemed to live. One man, apparently well-to-do, was mentioning a circumstance of some significance in the agent's management; but, upon perceiving that the shorthand writer who accompanied me was taking a note of his observation, he became alarmed, and said it would be ruin to him if he were known to have said anything about the agent, and requested us on no account to mention his name.

"On another occasion, and on the same estate, a remarkable incident occurred. A man who was a high class type of the Kerry peasant, commanding in figure, with an intelligent and even refined face, upon our meeting him on the threshold of his door (we had been told that his case was a hard one) drew himself to his full height, and, raising his hands earnestly, cried out, 'For God's sake, gentlemen, pass me by—pass me by!' We were startled. We afterwards learned that years ago he had given information as to the management of the estate to the representative of a southern paper in Ireland, since which it had been noticed that he had been made to feel the weight of the agent's ill will. For these reasons I reluctantly abstain from giving the names of the tenants whose cases I investigated, but I can assure your readers that I used every precaution to arrive at the truth in each instance. Occasionally lightheartedness and cheerfulness appeared amongst the tenantry, but these were rare; and the humour with which the Irish peasant is frequently credited has, if it ever existed, been stamped out of Kerry by the sad realities of their lives of want. With all this they have managed to preserve a certain dignity and grace of manner, and they are very intelligent."

Again he says :

" A further portion of the estate lies beyond Cahirciveen, on the coast road to Kenmare, near Waterville. Both portions possess many characteristics in common. The houses are in appearance inferior to those on the Kenmare portion of the property ; otherwise there is, I think, little difference. While, however, the same feeling in reference to the agency of the estate seems to exist here, I was somewhat surprised to find that a freer tone of criticism and a more independent attitude was assumed by the tenants than in the Kenmare neighbourhood. There they seemed literally afraid to call their souls their own. It is no exaggeration to say they spoke with bated breath, as if afraid agent or bailiff might hear them. Here they spoke out their complaints with greater freedom and boldness. The greater distance from the agent's eye perhaps accounted for the difference. Lord Lansdowne was unknown to them. The few who had ever seen him had done so upon the occasion of his attaining his majority. Mr. Trench had only been there once in the last five years, and then his visit had been short. Neither landlord nor agent had visited them in the time of their distress, although Canon Brosnan, the parish priest of Cahirciveen, had given timely written warning to Lord Lansdowne that the condition of his Cahirciveen tenantry was likely to be one of great suffering and privation. Practically, the control of this part of the estate is in the hands of bailiffs, of whom the principal one lives at Waterville. I was unable to find that any considerable money had been laid out by the landlord, and where it had been 1s. in the pound had been added to the rent as a permanent increase."

The special correspondent of the *Standard*, who manifestly was sent to give the landlords' views of Ireland, calls this kind of government peremptory, and actually gives from the very life of a land agent his account of his autocratic style of government, of which he is not a little proud :—

" As to the meddling by the tenants with the wood on the estate, Mr. Trench himself related an instance of his rigour. A tenant cut down a tree. He was remonstrated with, but his answer was defiant. Mr. Trench thereupon took away half his farm, *pour encourager les autres.* Another man, named John Sullivan, of Cuddudagh, was summoned before the magistrates for cutting boughs and ' spars ' and twigs to bind his thatch, which a violent wind had disarranged. His wife went to the agent's office to ask that her husband might not be proceeded against, but she was told that the law must take its course. The man was fined 12s., including costs. This story was furnished to me by a gentleman whose veracity I have no reason to doubt. As to the permanent increase of rent in consequence of the sale of lime, we have here an arrangement of a rather singular kind. Through the middle of the Lansdowne estate a vein of limestone runs. Until lately, many farmers had each his own lime kiln, as lime is extensively used to lighten the heavy, peaty soil. It occurred to Mr. Trench that lime could be made cheaper by having a central kiln, and, accordingly, it was erected. Lime was then sold to the tenants at 1s. 6d. per barrel, and the old kilns went out of use. Under this system some 6,000 barrels of lime were sold annually. But it was proposed that, instead of paying for each separate barrel of lime, a penny in the pound should

be added permanently to the rent, and the lime given without charge. The tenants appear to have approved of this
plan ; for, instead of 6,000 barrels, there was immediately
an annual sale of 12,000 "

As to the approval of the farmers, they had
Hobson's choice, and their approval of any
arrangement made for them would be neither
cared for nor asked. Mr. Russell gives a
sufficient proof of this in another of his letters
on Kerry :—

"See the easy fashion in which the rise of rent is accomplished. No independent valuation, no mutual negotiation.
The mandate of the agent goes forth. Some may grumble,
even grumble in a loud voice, but it is useless. They are
practically without alternative, they must submit. A fact,
to my mind positively shocking, was told to me by a gentleman, in every way reliable, in reference to this last rise. On
that occasion, when Mr. Trench had issued his commands
to his bailiffs, and had condescended to notify the rise to
some of the tenants, he said to my informant, ' I have done
two good days' work ; I have put £10,000 in Lord Lansdowne's pocket.' In other words, he had additionally taxed
the energies and the industry of Lord Lansdowne's Iveragh
tenants to the tune of £500 a year! Once more I ask, is
it remarkable that in Ireland cultivation is backward, that
poverty abounds, that discontent is wide spread, that social
progress is slow, that man so little responds to the efforts of
Nature for his advantage, that in conditions like these, thrift
and industry do not flourish ?"

The *Standard* correspondent gives an amusing account of the way in which a land agent prepared himself for the peremptory rule. He says, the land agent, whose name he does not mention, is an expert bicyclist, and that he has been spending a considerable time every day firing shots at a target as he flew by it on his bicycle. Who could not wish and pray that a just and more humane system of government should remove all this miserable terrorism?

I believe, if a careful inquiry were made, that it would be found in every place where agrarian outrages have been committed, or where whole-sale evictions have been made, that a system of terrorism, and unjust raising of rent, and other unfair levying of burdens on the people, have been the cause. If this is so, would it not be more just if less blame was cast on the people and more on the system?

The great middle class in England are unquestionably becoming enlightened on this point. Unhappily those whom enlightenment would benefit most are often the very last to obtain it. In a leader in the *London Weekly Despatch* of November, 1880, we find the following :—

"So, leaving the peasants to take care of themselves, he lent the gentry, at a nominal interest, as much public money as they chose to ask for, to be advantageously spent—while wages were uncommonly low—in improving their estates, it being well understood on all sides that the tenant would have to pay the interest on the debt to the government, and also a handsome profit interest to the landlord, and further-more a highly increased rent on the land so improved. Similarly we are given to understand that, if Lord Beacons-field were now in power, he would take a correct view of the present situation. He would straightway lock up the agitators, confiscate the plant of the *Nation* newspaper, put the *Freeman* in fetters, and establish martial law throughout the whole island, and then rest upon his oars and laurels. Unfortunately for these Tory optimists, Lord Beaconsfield is no longer in power. But in his place we have a minister who, although he consents to the doubtful experiment of prosecuting some of the Land Leaguers, is imbued with the foolish but popular, and indeed well-nigh universal, notion that "there is no smoke without some fire," and who has avowed his conviction that the somewhat thick smoke which at present obscures the Irish landscape has its origin in the fires of a long-smouldering and perfectly justifiable discon-tent with an iniquitous system of legalised oppression, which no nation of men, worthy to be so called, can be expected meekly to put up with ; and that the true way to settle the Irish question is not to hunt down the agitators, but to free the land."

Yet such is the force of opinion against Ire-land in England, that we find the following in another part of the same paper :—

"A TIME OF BLOOD.

"It would appear just now as if murder was in the very air we breathe. If we pass from Ireland, where peasants

go behind walls to butcher peers, and peers, sheltering themselves behind the powers conferred by iniquitous laws, pass
" sentences of starvation, sentences of death," upon hapless
peasants, we find, on turning our eyes to our own country,
that there is bloodshed all around. From nearly every part
of England the daily papers bring us accounts of murders.
To begin with the metropolis, there is the Finsbury Park
murder, and Acton supplies us with a crime of greater bru-
tality. From the Eastern counties came only the other day
the report of a terrible and most determined murder at
Audley End."

Now, in this paper, where there is a real
anxiety manifest to be just to Ireland, we have
the old absurd story of Irish peasants occupying themselves with butchering peers. During
the whole agitation only one "lord" was mur-
dered. Lord Leitrim's murder occurred before
the present agitation began, and yet the English
papers ring with accusations of Irishmen, as if
they were all murderers. As we have said before,
let it be decided, once for all, by law, as it was
actually the "law" in Ireland, not so many
years since, that the murder of an English landlord or land agent in Ireland is a greater crime
than a murder in England; and we should
know where we are. But until that is decided
it is better to keep to facts, and the facts are,
that the murders and other outrages in Ireland,
are far fewer than they are in England. Why,

then, are we to be perpetually taunted with them?

I think if it was known that there is rarely ever outrage, or disorder, or discontent in any part of Ireland where there has not previously been aggravated oppression on the part of the land agent or landlord, that it would go far to make the state of Ireland more correctly understood. And since there can be no possible gain to either party from ignorance, we do hope earnestly that the truth may become known. It may seem hard to say it, but it is true, that only those who have an interest in concealing the truth are anxious to do so.

The Galtee property of Mr. Buckley came not so long since into painful prominence because of an agrarian outrage. Here, in a few short sentences is, not the excuse, for there is no excuse for murder, but the plain manifest cause. Was the murderer, then, the only guilty person? Will there not be yet another tribunal where this terrible greed for gain will be judged, and where the sentence may be heavy?

"Amongst the witnesses examined before the Land Commission were the Rev. David Burdon, Mitchelstown, who submitted the following statement:—

"'I propose, in the first place, to state the relations

T

between landlord and tenant on the properties in the neighbourhood of Mitchelstown, and will begin with the

" 'I.—BUCKLEY PROPERTY.

" ' Mr. N. Buckley purchased his Galtee estate from an
English company, of which he was a member. A successful
manufacturer, he bought it, to traffic on it as on any other
commodity. Having procured the services of Mr. Patten
Bridge as agent, the property was re valued by a Mr. Waller,
and increases of rent ranging from fifty to five hundred per
cent. were imposed upon a wretched mountain tenantry,
whose sweat had made the wild, rocky, and slushy slopes of
the Galtees capable of producing anything. Under their
former landlords they paid little, and if they paid nothing
they could hardly subsist. Wretched hovels, rags for gar-
ments, turnips and Indian meal for food—such was their
condition. No wonder, therefore, the notices demanding
increased rent evoked terrible passions.

" ' I beg leave to hand in as evidence the affidavits of
about fifty of these poor people ; also tables showing old
rents and increases, copies of notices signed by Mr. Bridge,
and to point to the charge of Mr. Justice Barry in the trial
of Bridge *versus* Casey.

" ' This confiscation of tenants' improvements, and fearful
rack-renting, which was a beggaring of beggars, was evidently
a crying injustice and developed a fierce war.   The condition
of these miserable Galtee peasants is proved further by the
fact that an immense number of them, nearly 300, were receiving, from Dr. Delany and the charitable committee of
Ballyporeen, relief up to the 15th August last (I make a
present of the documents).

" 'II.—KINGSTON ESTATE.

" ' I come next to the Kingston estate. I must say the

management of the Kingston property contrasts favourably
with that of any other within my knowledge. The area
comprises about 23,000 acres ; rent about £19,000 a year,
average above poor law about twenty per cent. The farms
in the eastern portion are high enough, as the land is not so
good. In some few cases the rent is nearly double the
valuation here. Mr. Bridge, who was joint agent with Mr.
Sadlier before his translation to the Galtees, left his mark
upon some of the farms. It is calculated he raised the
rental nearly £4,000.

Such plain, undeniable statements speak for
themselves, and I am convinced if every case
where there has been outrage or where numbers
of tenants have joined in denouncing oppression,
were inquired into, that real solid ground for
their complaints would be found.

And here I will ask consideration of a few
remarks about the non-payment of rent. Irish
tenants are being held up to unlimited obloquy
and abuse in the English papers, because, it is
said, they have refused to pay their rents or
they have offered only Griffith's Valuation. In
the latter case, they are accused of taking the
law into their own hands. Now, I will ask this
question—is the Irish tenant to starve, in order
to pay his rent? But, you will say, there is no
question of starvation now. True; but there was
question of starvation at the beginning of this

year; in fact, to my own personal knowledge, far into the year. The consequence of this is, that the people are deeply in debt for the absolute necessaries of life to the small tradesmen in every country town in Ireland. Is the landlord then to get *all*, and is the shopkeeper to get none? If this is morality, it is nineteenth century morality. If it is to be the law for the future in Ireland, it would be better that the people be slaves at once; their masters would then, for their own sakes, feed and clothe them. It is certainly extraordinary the inconsistencies and absurdities to which people are driven when, from prejudice or ignorance, they can only look at one side of a question. No one has a word about the poor shopkeeper; all the pity is for the rich landlord. If any one must suffer would it not be better that the rich should suffer? Are they never to share in any national calamity? Are they to be allowed to turn it to their own profit and then to be condoled with as if they were martyrs?

But, it is said, how is the landlord to meet his annuities, and rent-charges, and what not? Well, how is the shopkeeper to pay for his merchandize? The landlord can get unlimited credit; the shopkeeper cannot. The shopkeepers have made many and great sacrifices for the people; most assuredly, very few land-lords have made any sacrifices.

Mr. Tuke says :—

"Without the money distributed by the Dublin Funds 'many would have starved.' The farmers around Carrick, and generally along the banks of the Shannon, have suffered most severely during the last season from the overflowing of the river. The loss could not be estimated at less than £50,000, much of which might have been saved, by proper arrangements regarding the drainage of the Shannon.

Where were the landlords? If they had spent half the time trying to help their tenants in such matters that they have spent in writing unmanly letters to the *Times*, about the non-payment of their rents, they would have bene-fitted themselves and the whole country.

Again, Mr. Tuke says :—

"The people, as we were told, were very poor, and were eating up their resources. Some are cottiers, *i.e.*, people who have a house and garden or small plot, say half to one acre and no more; but they are chiefly small farmers. Want of clothing, here, as elsewhere, very great. One very sad case, may be quoted—a small farmer, with about fifteen acres, a Protestant, who had been in good circumstances. A year or two ago the family were well dressed; children at school; and the older ones in the church choir. Now, the man is miserably dressed, and his family, six or eight children, in rags. They crowded around a miserable fire, cook-

ing the stirabout and Indian meal cakes ; all more or less
affected with skin disease, very bad and infectious, the result
of low diet ; all looked thin, pale, and wretched, and evidently wanted nourishment. 'It's no use prescribing,' said
the doctor; 'it's nourishing food they want. What's to be
done ?' ' Well,' said the man, ' I've sold the bullock to pay
the rent, and the bit of corn for meal, and even the goose
the wife sold for some little thing ; and I've only the wee
bit cow ind little calf left, and the pony to till the land.
What can I do? I suppose,' he added, in a desponding
tone, ' I must sell them also, and go into the workhouse.' *

Now, how is such a man to pay his rent, after
such a year ? He may sell the " wee bit cow "
and little calf and the poor old pony and clear
what is due. How is he to pay the rent next
year and to live ? Mr. Tuke adds : " It is most
painful to see cases of this kind ; and for one
seen there are probably hundreds unseen."[1]
Unseen to man, indeed ; but they are not unseen
to their Maker. Nor does He fail to see and
to note the cruel reproaches heaped upon a
hapless people, who have suffered such sacrifices to pay their rents and all their honest debts
as are only known to Him and to themselves.[2]

---

[1] *"Irish Distress and its Remedies,"* p. 37.

[2] I solemnly declare that I know cases in which respectable men have
lived on dry bread and tea, as their food, for months during this past
year, that they might be able to pay their rents and their debts.

Here is what Mr. Tuke has to say of the
condition of THOUSANDS OF FAMILIES. Here is
the verdict of a calm, dispassionate Englishman
—a member of the Society of Friends, a man
absolutely free from *all* party politics, a man
above all suspicion of partiality or prejudice on
any side. He writes of his visit to Meenacladdy thus :—

"Of the destitution and misery found in these bog-dwell-
ings, I feel, after a lapse of twenty-four hours, that I
can hardly bring myself to write. It is not merely the unusual distress of to-day, arising from the causes which I have
enumerated, but the every-day life, the normal condition of
hundreds, nay, thousands of families on the west coast of
Donegal, and of many other parts of the west of Ireland,
which oppresses me. But, on this normal condition—this
every-day contest with existence and hardship—I must not
dwell here."

Yes ; and here in Kerry there are thousands
of families in the same condition—a condition,
the consequence of this misgovernment of hundreds of years, a consequence of suppressing
every Irish industry, of neglect of our fisheries,
of contempt of our prayers, and of the irresponsible government of Ireland by landlords and
land agents.

And the people, forsooth, who can barely
exist, are to be taunted with not paying rents

after three years of awful distress and one year of famine. And they are to be taunted with offering "only Griffith's valuation" to their landlords, because they wish, when they can pay anything, to give at least part of what they owe to the shop-keepers. And, in order to terrify them into doing what they know to be wrong, in order to terrify them into giving all to the landlord and nothing to the shop-keeper, whose charity and credit has saved them from famine, they are to be served with " Dublin ejectments," and to have writs served on them at the very doors of the rent-office, if they are even one day late with their payments.

And then the agent will boast how he has terrified the people into submission, and taunt them with being able to pay if they liked, as he says he has proved by making them pay. Certainly, they have paid, but how ? By selling their stock; next year they *must* be bankrupt; what matter. He will eject them—another tenant will be found. The "estate" will get all the benefit. There will be a handsome "fine" paid by the new tenant, who is foolish enough to hope against hope, and to think he will succeed where his predecessor has failed.

And the shop-keeper is left to live on the verge of ruin, because he cannot be paid. A fancy picture, you will say! Would to God it were; but the imagination of "Friends" is not supposed to be very vivid, and here is a "Friend's" statement of facts:—

"The man, who seemed an industrious fellow, was working on the bog, in spite of the weather, seeking to cultivate a little ground for the coming season. He had 'no baste left, neither cow nor sheep, only three or four fowls.' He had been to Scotland for the harvest last autumn, but had come back without earnings, and now, in debt for meal and rent, he was beaten.

"A shop-keeper stated that he had over £4,000 owing to him, for meal or other articles, by the little cottiers and farmers around, the whole of which he had no doubt would be repaid if good times came again. His relatives—who are working hard for the poor at Burtonport, a few miles distant—had £10,000 owing them for meal alone, which they had allowed the people to have on credit. The credit system, is, indeed, universal here. At all times most of the people are in debt to the store-keeper, who is the little banker of the district, and, no doubt, charges 'full rates' for his small loans."

After describing the wretched condition of a poor widow woman, he says:—

"The woman, whose husband had been dead a few months, looked ill and weak, and was suffering from ophthalmia. In her arms was her last infant, a thin and sickly one, with hunger in its face, crying, no doubt, for the nourishment which the allowance of meal could not give. The only clothing on this and three other very young,

children consisted of small calico shirts, given them by the
priest, which barely covered the upper part of their bodies,
and showed how thin and poorly nourished they were.
. Why is not such a family cared for by the Poor Law?
may again well be asked. But, as no outdoor relief is yet
given, miserable and suffering as she was, the poor woman
could not bear to give up her house and 'bit of land,'
hoping to hold it on for 'better days,' when her children
might take it.[1] Since the husband's death the neighbours
had helped her to crop it; and what a miserable 'bit' of
land it was—covered with weeds and almost drowned with
water, a rood or two reclaimed from the bog by past years of
labour.

   "The man who gave the £125 for the tenant right told
me he had earned the money in America in seven years, and
that he could not obtain half this sum now for the tenant right.
' But,' he added, with emotion, ' this is my last year here;
it's no use, a man may as well lie down and die—we are
beaten—everything is against us; there are no roads you
see to the land—the bit of turf from the bog (about a cart-
load) takes me two days to carry upon my back ; I shall take
my wife and family away to Ameriky again.' When I asked
him why he had come back before, and bought the farm, he replied, with bitterness, '*Nature binds a man to his own
counthrey*—but I can't stand it any longer.' What true
pathos and sentiment there is in these men ! "

   True "pathos and sentiment!" Yes, truly, and

---

[1] This poor woman, and many other tenants whose rents are unpaid,
have, subsequently to our visit, been served with processes (County
Court summonses) for non-payment of rent due for one or two years,
but it is satisfactory to add that no evictions have taken place.

bitter agony. Will that man or his descendants love the step-mother that drove them into exile ? Can it be any matter of surprise not only that thousands of pounds were sent from America to feed the Irish poor in the Famine, but that they are also sending thousands of pounds to support an agitation, which is the only hope of obtaining such justice for Ireland as will enable the Irish to live in their native land.

CHAPTER XVII.

IRISH LAND AGENTS.

(Continued.)

"At present I am convinced that, under the guidance of Lords Cairns and Redesdale, the Upper House deliberately intended to set the English and Irish people by the ears, to increase the difficulties of government, and to make conciliatory legislation impossible or difficult. But I trust that the English people will see who is to blame for the present situation. —*James E. Thorold Rogers.*"

BUT, it will be said, what is the remedy? I must leave to politicians the discussion of such subjects, as far as legal enactments are concerned, but from a long and intimate acquaintance with the people of Ireland, I would suggest some social points.

It is said that thousands of the people cannot live on their holdings, even if they had them rent free; and yet, in the next breath, we are told how wicked they are not to pay their rents!

In a letter addressed to myself by the Marquis of Lansdowne, dated August 28th, 1880, he says:—

"There must always be some destitution among a class, unfortunately not uncommon upon my estate, men whose holdings would be too small to support them and their families, even if they were rent free, in a decent degree of comfort."

What a statement from one of the largest land-lords in Kerry, and indeed in Ireland.

And yet the remedy for this state of things is to serve them with ejectments, and to terrify them with " Dublin writs ;" to add to their burdens by making them purchase lime which they could easily make for themselves, and to give them employment and make them pay five per cent. in perpetuity on the outlay.

This is precisely what should *not* be done if the Irish are to live in Ireland—*noblesse oblige*—and yet there are, I fear, many hundred Irish landlords who, while their tenants have endured severe privations, in order to pay their rents honestly for years, yet when a famine came these gentlemen did not give one gratuitous sixpence to help them, and only concerned themselves with exacting their rents at the point of the legal bayonet.

Noblesse oblige, but it seems somehow to be forgotten where Ireland is concerned.

Mr. Russell speaks thus of what I fear we must call the advantage taken of the people in the Famine. The *Standard* correspondent, who appears to have been sent down expressly

to do away with any bad impression made by
Mr. Russell, could only admit that on this point
he was correct—

"I find that in the end of 1879 Lord Lansdowne offered
to his tenants drainage work on their signing an agreement
to pay a perpetual addition to their rent—1s. for every £1
given by him for such work, such addition to commence at
the end of three years.   In reference to this charge for the
repayment of public money advanced by the State on exceptional terms for the purpose, not, I presume, of benefiting
the landlords, but of aiding an impoverished country to sur-
mount dire distress.

"Lord Lansdowne obtained from the State £6,000,
which he will repay by a terminable assessment of £3 8s. 6d.
per cent.   The information we received was that the tenants
who had received part of these moneys for drainage, &c.,
have to pay as a permanent increase to their rent £5 per
cent. after three years, and that they had signed office-
agreements to that effect.   I hope there is here some misapprehension.

"I am not surprised that only a comparatively small
number of tenants applied.   Everywhere the feeling is that
the rent is more than they can pay, living in the barest
fashion, and they shrink from anything which will involve a
permanent addition to that serious burden.   Nor is this
wonderful, when it is recollected that if overtaken by misfortune, and so unable to pay rent, they may be ejected
without one penny of compensation, or, if they refused to
pay an increased rent, be turned out at the will of the landlord with only the, as they conceive, inadequate protection
of the Act of 1870.

Very general complaints exist as to the charges made by

the estate management for lime supplied to the tenants, which for the wet and boggy land on the Kenmare estate is an absolute necessity. The only substitute for it is fine sea sand and seaweed, and these are not effectual. It appears that Lord Lansdowne some years ago erected a large lime-kiln in the town of Kenmare for the purpose of supplying the tenants, and that from that time forward they were obliged to take the lime from him. I understand that Lord Lansdowne does not admit having prohibited the tenants using their own kilns, but undoubtedly the impression that he did so prevails in Kenmare. One would have thought, indeed, that lime so produced on a large scale would not only be better burned, but cheaper, and thus a benefit to the tenants. They do not seem to think so. These are the facts as stated to me. From the date of the erection of Lord Lansdowne's limekiln in Kenmare, he continued until this year to supply his tenants with lime at rates varying from 1s. to 1s. 3d. per barrel. Even at these rates the sale of the lime ought to have yielded a profit. Mr. Samuel M. Hussey, Lord Kenmare's agent (a gentleman of great ability as well as great experience), told me that at Killarney Lord Kenmare expected to be able to supply lime to his tenants without loss to himself at 1s. 3d. per barrel, and that owing to the facility at Kenmare for water carriage of culm, or slack coal, the lime ought to be burned at a considerably lower price there than at Killarney. In the spring of the present year (when, you will remember, the distress was at its height) the tenants were informed by the agent that if they required lime they would get it on signing the following agreement, a printed copy of which is in my possession:

" ' I   hereby agree with the Marquis of Lansdowne to pay annually after two years one penny per barrel, as an addition to my rent, for each and every barrel of lime that I take. And I hereby acknowledge having taken from the said Marquis   barrels of lime.

'(Signed)

'Witness

'Dated

" Simultaneously with the publication of this agreement the cash price of lime was raised by the agent to 2s. 6d. a barrel. This last statement, strongly vouched to me, I fail to understand. It seems remarkable. I ought to add Lord Lansdowne's is the only public limekiln for miles around Kenmare. When we consider that land such as that on the Kenmare estate requires lime every seven years, and as much as sixty barrels to the acre, if properly treated, it does not seem very surprising that the tenants should look upon the above agreement, as they unquestionably do, with suspicion as an ingenious device for raising their rent."

The *Standard* special correspondent, though he obviously holds a brief for the Lansdowne estate management, says :—

" Mr. J. T. Trench, the agent of this estate, with whom I had an interview to day, admitted the truth of several of these charges. . . . . In his remarks to me he took special credit for the firmness with which he manages the estate. If the tenant does not pay within a short time after the rent has fallen due he issues what is called a ' Dublin eviction.' This is a peremptory mode of proceeding, which, besides being more rapid than the ordinary process of law, entails an expense of 30s. on the unfortunate tenant. I have heard of a case in which this proceeding seemed to work peculiar hardship. A tenant named John Wren owed rent amounting to the sum of £2 11s., but although proffered before service of the writ it was refused unless £1 10s. costs were paid in addition."

On this subject Mr. Russell says :—

" Bitter complaint was made that even in cases within the jurisdiction of the county courts writs of ejectment are issued from the superior courts—what the tenants call ' Dublin writs.' These not alone necessitate the employment of a Dublin solicitor, either directly or through some local solicitor, but suggests to the minds of the tenants a fearful unknown field of expensive litigation. Even the initial costs often are, in proportion to the rent demanded, enormous, but yet the screw is so powerful that the effort will be made to pay, even if the payer is to denude his farm of the greater part of his stock, and himself of the means of turning his holding to account. I find that from Sept. 1st, 1879, to Sept. 1st, 1880, sixty superior court writs of summons in ejectment, exclusive of Quarter Sessions processes, were issued. Of these forty were issued about September, 1879, and twenty were issued in May of the present year. I have the list before me. The former comprised rent due up to May 1st (but by the custom of the office collected in July), and the latter twenty comprised rent up to May 1st, 1880. Excepting one case the greatest amount of rent due was two years' rent, or excluding the stale or fictitious outlying year, one year's rent. In the great majority of instances three half years' rent only were due, or, excluding the fictitious year, one half year's rent was due."

Further he adds :—

" While, however, the same feeling in reference to the

y

agency of the estate seems to exist here, I was somewhat surprised to find that a freer tone of criticism and a more independent attitude was assumed by the tenants than in the Kenmare neighbourhood. There they seemed literally afraid to call their souls their own., It is no exaggeration to say they spoke with bated breath, as if afraid agent or bailiff might hear them. Here they spoke out their complaints with greater freedom and boldness. The greater distance from the agent's eye perhaps accounted for the difference. Lord Lansdowne was unknown to them. The few who had ever seen him had done so upon the occasion of his attaining his majority. Mr. Trench had only been there once in the last five years, and then his visit had been short. Neither landlord nor agent had visited them in the time of their distress, although Canon Brosnan, the parish priest of Cahirciveen, had given timely written warning to Lord Lansdowne that the condition of his Cahirciveen tenantry was likely to be one of great suffering and privation. Practically, the control of this part of the estate is in the hands of bailiffs, of whom the principal one lives at Waterville. I was unable to find that any considerable money had been laid out by the landlord, and where it had been 1s. in the pound had been added to the rent as a permanent increase."

With regard to Kenmare, I can only say that my own experience confirms the above. I shall never forget the abject terror shown by a tenant of Lord Lansdowne's who came to tell me of his grievances, and who, I begged, would write the particulars for me. All this is attributed to the agent system of government here.

I cannot but add, in justice to both the Marquis of Lansdowne and Mr. Trench, that there seems to be an extraordinary amount of duplicity in this district, and I cannot attribute it altogether to terrorism. I believe the remoteness of the locality and the mode of government have produced a race apart. I have heard also that the Marquis of Lansdowne has exerted himself on different occasions to benefit the sons of his tenants by obtaining situations for them in the Civil Service, &c. For this I heard he received not only scant thanks but ingratitude. It is certainly, as I know personally, one of the characteristics of this place to take everything and to refuse even the return of common gratitude.

Now, I would ask the honest English trader what he thinks of all this? How can the Irish peasant be prosperous, when advantage is taken of him at every possible moment to increase his rent, and, even in a year of famine, to add to his burdens? How can he be attached to a landlord who does, or to a Government which permits, the continuance of such injustice—north, south, east, or west, it is still the same. We have shown what is done on other estates in Kerry. In Cork, we have shown how Lord Cork's tenants are deprived of the benefit of

English law, and from an old authority we give
an account of the state of Gweedore and Meenacladdy :—

"The 'New Cuts' being taken from the bog or mountain-
land over which the old tenants have been accustomed to
graze their flocks, a strong objection is felt to the practice,
which diminishes their rights whilst adding a little to the
rental of the estates. In this instance it will be seen that
one fifth (88 acres) of the mountain land has thus been gradually taken from the village rights. The extraordinary
diminution in the amount of stock held cannot fairly be
attributed to this cause; but, whilst having some effect,
must have arisen from losses in the wet season, and the
gradual reduction in the stocks caused by sales to pay debts,
purchase food, &c., in the three past years. Both the large
amount of stock stated to have been held in past good years
and the very great diminution must, I think, be exceptional.
My informant, who obtained these returns for me, says :—

"'It is a very startling document, in my mind. The
people have been wonderfully pulled down in circumstances
in the lapse of a few years. Some years ago the inhabitants
of Gweedore generally, as well as those of Meenaclaxddy,
enjoyed very extensive rights of grazing on the adjoining
mountains and moorlands. This right or privilege begat a
remarkable thrift in the way of providing stock. The young
folks who had been at hire, and the men who had gone to
England or elsewhere, put their earnings to buy sheep or
cattle. The yearly increase in the stock, the profits from
wool and its manufacture, and the profits from buying young
cattle, grazing them for a season or two, and then disposing
of them at a considerable advantage, constituted the happiness and prosperity of those simple peasant people. The

land was never remarkably fruitful, and *the arable* possessions of the people *were never sufficient to give them a subsistence.* These rights of grazing have been gradually lessened or taken from them by the landlords. ' New Cuts ' have been made, and the tenants for them obtained, against the counsel of all who had the interest of the people at heart, and the people have been gradually compressed into very small limits, and thus they have fallen from a state of comparative comfort to a state of abject poverty. This is true of every part of the whole territory of Gweedore, as well as of Meenacladdy, and I take it to explain the otherwise, to me, inexplicable document I enclose."

Everywhere, it is taking from the hard-working, patient slave. Nowhere, even in famine, was help given to him by those who had so long lived in luxury on his sweat and toil.

One of my earliest recollections was hearing an aged relative describe the magnificent scene which she witnessed from the peeresses' gallery in the House of Lords, at the trial of Warren Hastings.

She told me again and again—for I took no ordinary pleasure in her tales of "old times"—how each peer, as he gave his verdict, rose in his place, and, as he did so, having placed his hand upon his heart, exclaimed, " *Guilty* (or not guilty) *on my honour !* "

I fear if the truth concerning the management of Irish estates was known to the House of

Lords, and if it was called upon for a verdict
that "*guilty, on my honour*" would be the
response. Would it not be better if these
gentlemen would begin by admitting themselves
guilty, and try to remedy the ills caused by
their misgovernment, instead of calling out for
coercion laws for their unhappy subjects?

The *Freeman's Journal* says :—

"If Parliament assembled to-morrow and suspended the
Habeas Corpus Act, every tenant in the districts, where
personal liberty was suspended, would be at the mercy,
night and day, of the magistrate, who would probably be also
his landlord."

And, we may add, land agent. The absolute
despotic power which the Irish land agent
possesses in Ireland is not even imagined in
England. Not only is he lord of their lives,
as far as deciding on what they shall live,
but he is also lord of their liberty. The
land agent is, with rare exceptions, the magistrate and the chairman of the board of guardians. His brother magistrates are too often
selected because they are in some way or for
some reason pliable to his influence. At the
board of guardians he reigns supreme. I have
heard, on what I believe to be good authority,
that chairmen of boards of guardians take their
seats with their resolutions in their pockets,

read them out, and with contemptuous indifference demand, rather than ask, the assent of the Board. By a little adroit management—and a land agent is nothing if he is not adroit—the Poor Law Guardians are selected from names specially to the Chairman's liking. Either by fear, or by some judicious attention or solid advantage, he can manage so that there will be no opposition.

And the poor know all this too well, and are made to feel it all too keenly. Most assuredly, no land agent should ever be allowed a seat on the bench, or at the Board of Guardians. What! are men whose business in life is to get all they possibly can out of their dependents, who even, perhaps, boast of their tyranny, to be allowed to sit in judgment on those men afterwards?

How this works, let the following examples suffice to show.

We take the following from the *Cork Examiner*, November, 1880 :—

"A few days ago we had occasion to complain of the manner in which compensation is granted for so-called malicious injuries. The proceedings at two of the Road Sessions in the West Riding, within the present week, afford a very apt illustration of the abuses to which we desired to call attention. The applications at Bantry and Ballydehob were not numerous, and the amounts claimed were small,

but the spirit in which they were disposed of by·a section of
the Bench was remarkable. The law provides that where
the destruction of property is shown to be wanton or
malicious, the owner is to receive compensation for his loss,
according to the value of the property. The Sessions have
no authority to add anything to the award for the purpose of
converting it into a fine upon the locality, and punishing the
inhabitants for constructive participation in the guilt of the
incendiary. It is a mere question of compensation, and
nothing more. Let us see how the law has been administered by the western benches. We shall take the Bantry
Sessions first. Mr. Timothy Regan Harrington came forward to complain that his rick of hay, containing ten tons,
had been maliciously burned. He gave, so far as we can
discern, no evidence that the destruction was malicious, save
his own surmise. But the Bench were not in a critical mood.
Mr. Harrington was granted immediately the sum of £40.
We may assume that when Mr. Harrington estimated the
contents of the rick at ten tons, he did not understate the
quantity, and he is certainly to be esteemed a fortunate man
who can make £4 a ton by his hay in the neighbourhood of
Bantry. Dr. Armstrong was remunerated on the same
liberal scale for the loss of five tons of hay. The peculiarity
of his case was, that he frankly admitted his inability to
prove that the burning was malicious—as, he said, ' he was
unable to attach suspicion to any one.' But that slight
hiatus in his proofs did not in the least affect the action of
the Bench. The Chairman, Mr. J. W. Payne, had, in a
previous case, declared that he would not be a bit sorry to
put hundreds of pounds upon the people of the district in
which the fire had occurred, ' to punish them.' Is this the
spirit in which the law should be administered ? The moral
of the proceedings appears to be that the best thing that can
happen to a man with a rick of hay, or other combustible

commodity, on his hands is, that some one should come and burn it—rather a dangerous idea to get abroad."

So far for Bantry. The writer of the article then turns to Ballydehob, where a Mr. Holland applied for compensation :—

"So far as we can see, from the reports of the proceedings, no reliable evidence of the value of the houses was given on the part of the applicant, and three respectable witnesses, one of them the under-agent of the estate, produced for the ratepayers, proved that the premises had been for a considerable time mere ruins, and were not worth more than £7 or £8 at the utmost. In the face of this evidence, four magistrates—Messrs. Swanton, Fleming, O'Grady, and the chairman—and one cess-payer, Mr. J. Notter, voted for giving the applicant £30—just four times what the houses had been sworn to be worth. During the proceedings a voice called out, 'The magistrates should consider the poor people.' What was the response? The chairman replied, 'The poor people of the country must behave themselves. If not, I hope they will get powder and ball before long.' Verily, a discreet and humane sentiment on the part of a member of the Bench."

Are landlords and land agents in Ireland to be utterly irresponsible? Are they to be allowed to take into *their own hands*, not only whatever alterations they may please to make in laws made in England for Ireland, but are they also to be allowed to administer "justice" from the Bench at their own sweet will and pleasure? Is it any wonder that landlords are not loved, and that some land agents find adding as much terrorism as possible to their mode of governing the people the simplest and easiest way of carrying out this system of injustice.

Their only fear is the fear of public opinion. As far as that goes, in Ireland they are perfectly safe. They are masters of the situation. Complaints would be made in the county papers, and legal or other injustice may be exposed. What does it matter? It is not known in England, where, if even known and believed, it would be denounced. Hence it is that the action of the Land League has caused such absolute terror. Irish affairs are getting written about in the English papers. The truth is being told, and some of it, at least, is beginning to be believed. The day is dawning when Ireland will no longer be deprived of the benefit of English law, and when Irish landlords will be obliged to submit to it. Pity for them, they have not the wisdom to anticipate that day with a good grace.

The *Times* says :—

"We understand that Lord Monck, Lord Powerscourt, and others, are also inclined to approve some modification of the scheme known as 'the three F's'—fixity of tenure fair rents, and free sale—which has been already adopted by some leading representatives of the Roman Catholic Church."

Happily, there are some landlords in Ireland who are willing to allow justice to be done; and it is well worth noting that in every. such case landlord and tenant have lived on peaceful terms. Nor are land agents the only persons who press hardly on the people. I am far from wishing to assert that justice is unfairly administered on the whole in Ireland; but, certainly, the poorer classes often fare hardly in this matter, and are treated sometimes with rough and scant justice even by County-court judges. A gentleman who associates with the landlord or land agent, finds it hard to decide against him; above all, if the case has reference to land, wherein the lord of the soil seems to think he has a right to all, and the tenant has a right only to exist if he can. This has happily been noticed of late in England. The *Pall Mall Gazette* says :—

"County-court judges in Ireland have particularly delicate duties to discharge, and their absolute impartiality is at the present moment more than ever imperative. A case reported from an Irish county court this morning, in which a Protestant landlord was prosecuted for not giving notice of an ejectment to the relieving-officer of the district, hardly seems to have been dealt with in the true judicial spirit. The case·

was the first of its kind, and the defendant, an archdeacon
as well as a landlord, appears to have had no defence, and
was willing to pay the penalty. The Local Government
Board, however, refused to allow the prosecution to be withdrawn ; and when the case came on for trial the judge, holding that the neglect, if any, was that of the agent and not
the landlord, condemned the proceedings as vindictive, and,
regretting that he was obliged to inflict a penalty by law, he
refused to give any costs. It does not seem to be within
the province of a judge to inquire into the motives of a prosecution for an offence of which the law has marked the
exceptional gravity by fixing a minimum penalty. If the
vindictiveness is explained by the fact mentioned at the
meeting of the Land League yesterday that Archdeacon
Bland had evicted thirty-eight of his tenants, we are afraid
that the action of the judge will be construed as indicating
sympathy with the side of the landlords in the great agrarian
dispute. Let the administration of the lawbe swift and
stern by all means; but, first of all, let it be strictly impartial."

Certainly, those who are clamouring so loudly
for what they call justice, should be willing to
allow a share of it to others. There are landlords who have not troubles with their tenants,
because they have not treated them unjustly.

Mr. Leoni Levi, writing to the *Times*,
August 31, 1880, has the following platitude
about Ireland :—

"The great wants of Ireland are, I apprehend, capital,
confidence, and industry. Most unfortunately, at the pre-

sent moment both landowners and tenants are very poor. The landowners, or a great portion of them, harassed by debt and mortgages, will do and can do nothing to improve the land. The tenants, generally with large families and destitute of means, have as little power to do much for it. Little or nothing, therefore, is attempted ; and what is done is principally accomplished either by loans from the Board of Works or with money from money-lenders at high rates of interest. The total amount of farmers' capital in Ireland must, I fear, be very small, and the results are apparent in the comparative poverty of the land and the scantiness of its produce.

" But a greater want is confidence. How can capital flow into the country so long as the people are for ever wrangling on social grievances and indulging political discontent? Perfect safety of person and property and respect for legal rights are the first conditions of social progress. Want of confidence affects the cultivation of land in every way. The landowner has no confidence in the tenant, and the tenant has no confidence in the landowner, and so the land suffers. Unfortunately, there are too many reasons for this want of mutual confidence."

This is just the usual and most fallacious style of English reasoning. First it is admitted that there is no capital in Ireland, then we are told that we indulge political discontent, and that this is the cause why capital does not come to us from some unknown and mysterious source. How can a people refrain from political discontent when they have such serious political grievances ? and how can there be "confidence" when the one object of the "office" is to deprive the people of every possible means of accumulating capital? And yet the men who do this are to judge the poor on the bench, and to be their so-called guardians at the Poor Law Board. Guardians of the poor! One day they will have been shown to have been rather the taskmasters of the poor.

But you will say I exaggerate; again let me offer you facts. Here is from an English authority a statement of how capital is kept out of Ireland; for unless the poor farmer is allowed to make capital, how can there be capital. The *Daily Telegraph* correspondent, writing from Claremorris, says :—

"But it must not be supposed that Lord Sligo's tenants have no grievance against the 'office,' at which impersonal thing they hurl bitter words. It was the 'office' that took from them years ago the privilege of pasturing their cattle upon the adjacent hills. It was the 'office' which laid a tax of 25 per cent. upon the proceeds of the industry in making kelp. It was the 'office' which insisted that, while drift seaweed might be freely gathered, weed growing on the shore may not be had without payment. It was the 'office' which demanded half a crown per homestead for cutting turf, on pretence of making roads to the bogs, and left the' roads unmade. And it was the 'office' which, four or five years ago, raised the rents 25 per cent., established a new tenancy, and deprived the holders of the right to claim compensation under the Land Act for their improvements. The memory of these things is bitter, yet those who suffer by them will not say a word against Lord Sligo. Their expression concerning him is, ' Not a bad man ;' but they use very different language when speaking of the ' office' and its occupants."

Is it any wonder then the very name of a land agent is a name of dread, and that the office, wherever he issues his " writs," a word of many meanings, is spoken of with abject horror ?

It is from these offices that orders issue forth for the raising of rent ; it is from these that the will and pleasure of the land agent is made known to a people who know the " peremptory" methods that will be used to insure obedience.

It is in these offices that the poor tenants, if they dare come with a complaint, are browbeaten and terrified. An English friend, who spent some little time in Ireland not long since, told me that he passed some days in a rent office, I believe more for amusement than any other purpose. There are generally in those offices a number of young men who are training for future occupations as land agents, a most lucrative post. He said on one occasion a respectable old woman came into the office to ask some question, and the young gentleman, perhaps to show before this Englishman how they treated the " mere Irish," yelled and shouted

at her until he was almost deafened. He implored them to speak quietly to the woman, or
at least to hear what she wanted, but it was
useless, and the poor creature went away unheard.

In a letter to the *Freeman's Journal* from the
Rev. W. Dempsey, P.P., Camlough, the way in
which "addresses" are got up is significantly
illustrated. He says :—

" I am a tenant on the Marquis of Londonderry's estate,
and I never saw this address to him and the Duke of
Marlborough [two trustees of the Vane-Tempest estate]
until I read it yesterday in your paper, nor heard of it
until it had been despatched ; and I am sure that the great
majority of the tenantry have the same story to tell. The
plain truth of the matter is this—A committee was formed
for the ostensible purpose of raising funds for the relief of
the sufferers by the late explosion at the Marquis of Londonderry's colliery at Seaham. I subscribed, as did all, I
think, or nearly all, the tenantry on the estate. We were
asked to subscribe on the plea of charity ; but we had no
idea that we were in reality subscribing to a sort of testi-
monial to the Marquis of Londonderry, and much less that
our subscriptions would be made to serve a political purpose
by supplying an argument against the present land agitation.
Whatever may be said as to the propriety of making such a
collection at all under circumstances the most adverse,
I believe the majority of the tenants would say that the address was quite uncalled for, and that it by no means represents accurately and fairly either the real state of things on
the Vane-Tempest estate or their own views with regard to
the matters with which it deals."

Again here is another specimen of the manner in which land agents treat their dependents. At a meeting at Tipperary, where the Rev. P. O'Donnell, C.C., took the chair, a farmer begged to be allowed to state his case. He held 63 acres of poor land, for which he paid originally £61. In 1859 the rent was raised to £68. In 1865, when the landlord became of age, the rent was raised to £80, and in 1875 to £90, while Griffith's valuation was only £71. On asking an abatement of some kind he received the following letter from the landlord :—

" *29th August*, 1880.

"I suppose you won't pay. If I go down I will show you no quarter. Out you go."

" *4th Sept.*, 1880.

"I write to say that all negociations must now cease, so help me Christ Immanuel."

Again I quote an English authority, the special correspondent of the *Daily News*, as to how capital is " driven out of the country."

"The idea of any right which a landlord was bound to respect had not dawned upon them, and if it had, prompt vengeance would have descended on the village of Hampden in the shape of a notice to quit; and he, whose conception of the world was limited to his native mountains, would have been turned out upon them with his wife and children to die."

V

Another evidence of the style in which the land agents rule their masters' estates :—

"The first act of the new management was to 'sthripe the land on 'um,' that is, to mark it out into £5 holdings, each in one 'sthripe' or block. This arrangement, which to the ordinary mind hardly appears unreasonable, was considered oppressive by the tenants, who submitted, however, as was then the manner of their kind. They had still the moun·tain, and could graze their cow or two or their half-dozen sheep upon it, and they naturally regarded this privilege as the most valuable part of their holding, inasmuch as it paid their rent, clothed them, and supplied them with milk to eat with their potatoes.

"Satisfied with little, they rubbed on contentedly enough, only the more adventurous spirits going to England for the harvesting. Then came serious changes. The rent of the £5 holdings was raised to £7, and the mountain was taken away. The poor people protested that they had nothing to feed their few animals upon on the paltry holdings, of which a couple of acres might be available for tillage, a couple more for grass, and the remaining two or three good for hardly anything. An answer was given to them. If they must have the mountain, they must pay for it, practically another rise in the rent. To this they agreed perforce, and even to the extraordinary condition that during a month or six weeks of the breeding season for grouse, they should drive their tiny flocks or herds off the mountain and on to their holdings, in order that the game might not be disturbed at a critical period. I hear that for the last year rents have fallen into arrear, and that the beasts of those who have not paid up have just been driven off the mountain.

"I have cited this case as one of the proofs in my hands

that the country is not over-populated, as has been so frequently stated.

"'The people who in their little way were graziers and raisers of stock, have been deprived of their cattle run, and having no ground to raise turnips upon, cannot resort to artificial feeding. What was originally intended to serve as a little homestead to raise food on for themselves is all they have left, and it is now said that they are crowded together. It would be more correct to say that they have been driven together like rats in the corner of a pit."

Like rats in a pit! Here is an English account of landlord government of Ireland. And yet we are told that we are lazy and dirty and discontented and full of "sentimental grievances."

But let us see how capital is *kept out of Ireland* by the very persons who are loudest in their denunciations, and who are always writing letters to the *Times*, with hints of that mysterious capitalist who is always coming (on paper) but who never comes in person.

The same authority says :—

"I esteem myself fortunate in being enabled to describe what the life of the Connemara peasant is, under favourable circumstances. His abject misery in years of famine and persistent rain, when crops fail and peat cannot be dried, may be left to the imagination. Potatoes raised from the "champion" seed, introduced during the distress last year, are, if not plentiful, yet sufficient, perhaps, for the present, in the localities to which a good supply of seed was sent ;

but I should not like to speculate on the probable condition of affairs in March next. I have also spoken of such a peasant as has been fortunate enough to obtain work at nine shillings a week, esteemed a fair rate hereabouts. But, in truth, there is very little work to be had ; for the curse of absenteeism sits heavily on the West. Four great landed proprietors, who together have drawn, for several years past, about £70,000 from their estates in Mayo, Galway, and Clare, have not, I am assured, ever spent £10,000 a year in this country. As with the land itself, crop after crop has been gathered and no fertilizer has been put in. The peasant is now aware of as many of such facts as apply to his own locality, and this knowledge, coupled with hard work and hunger, has aroused a discontent not to be easily appeased.

"Thus arises a state of affairs against which the peasant, at last, shows signs of revolt. Physically and mentally neglected for centuries by his masters, he has found, within the last fifty years, neglect exchanged for extortion and oppression. To prevent the sale of the property, the owners or trustees must pay the interest on the incumbrances. Moreover, they, being only human, think themselves entitled to a modest subsistence out of the proceeds of the property. To pay the interest and secure this " margin " for themselves there is only one way—to wring the last shilling out of the wretched tenants, to first deprive them of their ancient privileges, and then charge them extra dues for exercising them ; or to let every available inch of mountain pasture to a cattle farmer, whose herds take very good care that the cottier's cow does not get " the run of the mountain " at their master's expense.

The correspondent of the *Daily Telegraph* says :—

" Smaller land-owners in the parish are either unable or

unwilling to treat their tenants with the leniency shown by
the Marquis, and on the property of one or two of these
evictions are now threatened. Their rents seem immode-
rately high, taking the Poor Law Valuation as a standard.
John Grady, for example, occupies land valued at £3 10s.
and pays £9 ; while Tom Ball has a still smaller holding,
rated at 30s., for which he pays £5 and taxes. It is manifestly impossible that these men can make a living off poor
land so heavily burdened—land brought under cultivation
by themselves or their predecessors, without the owner stir-
ring a finger or investing sixpence in its improvement. The
rent, in point of fact, has to be made up by labour in
England, and it is just this state of things which should be
borne in mind by people who are disposed to complain of
the Irish tenant's revolt. His life is often one of slavery for
the benefit of the man who owns the soil of a country where
agriculture is the only industry."

Here are Connemara and Kerry described by
English writers; and yet, English people wonder
the Irish are so discontented and rebellious.

But, even at the expense of possible weariness
to the reader, let me call attention to what
Canon Heany, P.P., writes about Downpatrick:

"The desolating system that has been pursued and carried
out in past times, upheld by the land laws of the country,
has at length forced the tenant farmers to seek temporary
protection under a Land League organization, rather than
be exposed to the risk of eviction under a capricious or a
rack-renting landlord. If there be anything unnatural or
unhealthy in this state of things, let those be responsible
who have persistently refused to recognise the just claims of

the tenant. The proprietor, no doubt, has rights which
must be respected and preserved. Individual property is in
the order and nature of things established by God, and forms
an essential element of human society ; but the tenant, too,
has his rights, derived from a source equally high and holy.
The labourer is worthy of his hire. Were the landlord himself to farm and cultivate his estate, and were the tenant
or tenants thereon to till it, in the capacity or condition of
labourers, he or they would not be deprived of the fruit of
their toil, nor doomed to starvation. What the Indian
planter even does for the negro should be done for the free
tenant farmers of the British Empire. Let the land be let to
the tenantry of Ireland for a fair and equitable rent, with
fixity of tenure, and every facility for honest purchase, when
the occasion arises. Let the tenant-farmers and people
press and insist on this, and let them not be deluded by
imaginary or impracticable schemes, which would tend more
to impoverish than improve the condition of our people."

Mr. T. D. Sullivan, M.P., at the Mullingar
Meeting, said :—

"A priest had told him of one poor man dying in the
Mullingar Workhouse who had once a happy home and a
virtuous family. He was thrown on the roadside, not for
arrears of rent, but because the landlord chose to clear the
farms. The misery and the shame of what he had been
reduced to was hard enough to bear, and the recollection of
the happy days he spent at home he could have forgotten,
but amongst the members of his family he had a daughter,
whom he left in that wretched abode. His daughter became
a wretch and she was lost. The poor father could have forgotten everything but that, and in his dying hours he could
not forget the author of his wrongs—the landlord who had

turned him and his children out of their land (cries of 'Shame, shame')."

Mr. Thomas Fenelon, of Ballyconnel, writes to the *Freeman* :—

"Among the many counts in the indictment which the Government have brought against Mr. Parnell and his companions, is one for calling on the people not to take any farm from which the tenant has been unjustly evicted. Now, I wonder what would Mr. Gladstone or Mr. Forster say if every priest and bishop in Ireland stated that they felt bound, in the interest of Christian charity, religion, and social order, to adopt the same course? What Irishman can be ignorant of the evils inflicted on the tenantry of the country by the hunger and thirst hitherto existing for land? I will give one instance of the cases that came within my own knowledge, and which I could count by the score since the general election of '52. An honest, industrious farmer, with his wife and children, struggles against a rack-rent by the constant labour of himself and family; living on the poorest fare, and clad in the cheapest and coarsest material, he is able to keep his chin over water for a time. A bad season comes, he loses a cow or horse, distemper gets among his pigs, on which he may largely depend for rent; fever or other sickness comes among his family. Any visitation of this kind is a terrible blow to a man staggering under a rack-rent. The rent-day comes round, he is not able to meet his engagement; the agent or landlord may not regret this for reasons known to themselves. Another gale day comes on, but this poor man from one cause or other is still sinking under the load. At last, perhaps, he owes two or three half-years' rent. During all this time some neighbour or other was testing his plans through the machinery of bailiffs, drivers, and agent. The work is now ready to hand, there is no one to blame, a visitation of Providence rendered this honest man unable to pay the rent, the landlord or agent can wash his hands and give the place to the land shark, who will clear up all rent due, and perhaps do a little more. Thus the tenant is deprived of his home, of the fruits of his toil and outlay, himself and family driven to the poorhouse, or obliged to labour in the service of others, because another man was watching, base enough, to rob them of their rights. The Land League says, and every honest man must endorse the saying, 'If there were no receivers, there would be no robberies.'"

The Rev. M. J. Clarke, C.C., of Kilmore, Belmullet, writes on the same day and date, November 5, 1880 :—

" In the early part of this week I was called to the townland of Clogher, situate in the parish of Kilmore, and about ten miles from Belmullet, to administer the last rites of the Church to an old woman whose years, I believe, number not less than eighty. A few days previous her son-in-law, a man named Keane, with whom she lived, together with his wife and a family of eight, were evicted from their home by a landlord of the middle-class type for the non-payment of an exorbitant rent. I say exorbitant, for on inquiry I find that the Government valuation of the holding is £3 10s., while the actual rent is £8, exclusive of rates and taxes, which the late tenant, contrary to stipulation, had been obliged to pay."

I omit his graphic description of the miserable scene.

He continues :—

" I inquired for the old woman whom I was called to

attend, and was conducted by one of the bystanders to the
spot where she lay. Towards the west side of the walls of
the house, and adjoining what was once the gable, is an
enclosure formed by the articles of furniture, which have
been huddled together for the purpose of making an attempt
at something like a dwelling. A few sticks, with some straw
spread over, serve the purpose of a roof, while an open space
is left on the side of the structure for an entrance. The
whole enclosed area measures about 14ft. by 6ft., and here,
God be praised, in this nineteenth century of enlightenment
and progress, in the midst of peace and plenty, is a poor,
honest, hard-working serf, with his family of little ones,
obliged to shelter themselves from the biting blast of a cold
November night. Shelter from their neighbours they cannot
obtain, for this most humane of landlords, whose tenants, I
am happy to say, are few, not content with carrying his cruel
designs thus far, threatened them with a similar punishment
should they take this poor family under their roof even for
one night.

"Here, I say, in this wretched spot, with the green grass
for her bed, did this poor old woman receive at my hands
the last rites of the Church ; and here, while I write, is this
destitute family obliged to live for want of a better home."

Mr. Lucas, writing to the *Tablet*, makes some
remarks which are an admirable commentary on
the above. He says :—

"The ' old fashioned notions about the rights of property,' to which he lays claim, were, I believe, held by my
brother who assisted in founding the Tenant League, in
order to put a stop to the habitual breach of those rights by
the landlords.

" In this view it was not tenants who refused to pay rack-rents who were dishonest, but the landlords who enforced them.

" That peculiar truth was new to Englishmen in these days, and is not generally acknowledged now, I fancy."

We take the following extract from a leader in the *Echo*, and we add that this clever device to throw the Poor Rate on the tenant is a usual proceeding of Irish land agents. Is it not time we heard a little less about the nobleman's "rights of property," and a little more about the poor man's right to live.

" Lord Ventry's Irish rental amounts to £30,000 per annum, and his tenants live in mud cabins without windows, sometimes without doors, the smoke making its escape as best it may through the door, or through a hole in the roof, for there are no chimneys. Here and there the houses are better, but in every case they have been erected, unaided, by the tenant himself, who not only has to pay for the cost of erection, but is in addition taxed for the improved yearly value by an amended rating valuation. Some idea of the condition of the people may be gathered from the fact that during the recent scarcity 4,000 were receiving relief from charitable funds, towards which Lord Ventry did not think it necessary to contribute. An ingenious contrivance which finds favour with his agent deserves notice. The law enacts that where a valuation is under £4 the landlord must bear the whole Poor Rate. In this district the rents, or many of them, are very small, so the agent groups together in one receipt for rent several persons, and, by making them severally answerable for each other, adds to the landlord's security, whilst compelling them to pay that proportion of the Poor Rate they would otherwise escape ! . . . . . And people marvel at the thousands who crowd to listen to Mr. Parnell, and English landlords make the cause of Irish landlordism their own, and even the liberal-minded murmur that whatever may have been wrong in the past was redressed long since ! Was it ? Scan Europe from Brest to Astrachan, and where is the tiller of the soil so utterly helpless as in Ireland ? Even the Turk only plunders intermittingly. Coercion ! let us have coercion ! shrieks the Tory. Well, it may come to that in the end. It is what we have fallen back upon any time since the Union ; but there is no statesmanship in the acts of force. Justice Fortescue once said that nothing makes a people rise against their rulers but a lack of goods or a lack of justice. Ireland has long lacked both, but the concession of the one will be followed by the advent of the other. May it be Mr. Gladstone's lot to crown a splendid career by the completion of the work with which his name is already imperishably connected ?"

CHAPTER XVIII.

THE FAMINE YEAR AND SENTIMENTAL GRIEVANCES.

" English and Scotch landowners in bad seasons bear their share of the depression, by abating a considerable percentage of their rents."—R. Mahony, J.P.

HE above sentence is taken from a pamphlet addressed to the Right Hon. W. Forster, M.P., by Richard Mahony, Esq., J.P., Dromore, Kenmare. The object of the pamphlet apparently is to impress Mr. Forster and the public generally with the extraordinary virtues of Irish lords, and the fearful ingratitude of the Government towards them. He commences with Socrates, and ends not, indeed, with an offer to poison himself, but with a wild offer or threat, it is difficult to tell which, of going to an unknown district in some free land, " where enterprise is not discouraged, and where life and capital are secure." Why not stay at home, and allow laws to be made which will encourage enterprise, and thus secure life and capital. But to do this neither life nor capital

PATRICK EGAN.

must be longer at the mercy of a class of men
who will not save the lives of their tenants whenever a God-sent calamity overtakes them—and
who rack-rent all their capital from them, and then
taunt them with being paupers. He says the
landlords are a "garrison," (p. 52,) which is quite
true, and that they have "defended themselves
honourably," which is partly true. They have
certainly defended themselves, and that somewhat rudely, but some persons may question the
honourable nature of the defence. It would be
impossible to notice all the wild writing in this
curious production, which includes the following
remarkable observation :—

" When Socrates, falsely accused, and adjudged guilty by a
large majority in a popular assembly, was permitted to award
his own sentence, he gave his opinion that he ought to be entertained honourably during the rest of his life at the public
expense. The government of the day, however, came to
the conclusion that he should drink hemlock. Not long
afterwards they discovered that they had killed the wrong
man.

" There are people recklessly impeached every day
before popular assemblies in Ireland, who, if not as wise as
Socrates, would certainly, before a fair tribunal, be found as
innocent of the crime of which they are accused."

Whether the English Government will be induced by this touching appeal to pension off

and feast luxuriously the Irish landlords for the rest of their lives remains to be seen. Possibly some of Her Majesty's Ministers may think that if these same landlords had tried to feed their tenants even with the poorest food during the late famine, and if they had followed the example of English and Scotch landlords by "abating a considerable percentage of their rents," that they would have been more worthy of perennial banquetting. But this was precisely what Irish landlords did not do. The most lamentable efforts were made to deny the distress until it was past denying, and even then the most miserable and contemptible subterfuges were made use of to make it appear less than it was, or, if that was not possible, to make it appear the fault of the people.

It was the fault of misgovernment. It was the strongest proof that could possibly be given of the fearful *normal* state of destitution in which the people live, and it should arouse the deep sympathy of every Christian heart. What! because one of the commonest articles of food fails, the whole population are plunged into famine. Why? because the people are *normally* in such a state of poverty that a potato stands between them and a famine—a potato which is an accompaniment to the meal of the same class in England, and not as here the meal itself. Could any-thing prove better the wretched state of the country ?

But it is all their own fault. How easily said, and how untrue. Ireland has been deliberately and cruelly prevented from having any other food, because the manufactures and industries which are needed for the ordinary well-being of every nation have been denied her. Let me again quote from Mr. Russell's letters, and let it be noted that these are not matters of opinion about which there may be a dispute. No ; these are matters of fact about which there can be no dispute.

"As to the commercial laws. In 1660 Ireland's proximity to America, and the good quality of its natural harbours, had caused a considerable Irish colonial trade to spring up, but by legislation in 1663, the importation of any European article into an English colony, except from England, and in English ships, built and manned by Englishmen, was prohibited. This was capped, in 1696, by an express provision that no goods of any kind should be imported direct from the colonies into Ireland. About the same period the ex-portation of Irish cattle was becoming a source of wealth to the country ; but upon the complaint of English landowners that thereby their rents were being affected, laws were enacted, in 1665 and 1680, prohibiting the importation from Ireland, not only of cattle, but also of butter and cheese. Upon this, Ireland, striving to accommodate itself to this harsh legislation, turned to extensive sheep farming. In a few years a flourishing trade in woollen manufactures existed.

Again English jealousy was aroused.   Export duties were imposed.   But even these failing utterly to crush the trade, the Irish were, in 1699, prohibited from exporting their woollen goods to any country whatsoever.   This was a sad blow.   Between 20,000 and 30,000 operatives had been employed in this branch of trade alone.   The linen trade had existed, in some small degree, as early as the fifteenth century, but, by 1700, it had risen to great importance.   In 1705 the Irish were first allowed to export their white and brown linen to British colonies ; but they were forbidden to bring back any colonial goods in return.   In this linen trade England was no competitor; but it was feared that the Irish would supersede the Dutch linen, and so cause jealousy in Holland.   Accordingly, attempts were made to restrict the manufacture to the coarsest kinds.   But these attempts ultimately proved unavailing.   Even as to the fisheries, it is almost amusing to read that, about the beginning of the eighteenth century, petitions from Folkestone and Aldborough were considered in Parliament, complaining of the injury done to the fisheries of these towns 'by the Irish catching herrings at Waterford and Wexford, and sending them to the straits, thereby forestalling and ruining your petitioners' markets.'   There was even a party in England desirous of prohibiting all fisheries on the Irish shore, except by boats built and manned by Englishmen !

Here we have in a few sentences the cause of Irish famines.   What wonder if the Nemesis should come from America where the Celt has "gone with a vengeance."   The *Munster Express*, in an article headed " Ireland's Decay," says :—

" The Registrar-General has issued his report of the

annual stock-taking of Ireland, and it is a dismal and depressing document. *Decrease* is written in every page. There is a decrease of 40,609 acres in the area under crops; there is a decrease of 14,837 in the number of horses and mules; a decrease of 2,594 in the number of asses; a decrease of 146,752 in the number of cattle; a decrease of 456,542 in the number of sheep; a decrease of 223,149 in the number of pigs; a decrease of 13,155 in the number of goats, and a decrease of 356,106 in the number of poultry. This document tells of the gradual decadence in Irish farming. The land devoted to cereal crops, which in 1847, occupied 3,313,579 acres, or one-fourth of the arable land, has gradually lessened, and in 1880 was only 1,766,424 acres, or less than one-eighth of the arable land. Notwithstanding the supply of seed, there is a diminution of 21,943 acres in the area under potatoes; and in green crops there is a dimunition of 25,388 acres. The return shows very painfully the effect of the past season, and the action of the landlords upon the tillage of the poor—their asses, their pigs, their goats, and their poultry, have all diminished in number. Notwithstanding the continued boasts of great prices for dairy produce, there is a decrease of 67,985 in the number of milch cows, and of 108,096 in the number of calves; in 1859, the number of milch cows in Ireland was 1,690,339; in 1880, it was reduced to 1,396,833. The decrease is 293,556. These figures show that dairy farming cannot be so profitable as those who argue in favour of high rents wish to make out, but which they are unable to prove. It is usually calculated that each milch cow should return £10 a year, and the annual loss to Ireland upon the diminished number of milch cows would be nearly three millions sterling (£2,935,560). The alleged increase in the price of butter does not compensate for this loss. The porcine race has gone down from 1,621,443 in 1871, to 849,046 in 1880;

W

the diminution is 772,397, or about 48 per cent. The number of breeding pigs, those of one year old and upwards, which was 322,982 in 1859, has been reduced to 115,309 in 1680. The pigs under a year old, from which the market supply was drawn, has diminished by 650,857. If these animals were in the country they would, when fat and fit for killing, represent from two to two and a-half millions sterling. We miss from the return an account which used to appear in former numbers—the Emigration from Ireland. Irish Farming is perishing under excessive rents."

And the only remedy that can be suggested for all this by sapient Irish landlords is emigration. Get rid of the people! and will that fertilise the country? will that reclaim waste lands? will that re-establish fisheries? will that open up new industrial resources? Was there ever a wilder absurdity? Because, let us say, ten men cannot make the land sufficiently fertile or profitable for existence, send away five of them, and who is to do the work of the five sent away? To such absurdities are men driven when, in their miserable selfishness, they can see no interest but their own.

The special correspondent of the *Standard* says :—

"There are several ways in which it may be shown how impracticable it is for a family holding a small farm, and unable to pay their rent, to continue to live upon it as human beings, even in the worst condition. The average

number of persons in an Irish family is six; the average
cost of maintaining a person in a workhouse is £9. Unless,
therefore, a man clears an average of £54 annually, in addition to his rent, he must sink with his family to a measur-
able condition below that of the inmate of a workhouse.
Again, let us take a farm of sixty acres, say, in the neighbourhood of Kenmare. Kerry farms are not estimated by
acres, but by being in pasturage. The sixty acres represent
'cow's grass,' the greater portion of the country grass for
ten cows, which yield from ten to twelve firkins of butter,
selling at an average price of £3 per firkin, thus making,
say . £36. Four calves are sold for 30s. net. A porker, or
'bonnive' costing £1 16s., is sold, at the expiration of five
or six months, when fattened, for £3 or £4, but, as was remarked to me, a pig in Ireland is really an investment in a
Porcine Savings' Bank, the instalments being the sums spent
in feeding stuffs, until the 'gintleman' is ready to pay the
'rint.' A few young sheep are bought for 15s. or 20s. each;
money is spent in fattening them, and they are then sold at
about £2 each. Against these figures have to be placed
the rent, £15, the poor rates—which are sometimes, as I
have shown, 4s. 6d. in the pound—an average of £1;
county cess, £2; meal, &c., for the support of the family,
£15; feeding stuffs for cattle, £3 10s; to say nothing of
clothing, education, religious, and miscellaneous expenses.
The problem is—can such a family ever better their condition?"

The landlord says, get rid of them. But
when they are got rid of, what then? If there
is *no other* remedy for Irish misery and destitution but to fling them out on the streets of New
York, and so get rid of them, what are we to

say of the statesmanship of such a proposal?
A Red Indian might shrink for shame if such a
suggestion were made in his hearing.

And yet this is the only remedy we hear of
from the vast multitude of Irish landlords. But
it has been tried here in this very district of
Kenmare.

Mr. Stewart Trench flung 5,000 unhappy
people on the streets of New York after the
late famine, and to-day his son and successor
in the agency has only the same plan to suggest.
One might have thought that when the experiment had so signally failed before, and
had met with the reprobation of every man of
common humanity, that it would not be again
suggested.

And the Irish people are expected to act
with devoted loyalty to men who, in the time
of famine, not only will not help them, but will
actually try to prevent others from helping them,
and who would fling them into the emigrant
ship like cattle, if they dared.

As there certainly must be some one left to
till the land in Ireland and to pay the rent,
clearly if the Irish are driven out other people
must be brought in. This is an experiment
which has been tried before, but there are some
persons who can never learn from experience.

Let the Irish landlords get rid of their tenants and bring over English settlers. If they do, a very few months will settle the land question. English farmers will not live on Indian meal, or any other meal, in order to pay rack rents.

The *Times*, the English landlord organ, said lately, in a passing gleam of justice :—

"In the details of Irish destitution there is generally, not to say always, an omission that would never be found in any corresponding details in this country. Where is the landlord? If a population were found in any part of this island hugging the soil, fighting for patches, living like pigs, and every now and then clamouring for somebody to tide them over their difficulties, we should at once ask for the landlord. No title, no political influence, no personal merits, would protect him from a very unpleasant intrusion into his private affairs. If he pleaded that he could not help it, the public would soon see that his hands were at liberty."

This is what the Land League says. But what is flat blasphemy in the private soldier is only a rough word in the colonel.

And it is not in Kerry or Connemara alone that this dire poverty exists. The Rev. E. Sheehy, C.C., speaking at the Kilmallock meeting, said :—

"It had been stated, and that statement had been repeated, that the agitation for the abolition of landlordism, started in the sterile and poverty-stricken district of Connemara (cheers for Connemara), would close, and would not receive the support of the endorsement of the other provinces of Ireland. They were assembled there to-day, people born, cradled, and nurtured in the golden vale of Ireland. It was not merely Connaught to-day, but Kilmallock, that spoke in the name of the sacred principle of a free land for a free people (cheers). He had had an extensive ramble through this wide earth, and he had not seen anything to compare with the luxuriant richness of that golden vale of theirs. Yet, what had they on its fertile bosom? They had fat cattle and famishing Christians (cheers.) They had emigration schemes and cattle shows."

The following were present at this important meeting:—

"Rev. M. Clery, P.P., Bulgaden; Rev. E. Clifford, C.C., Kilmallock; Rev. E. Sheehy, C.C., Kilmallock; Rev. Mr. Enright, P.P., Rockhue; Rev. Mr. Costello, C.C., Rockhue; Rev. Mr. Canick, P.P., Ardpatrick; Rev. T. O'Reilly, C.C., Charleville; Rev. J. Conway, Rev. Canon Slattery, P.P., Hospital; Rev. J. Fitzgerald, C.C., Bulgaden; Rev. J. Gubbins, Kilmallock; Messrs. William Henry O'Sullivan, M.P., Michael Ryan, J.P., Bruree."

The Chairman, the Rev. M. O. Cleary, P.P., said:—

"He would say the cause of murders was the half-hearted, deaf ear the English Government had lent to the grievances of the country.

"There was bloodshed in the matter of the tithes, and O'Connell did not charge himself with that bloodshed, though he was agitating against the tithes (hear, hear.) He

did not fear to raise his loud voice and tell the Government
their grievances, for he was the vindicator of the people's
rights (cheers.) The land question was now the leading
question, and it had been stained with blood, but had it not
also been stained by the wholesale murder of gigantic evictions that filled the emigrant ships and crammed the grave-
yards? For he remembered when a Protestant minister, the
owner of a grave-yard, had to stop interments, for the place
was choked with the dead victims of evictions."

I do not think the people can be induced, and
they can scarcely be compelled, to leave Ireland
wholesale. But what is the result of the present efforts to get rid of the population in that
way? Again, I give English authority. Lord
Emly can scarcely be claimed as one having
"national" proclivities in any sense. He said
in the debate on the Relief of Distress
[Ireland] Bill in the House of Lords :—

" There were, however, districts in which there had been
distress for many years, and which was not owing to bad
harvests, but to the poorness of the soil and over population.
Those districts extended along the west coast of Ireland—
from Donegal, Mayo, Galway, Clare, Cork, and Kerry, and
comprised a very considerable population. The hon. member for the county of Waterford, who was a Fishery Commissioner in 1876 and 1877, and having to dispose of certain
loans, had to make himself acquainted with the condition of
the people on the coast of Galway; that hon. member, in one
of his fishery reports, said that the holdings of the people
there were miserably small—one or two acres—and that in
the best of times the people were in a state of semi-starvation,

that their lodging was miserable, that they had not got clothes to enable them to go to Mass; and that they had all those scorbutic diseases which arose from a constant want of food. Passing on to Mayo, he saw an account written only lately in a very able manner by Mr. Fox, and addressed to the Dublin Mansion House Committee, in which that gentleman said the great evil of the times in Mayo was not the question of rent, but other evils; that their holdings were too small, and deficient in quantity and quality. This was a question of special importance now, because when there was a prospect of a good harvest, and the distress in other parts of Ireland was passing away, the normal condition of the west coast of Ireland would be forgotten and left without remedy. Mr. Parnell seemed to think that the only remedy would be for the population to move to the fertile plains of Meath, but he did not think that the Meath farmers would believe in that. In his opinion the best remedy would be found in assisting families to the colonies. There was one objection to assisting emigration, and that was a most powerful one, viz.—that assisting emigration interfered with voluntary emigration, and that it would dam at once the spring from which great sums of money now came from America for emigration. But in his opinion the emigration which was now going on was an almost unmitigated evil. Families did not emigrate, and the very poorest could not emigrate. He himself only the other day, at Queenstown, saw the class of persons that were emigrating. He went on board an emigrant ship and saw them. The persons who were emigrating were the very bone and sinew of the country—young men and young women well clothed and apparently respectable in every way. It appeared to him that that kind of emigration was a distinct loss to the country. They did not wish to get rid of that class of persons, but the very poor and miserable, who might find homes in the colonies, and be very comfortable. Such a state of things as that which he had mentioned was a disgrace to this country, and it was their bounden duty to attempt to redress it (hear, hear).

No doubt the colonies will know how to be grateful to the noble lord for his charitable suggestion. If the subject were not so grave, it would be simply amusing. The aged, the miserable, the worn out, are to be flung out of Ireland; the young, the strong, are to remain until they also are worn out and sinking under the burden of making bricks without straw. It is no wonder that Ireland has not much faith in English legislation.

I was speaking to a gentleman who owns vast estates in different parts of Ireland, and calling his attention to the miserable fare of his tenantry, and to the amazement of some English friends who discovered that they *never* eat meat of any kind, nor even fish, that their sole fare was Indian meal or potatoes. His reply was not made in any unkind spirit. He said:—"Are not potatoes and milk good enough for them?" I replied:—"You know very well that most of them cannot get milk."

Now, I ask, dare any English gentleman say this of the farmers on his property; and why are the Irish to live on poorer fare?

Then we are perpetually told that the Irish impoverish themselves by drinking whiskey. I hope I shall not be considered an advocate for drink if I say, why should they not drink whiskey? The Englishman drinks beer and gin and the Irishman drinks whiskey. No doubt, it would be better for both if they drank water. But, if the millennium of temperance has not come, why is the Irishman to be selected as a special object of scorn and reproach, because he uses his national drink? And who gives it him? Who, I had almost said, refuses him anything else? Who, I had almost said, forces this vile drink on him? Who, but the very land agents of these landlords, who are so busy denouncing the Irish for drinking?

It is they who license so many public houses. Why do they license every other house in some miserable little village? Truly, every honest industry is snatched from the people's hands, and the cup of destruction is pressed on them.

In a letter of Lord Fitzmaurice's, he accuses the people on his brother's (Lord Lansdowne) property, at Cahirciveen, with "habitual drunkenness;" and yet, Mr. Russell tells us, they had been imploring in vain for a supply of water!

"One other matter I must mention : it is a subject of bitterness at Cahirciveen. This town has now a very defective water supply ; but, lying at the base of a range of hills, there is ample water-shed easily available, and, at the small cost of about £700, capable of supplying the town at a high pressure. The town was willing to bear one-half the interest on this expenditure of capital, but the college would not bear the remainder."

Perhaps, if the people were supplied with water, and a few, at least, of the public houses closed, we might hear less of drinking.

Dean Dickinson, like too many men of his class, has lately brought forward the stock story of the famine being all the fault of drinking and of drunkenness.

The Rev. Mr. Wingham, a Protestant clergyman, has well replied to this miserable calumny in a letter to the *Ballinasloe Western News :—*

" SIR,—I read for the first time, in your paper of the 30th ult., the astounding remarks recently made at a Dublin meeting by Dean Dickinson, and in support of which, it appears, he gave me as one of his authorities. I know not what information he may have gleaned elsewhere, during his temperance tour in the West, but, so far as I am concerned, I utterly repudiate the statement he is reported to have made. So far was I from saying that the 'cry of distress was a wholesale fraud,' I assumed, in my conversation with him (what no sane man could deny), that wide-spread distress existed. I instanced the localities in this province on which the famine had fallen in its direst form, in consequence of failure—not only at home but in England and Scotland— depriving many thousands of the employment by which, in

ordinary years, they are enabled to eke out a scanty subsistence. These statements do not seem to have made any
impression on the Dean ; for he is reported to have made
the extravagant assertion that, 'so far as real distress was
concerned, it seemed that the majority of it—nine-tenths of
it, perhaps—was caused by the drunken habits of the people,
political agitators, and idleness.' It is little wonder that a
statement such as this should have occasioned the deepest
indignation, and called forth loud and energetic protests."

One of the usual charges against Ireland is,
that the people are "ungrateful." So frequently
is it reiterated that it is actually believed. And
though no one can point out any particular reason
why we should be grateful to England, it does
not matter—the charge is persisted in all the
same. It, might be supposed, indeed, that the
English Government and the Irish landlords
had wearied themselves pouring forth favours
on a people who, in return, did nothing but
rebel. But between Ireland and England
there should be no question of gratitude—the
idea is simply absurd. We do not court and
we do not ask favours ; but we ask and we do
not get justice. Why should we be "grateful" for
help in the Famine Year, for example ? Is not
Ireland part of the United Kingdom ? Yet we
are told—the Irish are so ungrateful for all that
was done for them last year.

I am very unwilling to criticise what was

kindly meant; but truth has higher claims than compliments. I am afraid it must be said truthfully—that England did very little for Ireland, and that same little was done very grudgingly. Again and again the English papers rang with denials of the distress. What did the English Government do for Ireland in that famine? Nothing. We were, indeed, allowed to tax ourselves with a "Seeds Potato Bill,"—a Bill which never would have passed the House of Lords had not its noble legislators known well that, if they did not make some effort to provide the people with potatoes to plant, they might look in vain the next year for their rents.

The Queen, it is true, gave £500; but three millions were spent in India, to give her the empty title of Empress of a people who do not show much love of English Government. Almost at the same time, the very same sum was given by a gentleman in London towards the election expenses of Mr. H. Gladstone, and many sums of scarcely less amount were in his subscription list. No; Ireland is not ungrateful; but, when a fearful national calamity comes, and when its existence is denied, and intentionally denied, for political or other purposes, and when the assistance given is doled out with grudging reluctance and incessant reproach,

even were it in proportion to the need, there
was small claim for gratitude.   Had such a
calamity occurred in any part of England, we
know what expressions of sympathy, at least,
would have been used by the majority of the
people of England.   All the royal sympathy
we received was from the Duke of Edinburgh,
who "wished" the people of Arran had blankets;[1] and I suppose we ought to be grateful for
royal wishes.

Nor can it be forgotten that the food given
was of the very coarsest kind.   Even the vile
suggestion was made in an English paper

---

[1] At the meeting of the Mansion House Committee, April 8th, 1880,
the following official telegram was read and published in the *Freeman's
Journal*, April 9th:

"His Royal Highness the Duke of Edinburgh, yesterday, visited
North Arran and the villages of Kilronan and Killaney.   In the latter
he found abject misery, many people with little clothes to cover them,
and houses visited without food, fuel, or furniture.   The beds and bed-
clothing would require the pen of Charles Dickens to describe them.
The Committee expressed their gratitude to the Mansion House Committee, and stated that, but for the grants sent there, many deaths from
starvation must have occurred.   On our way back to Galway we visited
Costello's Bay, and hope on Saturday, or early next week, to send a
supply of clothing there, as it is much wanted.   The Duke expressed a
wish that every house he visited should have a pair of blankets that
night."

The blankets given out by the Dublin Committee were hardly fit for
horse cloths, at least those that I saw, and, I have reason to believe, the
same kind were sent everywhere.

that this food, which in England would hardly be given to dogs, should be made in some way unpalatable. Throughout the whole business the Irish were treated as if the famine was solely their own fault, and as if to give them anything was an act of grace to felons. Nor could the Irish people fail to note the difference both in spirit and in food between the relief given to the Turks and to them, as the following will show :—

TURKS.	IRISH.
Graphic, July 10th :—	*Freeman's Journal,* July 10, 1880 :—
" Good strong soup is given out twice a week, and biscuits on other days. As the time for distribution draws near, a certain number of the people are told off for bearing the soup, and enter the huge kitchen, where seven seething cauldrons are placed upon a trough of fire ; from here they march out, each carrying a bucket of the hot liquid which is to vanquish for the moment the terrible cold benumbing the poor dwellers of the khan."	" Outdoor relief has been given with such an illiberal hand by the Castlebar guardians, the weekly allowance for a large family being in many instances only two stones of yellow meal. Hundreds of our people are without employment, and their cry is 'Food or labour!' yet labour or food will be slow to come unless you take instant action, and step in to stand between the people and death."

I had some idea of giving extracts from the

reports made to the Duchess of Marlborough's Committee and to the Mansion House Committee, but I fear it would occupy too much space. I fear also that those who were determined to believe that famine in Ireland was not as severe as it was would hardly be convinced even by such high authorities as a Royal Duke, Lord Randolph Churchill, Major Gaskell, and others. I append, however, an extract from a report from Major Gaskell, read by Lord R. Churchill before the Duchess of Marlborough's Committee, in March, 1880. He said, speaking of Donegal :—

"The ties of association or tradition must be strong, indeed, which bind a superior race so fast to a home unattractive from all points of view except those of sentiment and romance. The harvest of the sea, no doubt, contributed more than that of the land to feed and clothe the forefathers of the present generation. Fishing and manufacture of kelp must have been lucrative up to a comparatively recent date. But of late years the price of kelp has been less remunerative, while fishing has declined owing to the wearing out of tackle and the inability through gradually increasing poverty to replace it. The only market the fishermen have is the chance one of a passing steamer, which must be intercepted by the row-boats in the open sea. To row out into the Atlantic in a 20 feet boat is no light matter. The boat must be good, and the crew steady ; and so they are. But a trade so costly and full of risk was profitable only under favourable conditions of weather and demand, and both were adverse in 1879. Besides making kelp and fishing, the population of the Rosses and the neighbouring islands have been in the habit of adding to their means of livelihood by farm labour abroad in the summer months. Each year, as soon as the seed potatoes and oats have been planted, almost all the able-bodied males emigrate to Scotland, whence they return after the harvest with varying amounts of money per head, the average being £6 or £7. Last year the labour market was so dull that £5 among three was about the highest sum saved, and was looked upon as a fortune. Few brought home anything, and many nothing at all; while quite half the emigrants were so much worse at the end of the summer than when they started, that their passages were paid by their more fortunate, thou still poor, companions. Thus, book debts to tradesmen which would have been paid in whole or in part with the summer's earnings, were not met at all, and credit—the fabric, almost baseless, upon which this light-hearted, sanguine people have lived for years—collapsed."

The *Times* gave the following letter from the Duchess of Marlborough's Committee in March, also :—

"The normal state of the peasantry of the wild parts of the west appears to be an almost utter want of clothing except coarse rags, and of covering except old sacks. Major Gaskell mentions in his report that he hardly ever saw in Donegal such a thing as bed-clothes. People were all lying on heaps of straw, their only covering being some old bags. In Clare, Captain Fletcher, another inspector, says the same, and that any kind of rough material fit for bed-covering would be an enormous boon. Thousands of children all through the country have been kept from school

by want of clothes, and are described very much as Zulu
children. In the islands, the case is still worse, some of the
people being described as perfectly naked, with the exception of an old rag or shawl about them."

When, according to the Duchess of Marlborough's report, the *normal* state of the west
of Ireland was such, what must it not have
been when the only crop failed? And, I know,
that in many parts of Kerry the normal state of
the poor is the same.

" At the annual dinner of the Geographical Society, which
was held June 1, 1880, his Royal Highness, the Duke of
Edinburgh, who presided, spoke as follows on the subject
of Irish distress :—

" 'Your Excellencies, my Lords and Gentlemen—I thank
you most heartily for the kind manner in which you have
drank my health. I am deeply sensible of the kind expressions used with regard to what I have been lately doing on
the coast of Ireland, and I will take this opportunity of saying a few words on that subject It has been believed· by
many that the extent of the distress on the west coast of
Ireland is greatly exaggerated ; that the relief administered
has not in all cases been necessary ; but I can confidently
state, as the result of what I have seen, and from an intimate
knowledge of how the relief has been granted, that *the distress in the main has not been exaggerated. It has been excessively
severe, and that it has not reached the point it reached at the
time known as the "Irish Famine,"* is due entirely to the fact
THAT PREPARATIONS FOR MEETING IT HAD BEEN TAKEN IN
TIME. I cannot refrain from expressing my sense of how

much that taking in time was due to the charitable exertions
of the Duchess of Marlborough. It has been a great pleasure to me to be associated with her Grace, as well as with
many others in this beneficent work.

" ' *We have also to thank the citizens of America for the great
and generous help they have sent to Ireland* (cheers). It was
my good fortune to be able to be at Queenstown to assist in
the distribution of that magnificent cargo which was sent
from America (cheers). I must say that the distress is
not over yet, *nor will it be over for at least two months and
a half,* when the first crop—the potato crop—will be gathered
and is followed by the general harvest. Until then, in many
cases, *actual relief by feeding the population* in some portions
of the west of Ireland, including the islands, must be continued. *Otherwise the starvation which would have occurred
in the first instance but for such relief will occur ;* yet I hope
all those who are here this evening will bear in mind, and
tell others who are charitably inclined, that the time has not
yet passed when much good may be done by sending subscriptions to those great funds which have already done so
much to relieve the distress.'"

· And yet, in the face of this statement, there
certainly was no warmth in the efforts made to
relieve the distress, and none of that cordial
giving which might have been expected.

It was, indeed, from the Irish in America,
in Australia, and in India, that the most sums
of money came which saved the people from
death by starvation.

A Protestant clergyman said :—

" There are whole townlands absolutely depending upon the meal supplied by the Moylough committee, but for which the people would be in dire starvation."

Dr. Dickinson having made the false charge,

".That nine-tenths of the poverty was caused by the drunken habits of the people, political agitators, and idleness,"

Dr. Sigerson replied :—

" It was my duty, in company with Dr. Kenny, to make a careful investigation into the condition of the people of the western province, from its northern to its southern boundary. Having thus become intimately acquainted with the domestic circumstances of the inhabitants in widely varied districts, and attentively observed their conduct everywhere, I declare that it gives a shock to the moral sense, as of an outrage committed, to hear idleness and drunkenness imputed to them as the causes of their poverty.   Nowhere have I seen, not even in France, a population more free from any sign of intemperance, more generally and thoroughly sober. During a month spent entirely amongst the people, in the wildest parts of Connaught, I have never heard a discourteous word, nor seen a drunken man.   The solitary exception to the rule, so far as the last element is concerned, happened in a town where assizes were being held.   In the rural districts, even in those houses where fever-stricken patients so much required them, no stimulants were to be found in the homes of the peasantry."

CHAPTER XIX.

INDIA AND IRELAND.—POLITICAL ECONOMY IN IRELAND.

" We think we are the only good colonists in the world ; on the contrary, we cannot train or teach ; we can only multiply and spread. . . . We have developed India for the usurer, Ireland for the landlord, other parts of the world for the Manchester man, or the London man, or the outside man generally, not for and by the native."—*Far Owl*, Colonel W. J. Butler.

IT is, I think, the great misfortune of all English colonial government that her colonies are treated as places out of which all that is possible is to be got, and to which as little as possible is to be given. Ireland is by no means the only colony under British Government which has met with this fate. The further the colony is from England, the better chance there is of its being allowed to prosper. If Ireland were as far from England as Australia, it would be in a happier condition. Yet there are Englishmen who are not without some gleaming of this painful truth, as the extract given above will sufficiently show. This policy is neither wise nor honourable. It must end inevitably in failure and disgrace.

I believe it arises from two causes. First, from the natural desire of the human heart to possess wealth and power; the consequence, where this desire is given no check, either by law or public opinion, must inevitably be a system of petty tyranny and unjust government. The second cause from which this evil arises, or rather, perhaps, I should say, which occasions its continuance, is the excessive pride which the English have in their own form of Government.

When the English people hear that injustice is done in any dependency they will not believe it. When they hear that a colony is discontented and living in smouldering rebellion, they, without further inquiry, are certain it is the fault of the people. Would it not be wiser, as well as more in accordance with justice, to be willing to inquire calmly and dispassionately ?

Not long since, a writer in the *Commune* said, the Englishman was the subject of the Queen, and the Irishman was the subject of the Englishman. Never was there a truer saying. Ireland virtually is not governed by the Queen; it is governed by English, or Anglo-Irish lords, who scarcely care to conceal their contempt for the people, or for their religion—who treated them with most persistent cruelty until the world cried shame on them.

Never was there a more loyal race than the Irish, and never was there a people more persistently accused of disloyalty. The reason is not far to seek. You cannot expect a people to be loyal to a form of government which allows them to be oppressed, which persistently refuses to hear their complaints, and which will only believe the word of those who oppress them. It is less trouble certainly, for the present, to take things for granted and to believe one side only.

It cost three millions of money to have the Queen proclaimed in India by the empty title of Empress. If she had signalized her reign in Ireland by some great act of beneficence, such as ancient monarchs would have done, by reclaiming waste lands, and planting on them a happy and grateful people, she might have been proclaimed Empress of the hearts of the people at one-half the cost, and undoubtedly her name would have descended to posterity with far more glorious fame.

The great Anglo-Irish lords, and the great Anglo-Indian lords have acted on a uniformity of principle, or of want of principle, producing a uniformity of results, which might well give cause for serious reflection.

No doubt they are all honourable men (in England) but in India and in Ireland how differently they act. Take for example in Ireland the case of one territorial lord, the Duke of Leinster, through all whose vast property of 68,000 acres, no one, be he peer or peasant, can obtain possession of a farm unless he signs the Leinster lease, and contracts himself out of the benefit of the Land Act. Yet we are perpetually told that Ireland is governed by the same laws as England. Here is yet another evidence that while England is governed by the Queen, Ireland is governed by Englishmen. Here is another evidence of that wonderful freedom of contract of which we hear so much, and of which we see so little. Here is an explanation of the wild letters of the *Times* and the *Standard* and the *Daily Telegraph* about Irish outrages, and the wonderful benefits conferred on Irish tenants by their landlords. These landlords naturally wish to continue the exercise of their arbitrary and despotic power. Hence their cries when they find this *imperium in imperio* threatened.

The Very Rev. Dr. Walsh, President of Maynooth College, has written on this subject fully to the *Freeman's Journal*, and has happily given evidence also before the Land Commission. When gentlemen could meet with such treatment, what can the poor expect?

" 1. My evidence regarded chiefly, I may say almost exclusively, the case of this college and the eviction of its trustees from their college farm of Laraghbryan, as an illustration of the peculiar view of landlord rights held by his Grace the present Duke of Leinster. The trustees of Maynooth—that is to say, the four archbishops and twelve of the bishops of Ireland—were evicted from their holding because, though consenting under compulsion to pay the increased rent demanded, they could not consent to sign the form of agreement unhappily known as the 'Leinster' Lease. I need not burden your columns with a detailed statement of the ingenious devices embodied in this document for practically abrogating, so far as it was possible for legal ingenuity to do so, the provisions, inadequate as they were, of the Land Act of 1870. But I think it right to state that I hold in my possession a letter from his Grace's agent to the secretary of the Maynooth trustees, in which the agent expresses his opinion that there must be 'some misapprehension on the part of the trustees as to the terms of the lease,' inasmuch as it was a strictly legal document, and had, in fact, been drawn by two Queen's counsel expressly 'to meet the provisions of the Land Act of 1870.' In my evidence, it is hardly necessary to add, I brought this noteworthy statement under the consideration of the Commissioners. I trust that the disclosure of it may lead the Ministry, who are now responsible for the Government of this country, to see that it is a hopeless task to attempt to meet the difficulties of the great crisis that is before them if they confine themselves to the framing of a Land Act, the pro-

visions of which can be 'met,' that is to say, evaded and
neutralised, by the ingenuity of counsel, however learned
in the law.

"2. In the second place I felt called upon to put before
the Commissioners, as also illustrated by the dealings in
connection with the Leinster Lease, another main source
of the now admitted failure of the Land Act of 1870. The
Act went upon the supposition that tenants of holdings
valued above £50 a year enjoy 'freedom of contract,' and
should therefore be left without legal protection. There is
an obvious fallacy in this. 'Freedom of contract,' no doubt,
exists to this extent—that the persons in question are
rational beings, with full liberty of action, and, it may be
conceded, notwithstanding the difficulties of their position,
in the undisturbed possession of their faculties, so that they
fully comprehend the nature of the contract into which
they are called upon to enter. But in any other sense
'freedom of contract' is for them an empty name. The
possession of a farm may be for such a tenant a *sine qua non*
of decent subsistence. It may even be his only means of
livelihood outside the walls of a workhouse. But on the
Duke of Leinster's estate of 68,000 acres he cannot obtain
a farm of any size, however small, at any rent, however
exorbitant, without signing the 'Leinster' Lease. Is it any
wonder that an Act should to so large an extent have
broken down which went upon the theory that in such cases
'freedom of contract' existed in any sense worthy of the
name? Our trustees exercised their 'freedom' by stead-
fastly refusing, as in the interest of the tenant farmers of
Ireland they were surely bound to refuse, to sanction by
their signature the 'Leinster' Lease. The result was eviction.
Let us hope that the official statement of this transaction,
which will soon be placed before Parliament in the report
of the Commission, will have the effect of convincing the

Legislature that a 'freedom of contract' which can be exercised only under a penalty that for a tenant farmer means absolute ruin, is not again to be relied upon as a plea for the insertion in a Land Act of clauses enabling any landlord in Ireland to coerce his tenants into a forfeiture of the rights to which Parliament considers them entitled.

"3. I did not fail to explain to the Commission that the proceedings which resulted in the eviction of the trustees had their origin in a demand made in 1877 for an increase of rent—the rent demanded being determined merely by a valuation of the land as it then stood. Until after repeated pleadings, as if mercy, and not justice, were in question, no allowance was made for the numerous and costly improvements which had been effected by the College during the lifetime of the late Duke, and in implicit reliance on the good faith of the house of Leinster. The extraordinary and all but incredible circumstances of this valuation are detailed in my evidence. I shall merely mention here that the hesitation of the College authorities to accede to a demand manifestly unjustifiable was described by the Duke's agent as an unwillingness on the part of the bishops to pay a fair rent to the landlord !"

Just so. It is so easy to say when there is question of the frequency of eviction in Ireland and of refusal to pay rent, that the unhappy victim of landlord cupidity would not pay his rent. No one cares to inquire whether would not, should be could not; and English gentlemen exclaim in indignant amazement at these wicked Irish who repudiate their just debts. Let us hope that they will yet exclaim in indignant wrath at those noble landlords who have thought it scorn to abide by English law where their Irish tenants were concerned.

It is to be wished, indeed, that Dr. Walsh's letter might be circulated from end to end of the British dominions. But since this is scarcely probable, I give another extract of considerable length.

"4. No better illustration could be found than is thus presented of the truth of a statement which is very commonly put forward, but in an entirely opposite sense, by many opponents of the tenants' claims—that 'Griffith's,' that is to say, the Government valuation, is not a fair standard for rent. Mr. Murrough O'Brien in an interesting paper in the 'Journal of the Statistical Society of Ireland,' (July, 1878), lays down this thesis :—'The public valuation is no guide to the fair rent between landlord and tenant ; and this should be expressly stated in any future Valuation Act.' And why? Is it because the valuation is, as we are so frequently informed, 25 or 30 per cent. below the fair value of the land? Not at all. But for a very different reason, which, strange to say, obvious as it is, seems altogether to have escaped the attention of many who should be deeply interested in giving prominence to it. The reason is thus stated by Dr. Neilson Hancock. In 1852, when the valuation was made, the tenant's claim to his property, at all events in the improvements effected by him, which has since been recognised by the Land Act of 1870, was ignored. The valuation, then, was made—fairly enough for the purposes for which it was intended, as a basis of taxation—by taking the value of the land as it stood.

But, as the Act of 1870 has since declared, the property, thus valued was in reality the property of two distinct owners. There was the property of the tenant in his improvements, as well as the property of the landlord in the soil. Each was a valuable property, and was therefore no doubt justly liable to taxation. But taxation is one thing, and rent is another. And as Dr. Hancock puts it, in his paper in the *Fortnightly Review*, of last January :—

"The Irish tenement or Government valuation of 1852 is not fitted to determine a fair rent, or rent on scientific principles, for the obvious reason that the legal ownership of improvements was unsettled in 1852. The valuation includes all farm buildings, and certain specific tenants' improvements, if made more than seven years before valuation or revision, and includes other tenants' improvements. If the valuation were revised up to date, on the existing principles of the Act, and were right in other respects, it would, if taken as a conclusive guide, lead to a demand for rent that would confiscate the tenants' improvements."

"I trust that my evidence may have the effect in calling more attention to this important aspect of the Government valuation of land in Ireland, than, somehow, it has hitherto attracted. I refer to the matter now, merely for the purpose of noting that the method adopted on the Leinster estate in 1877 to determine the rent to be paid for our college farm was that which is thus described, in a calm statistical essay by a very deliberate writer, as 'confiscation.'

"5. There is but one other section of my evidence to which I think it of any present advantage to ask you to give publicity. I thought it right to call the attention of the Commissioners to some incidents of the debates in Parliament of 1870, on the Land Act of that year. They go to show how necessary it is that evidence, copious and unassailable, as to the dealings that have taken place in Ireland between landlord and tenant, even since the passing of that Act, should be placed before Parliament if we wish the

Legislature to deal with this great question of the Irish land
in a way that can be regarded even as a temporary settlement of the difficulty.   I will ask you to reproduce two of
the passages to which I thus referred.   In one of the debates in committee of the House of Commons, a motion
was made to exempt all 'leaseholders' from the benefit of
the compensation clauses.   And when Mr. Gladstone resisted the proposal on the ground that in this way 'a lease
for a year and a day' might be made a bar to compensation,
an eminent Conservative statesman who had previously been
a member of three Ministries, each time with a seat in the
Cabinet, and who was subsequently a Cabinet Minister in
the late Conservative Administration, protested against Mr.
Gladstone's argument, declaring that he wished—

To say a word in favour of the common sense and understanding of
the Irish people. If the tenantry of Ireland were offered leases for a
year-and-a-day they would refuse them. The tendency of Parliament
to legislate as if the people of Ireland were a set of the most incapable
and helpless savages was to him a matter of regret and astonishment.
To say that the tenantry would be compelled to accept leases for a-year-
and-a-day, or any such term, was to impose upon the credulity of the
Committee—("Hansard," vol. 200, p. 1070).

"Now the "Leinster Lease," which I had the honour of
laying before the Royal Commission on Monday, as the
document sent by his Grace's agent, for the signature of our
trustees, is a lease 'from year to year.'   Is it too much to
hope that the noble lord, whose words I have just quoted,
will express his opinion of it, when it comes under the notice
of Parliament, in words no less emphatic than those in which
he ridiculed—as unworthy of the serious attention of the
House—the idea that such a lease could be forced by any
Irish landlord upon the acceptance of any body of Irish
tenants?

" Another extract and I shall bring to a close this long demand upon your space. In a debate in the House of Lords, when it was proposed to exclude from the benefits of the Act all tenants the valuation of whose holdings was over £50 a year, Lord Cairns supported the motion of the peer, Lord Bessborough—the brother of the Chairman of the present Commission—whose proposal was, that no such limit should be placed. In his speech on that occasion, Lord Cairns assured the House that—

He regarded the question simply as a theoretical one. Everybody acquainted with Ireland would bear him out in saying, that the idea of ejecting a tenant in that country at upwards of £50, as long as he paid his rent, never entered into the mind of any Irish landlord. Therefore, to provide for consequences that were to happen on the hypothesis that a tenant paying £50 rent was evicted capriciously—was providing for an event that never had occurred and never would occur—(" Hansard," vol. 202, p. 1443).

" The evidence in the Blue Book of the Commission will, no doubt, change Lord Cairns' views on this subject, at least so far as the Leinster estate is concerned. Will it induce him to contribute the aid of his powerful advocacy in convincing his brother peers of their duty to concur in the enactment of such legislation as will make it impossible that such things can again occur in Ireland ?"

No wonder, then, that the Irish nation should ask that what is being done in India and what has been done in the western provinces of Portugal should be done for Ireland. We frequently hear Irish landlords declaring that they are the best friends of their tenants ; that their tenants believe so, if they were not dis-

turbed by "agitators." What folly! It is a
folly they can scarcely believe themselves; but
which, unhappily, they can persuade others
to believe. An agitator who had not cause for
his agitation never yet obtained a continuous
hearing. Ireland has been for centuries the
land of agitators; but only because England
is so slow and so niggard in hearing and helping the cause of an oppressed people. And
yet, I do not blame all Englishmen. The truth
has been hidden from the honest multitude by
the dishonest few.

The fact that every colony under English
government has serious cause of complaint
should surely open the eyes of the masses to
the truth. Far from being indignant, because
the Irish speak hardly of English injustice;
they should rather speak hardly of those who
have caused the name of England to be sullied
in the mire of their own greed and selfishness.
The *ryot* in India—the peasant farmer in Ireland—had precisely the same cause of complaint
—a continued oppressive system of exaction on
the part of the landlords, who represent English
government, and who are, therefore, solely
responsible for the ill name which England has
got. What millions of money have been expended! what torrents of blood have flowed!

in order to keep up a system of persistent injustice. How long was it before the masses in
England could be got to see the injustice of the
slave trade, and how very soon the iniquity was
abolished when they did know it.

There is the strongest possible analogy
between India and Ireland—the population of
both are agricultural, and both are conquered
countries, the inhabitants of which have always
been looked down upon as socially inferior to
the English people.

The conquerors were masters of the land, and
a few of the natives who assisted the conquerors
were allowed some little share of authority; but
these latter were obliged to pay the Government a certain revenue, which they extracted
sometimes with torture and unheard of cruelty
from the *ryots*, who were a class corresponding
with the Irish peasant or tenant farmer.

This was the ryots' rent, upon which, after
paying the revenue, the zemindar or landlord
had a good profit. But the zemindars quickly
broke through the prescribed sums to be levied,
and while they paid only as much as the
Government stipulated, in the first instance,
they extorted from the unfortunate slave, the
ryot, as much as they wished. The ryots thus
became the most rack-rented people on the face

v

of the habitable globe; and so they remained ·
to the present hour.   It is calculated that the
yearly income of the zemindars of India has
swelled under this nefarious system from
£750,000, which it was worth in the beginning,
to at least £10,000,000.   Now, if we change
the names ; if we read for zemindar Irish landlord, for ryot of Bengal peasant of Galway, we
have a strict parallel between Ireland and
India.

But the Government report on the state of
India is of so remarkable a character, that we
give an extract from it here of considerable
length.

The report runs thus :—

"Report to Her Majesty's Secretary of State on
the Condition of India

"3 St. James's-square, 31*st* *October*, 1879.

" My Lord,—In the letter of Lord Salisbury to the Home
Secretary, in reference to my appointment as a member of
the Famine Commission, he said that (apart from my special
duties as a member of that Commission) advantage to the
Indian cultivator might be anticipated from my inquiries,
and from the advice which I should be in a position to
tender to the Government.   It is, therefore, my duty to
place before your lordship the views which I have formed in
regard to the condition of the vast population of these
countries for which we have made ourselves responsible.

"The available good land in India is nearly all occupied. There are extensive areas of good waste land, covered with jungle, in various parts of the country, which might be reclaimed and rendered suitable for cultivation, but for that object capital must be employed, and the people have little to spare. The produce of the country on an average of years is barely sufficient to maintain the present population and make a saving for occasional famine. The greatest export of rice and corn in one year is not more than ten days' consumption of its inhabitants. Scarcity, deepening into famine, is thus becoming of more frequent occurrence. The people may be assumed to increase at the moderate rate of one per cent. per year. The check caused by the late famine, through five million of extra deaths, spread as it was over two years and a half, would thus be equal only to the normal increase over all India for that time. In ten years, at the present rate of growth, there will be twenty million more people to feed, in twenty years upwards of forty millions. This must be met by an increase of produce, arising from better management of the cultivated area, and enlargement of its extent by migration to unpeopled districts, and by emigration to other countries. We are dealing with a country already full of people, whose habits and religion promote increase without restraint, and whose law directs the sub-division of land among all the male children. As rulers, we are thus brought face to face with a growing difficulty. There are more people every year to feed from land which, in many parts of India, is undergoing gradual deterioration. Of this there can be no stronger proof than the land revenue in some quarters is diminishing. It is unsafe to break up more of the uncultivated poor land. The diminution of pasture thereby already caused, is showing its effect in a lessening proportion of working cattle for an increasing area of cultivation.

"The pressure on the means of subsistence is rendered more severe by the moral disorganisation produced by laws, affecting property and debt, not adapted to the condition of the people. In most parts of India, as shown by the late proceedings in the Legislative Council on the Deccan Ryots Relief Bill, and as is plain to any careful observer in the country, the people are not only dissatisfied with our legal system, but, while the creditor is not much enriched, the debtor is being impoverished by it. Those British officials who see this, feel themselves powerless to influence a central authority far removed from them, subject to no control of public opinion, and over-burdened with details with which it is incapable of dealing. ·

" We have introduced a system the first object of which, for a Foreign Government, is necessarily the subjection of the people.   This is rendered possible by the religious difference between the Hindoos and Mahommedans which prevents their union against us, and they are in such proportions that the larger number of the first prevents the more warlike character of the second assuming predominance. We are accepted as the arbiters of justice to both, and the protectors of the weak against the strong.   A handful of Englishmen could not hold these multitudes on any other principle.   The strength we wield is a powerful army, now by the aid of railway and telegraph capable of rapid concentration on any threatened point.   And we govern through British officers stationed in every district of the country, who, under the supervision of the respective Governments, administer the law, command the police, and superintend the collection of the revenue.   Native officers are employed under them, both in the Judicial and Revenue Departments, in large numbers, to whom the drudgery of government is committed.   The whole number of such officers, not reckoning the Native army or police, is not more than one in ten thousand people. The English officers are not one in two hundred thousand, strangers in language, religion, and colour, with feelings and ideas quite different from theirs, and enforcing a system of law, the justice of which they are slow to comprehend, while its costliness and delay are manifest.

"By our centralising system we have drifted away from the patriarchal method of rule common in the East, where the populations are agricultural and dense, under which the management of the people is left to their natural leaders, the head men of the villages, hereditary or elected by the people, who are recognised by the community, and who administer justice and preserve order, and are responsible for the public revenue. We have superseded this by discrediting the head men, and in Madras and Bombay by an attempt to bring millions of small landholders into direct contact with the Government, through Native officials of a low type (for the higher class of officers rarely have time to see them), and with a theory that our European officers, so few in number, will be able personally to supervise this arrangement, which is physically impossible. The head men, no longer recognise or treated as leaders, and seldom communicated with, except through the lower class of Native officials (who are said to be apt to take advantage of their position to extort bribes), become distrustful to us, and are distrusted by us. I rarely met a civilian in India who did not speak of the head men with distrust. The British merchants who carry on their great business in India make no similar complaint of the Native merchants, whom they find upright and honest. Our officers do not know the Natives as they used to do when our government was less centralised, and they are every year becoming more strange to the people by the increase of indoor judicial duties, and the frequent changes from one locality to another.

"Following out our English ideas by collecting the land revenue in the convenient shape of money, we superseded the old principle of taking it in kind, in certain proportions of the produce, according to the value of the land. This is an ancient and common principle in all countries, both East and West, and prevails still in most Eastern States, and in many parts of Europe in the *métayer* system. It is specially suited to small cultivators having little or no capital, and it carries within it a natural check on over-population. For, when payment of rent is made by a share of the crop, the cultivator, if he finds that his land requires rest from over-cropping, lets it rest in fallow, as he saves in rent when he leaves the land idle. He must thus hold a larger area than he requires to keep under crop, and this operates against over-density of population. The share of the owner is greater in seasons of abundance, and when the crop fails the cultivator is not called to pay what he does not possess. The owner is also interested in rendering the land productive, and is more ready to co-operate with the cultivator in such improvements as are calculated to increase the income of both. And there would not be now the same difficulty in India as in former times in realising the owner's share, as roads and railways have opened up markets where it can be readily disposed of. The European officers say that it would be impossible now to revert to this system, because the detail would be overpowering, and the opportunities for oppression by the lower class of Native officials, and of fraud by the cultivators, would be largely increased. This may be true under foreign rule like ours, but it possessed two qualities of great value; first, a self-adjusting action of re-assessment, instead of the arbitrary re-assessments which are now the cause of great cost to the Government and much annoyance to the people; and second, a comparative independence of the money lender, who has become the source of most of the litigation which has since overspread the country. There is the best proof of its success in the fact that, while those Native Governments who thus levy the revenue obtain a land rent twice that of ours, the people are not only able to pay, but, with the exception of the money lenders, rarely show any desire to seek easier terms by passing into British territory."

In other words, the natives of India know how to govern their own country very much better than their English conquerors. The "native merchants are upright and honest." The "first object of a foreign Government is the subjection of the people." This plan has already failed in India and in Ireland; might it not be wise to try, by way of experiment, making the welfare of the people the first object? No wonder that the people of India are "slow to comprehend" the justice of English law, and object to its costliness.

The right of the cultivator to mortgage the public land has made him the slave of the money lender. Government rent must be paid on the day it becomes due; it is rigorously exacted by the officials, and as the Bunyia is the only capitalist within reach, the cultivator gives a charge on the land, and hands over all his crop to the Bunyia as a security for cash advances. An account is opened, the cultivator is credited with the value of his crop at the low price prevailing after harvest, and from week to week, as he requires food or seed, it is doled out to him, and he is charged at the retail price fixed by the seller, with interest at a rate proportioned to the risk. Difficulties and disputes arise, the courts are appealed to, litigation begins, the pleaders find employment, and the time and attention of the civil officers, European and Native, are occupied in adjusting questions which otherwise would not have arisen. The law necessarily enforces contracts, and in all parts of India the courts are crowded with litigants, the losing parties being generally the cultivators, who, when reduced to extremities, sometimes resort to riot and bloodshed, as in Sonthal and the Deccan.

Ireland again ! Is it any marvel that there is "riot and bloodshed" in India? Captain Sherrard Osborne says of the Lascars who inhabit the hilly regions of India :—

" I defy any nation to produce better sailors ; they possess all the qualities which make a sailor valuable. Treat them kindly, and they will serve you faithfully ; outrage their sense of propriety, grind them down, cruelly illuse them, and they become your open flatterers and your concealed implacable foes !"

And later on the writer made the admission that if the land was properly cultivated there would be no fear of excessive population; and more important still, "that the financial state of the country would be gradually strengthened by the growth of its agricultural prospects." A Conservative Government did a good deal for India in this direction, but a Conservative English author, Sir Stafford Northcote, has no other remedy for Ireland except to call any attempt to improve our agricultural condition "Force, fraud, and folly." We have had force for our rule in Ireland rather too long. The less gentlemen in his position say about fraud the better, since it is gentlemen in his position who have committed the virtual fraud of depriving their tenants of the benefit of the Land Act. As to the folly, it is to be hoped that such gentlemen will not bewail their own folly in refusing justice to Ireland when it is too late; or should justice be given, that they will not bewail their own folly in not joining heartily with those who gave it. Justice is no favour; it is a right.

Coercion has been tried in India also. With what success I leave it to the able pen of the Rev. M. Columb, P.P., to tell :—

"COERCION—*THE SATURDAY REVIEW.*"
TO THE EDITOR OF THE FREEMAN.
" KILLASHEE, *Nov.* 12.
"SIR—As the *Saturday Review* in its deep anxiety for

the protection of life and property in Ireland cries louder
for coercion than all its contemporaries, it may interest your
readers to learn from the *Saturday's* own columns how very
effectually, in practice, the lives and property of her Majesty's
subjects are indeed protected by good coercion bills.. For
the history of the introduction and nature of one such
good bill I beg to refer your readers to the issues of the
Saturday of the 23rd March and the 6th July, 1878, respectively. In these two issues are discussed the provisions
of the Indian Coercion Bill just then passed—a bill which
garotted the whole of India in so gagging the Press that
nothing dared be published in an Indian paper that had not
first got the *imprimatur* of some Government official. To
see now how effective in protecting life this good coercion
bill proved in India, I would refer your readers to the
Saturday's issue of the 31st July last, in which it is plainly
stated that under the protection of this unmistakably good
Coercion Bill five millions of her Majesty's subjects happened to die of famine. Only five millions! Of course,
under all the circumstances, we here in Ireland, who know
so well how beautiful always is the rule of the British
abroad, must hold that the death of these five millions ..as
a miserable euthanasia. Thousand times better for them
die thus of famine, protected by a good Coercion Bill, the
loyal subjects of the great first Empress of India and her
Grand Vizier, Ben Disraeli, than live under some home-
ruling, unpaternal Eastern potentate, who might either de-
moralise them at such a crisis by relief or by employment
on some public works—such, for instance, as the building
a great wall between them and China, to prevent the traffic
in opium, or the construction of some other scientific
frontier; or, worse still, might lead them out to make
wantonly wicked war on their peaceful neighbours in

Afghanistan, Burmah, or Beloochistan, and thus get many of them put *hors de combat.*"

After speaking of what would have been done by the "unspeakable" Turk for the help of a starving people, he goes on to say :—

" To learn now from the same enlightened authority how equally efficacious this same coercion bill proved in protecting the property of her Majesty's subjects, I would direct your readers in the first place to the *Saturday's* issue of the 21st August last, where it is shown that under the protection of this Coercion Bill only nine million pounds sterling of the taxpayers' money came to be unaccountably lost by the sapient satraps of India, who two years previously 'passed unanimously at a single session' this Coercion Bill for the protection of life and property.

" Wonderful therefore, must we all admit coercion to be as a means for the protection of life and property for have we not learned from the *Saturday Review* itself that under the operation of one thoroughly effective coercion bill only five millions of her Majesty's subjects died of famine ; that only nine millions of her Majesty's revenues got lost, never to be found ; that only twenty millions were 'wrongfully wasted' from her Majesty's lieges by iniquitous landlords ; and lastly, I may add, only one cruel, costly, wicked war begun for her Majesty but not quite finished. Such being the beneficent effects of coercion, no one that knows the *Saturday* will wonder that in the plenitude of its abiding benevolence for the people of Ireland it so persistently implores the Government to give us, too, a good Coercion Bill to protect, forsooth, our lives and property, even as the Indian bill protected the lives and property of the people of India, or even as the Coercion Act of '46, belauded by the *Saturday*, did indeed protect the lives and property of our countrymen, as the two millions 'gone with a vengeance,' the auxiliary workhouses and the existing Landed Estates Courts unmistakably prove.

We give a few further extracts from Mr. Caird's report, which speak for themselves :—

" Native Indians should be more largely employed in the administration of the country.   All details of judicial, revenue, and executive business should be left to them. . . . . . . It is by the concentration of responsibility and authority in each province, and the fuller development of native talent, that we may reasonably look for such a gradual growth of prosperity as will strengthen the people, and enable them to accumulate from the surplus of good years a reserve stock to meet the demands of scarcity. When English laws introduced by the British into India are unsuited to the country and to the people, who are dissatisfied with our judicial system.   This system plunges the mass of people into debt ; it ruins debtors without benefiting creditors.   Pleaders should be excluded from petty courts of justice ; and the fees on petty litigation should be abolished. As far as possible, civil causes should be decided by local juries (panchayats) and local notables.   If in this way Natives were more largely employed, and if Native methods were followed, towns and districts of British India might vie with the happiness and liveliness now so apparent at the capitals of Native States.

" But it seems to me that it is now our duty to face the questions of principle which are involved in our connection with India.   What do we aim at there ?   Not certainly to hold 200 millions of people under subjection, tempered only by the will of England."

I will only add that there was a report on the report, in which the English landlords in India assured the public that they were the true benefactors of the people, famishing notwithstanding, and that the people were only too happy and too content under their rule, rebellious notwithstanding!

The following extracts do not require observation:—

"M. W. W. Hunter, C.I.E., Director-General of Statistics to the Government of India, delivered to the members of the Edinburgh Philosophical Institution, in Queen Street Hall, the first of two lectures on "What the English have yet to do for the Indian People."

From this lecture, published in the *Times* [Nov. 1880], I give the following extracts :—

"In districts where the soil is poor or the rainfall uncertain, the people have always had to depend upon village usurers for the capital necessary to feed them till the next harvest, and to conduct the operations of the agricultural year. Amid the tumults and insecurity under the old Native Governments, the usurers lent comparatively small sums. If the peasant failed to pay they could not evict him or sell his holding, because, among other reasons, there was more land than there were people to till it. The Native Government, moreover, could not afford to lose a tenant, and so the bankrupt peasant went on, year after year, paying as much interest as the usurer could squeeze out of him until the next Mahratta invasion or Mahomedan rebellion swept away the whole generation of usurers, and so cleared up the account.

"Under our rule there is no chance of such relief for insolvent debtors, and our rigid enforcement of contracts, together with the increase of population, have, in many ways, rendered life harder for the peasant ; for the peasant's holding, under the British Government, has become a valuable property, and he can be readily sold out, as there are plenty of other husbandmen to step in. The result is two-fold. In the first place, the village usurer lends larger sums, for the security is increased ; and, in the second place, he can push the peasantry to extremities by eviction, which was unknown under native rule.

"In certain districts of Southern India the people are sometimes driven by misery to take the law into their own hands. They kill the village usurer, or burn down his house with his account-books, and, perhaps, himself in it. But this offence, which was a common one under native rule, now brings upon the perpetrators the inflexible arm of the British law. Of late years there has been an agrarian agitation in Southern India, similar, in some respects, to the agrarian agitation in Bengal. But in the south (where the Government has kept the land under its own control) the revolt has been against the usurers, while in Bengal it has been against the landholders.

"In Southern India the demand is for legislative restraints on selling out the husbandman ; in Bengal it is for legislative restraints on the enhancement of his rent. The sad result seems to be that, whether we give over the land to a proprietary class, as in Bengal, or keep it in our own hands, as in Southern India, the struggle for life grows harder to large sections of the people.

" Our first attempt to ascertain and define the Land Laws of Bengal is embodied in the Cornwallis Code of 1793. The difficulty, at that time, was where to get tenants, not how to raise their rent. Enhancement was not a practical question, and it finds no mention in that code. So far as can be inferred from the spirit of its provisions, the Indian Legislature seems to have assumed that the proprietors were thenceforward to pay the same land-tax for ever to the Government, and that the tenants were thenceforward to pay the same rates of rent for ever to the proprietors. But, before the middle of the present century, rents had been enhanced to such a degree as to threaten an agrarian dead-lock. It was found absolutely necessary to revise the land laws, and 1859, the year after the country passed under the Crown, is memorable in Bengal for the second great Land Code. The enhancement of rent had meanwhile grown into the great problem of the day, and restraints upon enhancement form the most important features of the Land Code of 1859. But, in spite of the provisions of that code, the increase of the people and the natural operation of economic laws have led to a still further rise in rent. The peasantry resisted by every legal means, and, in some parts, combined to ruin the landlords by refusing to pay rent at all.

" Their attitude was, in certain respects, similar to the position of the Irish peasantry at this moment. The Indian husbandmad has, however, a power of pacific combination and of patient, passive resistance, which the Irish cottiers have not yet developed. The most peaceful district of Bengal, Patna, was, for some time, in a state of agrarian revolt. But it was a revolt conducted, as a rule, according to the forms of law. With the exception of a few local and quite insignificant ebullitions, the husbandmen simply said : ' We shall not fight, but we shall not pay. Every single rent which you landlords collect shall cost you a law suit, and we shall contest each stage of every law suit, from the institution of the plaint to the final order for selling us up, by every delay, appeal, and other weapon of chicanery known to the law.   You will get your decree in the long run, but, in the meantime, you will be ruined.   For ourselves, we are as badly off as we can be, and it is better for us to sell our last cow to fight you in the courts than to pay your rent.' Among a people of small cultivators it is simply impossible to collect every petty rent by a law suit, and such a combination really did mean ruin to many of the landlords.   The Government, while it declared that it would maintain public order, counselled private concessions.   Some sort of compromise was arrived at, and the Legislature obtained a breathing space to again consider the whole questions involved.   The result is a new Land Code, the draught of which has just reached England.   In this code the most prominent question is again the enhancement of rent, and its provisions are more stringent than ever in favour of the tenant.

"In 1859, the Government practically said to the zemindars :—'We created you as a proprietary body in 1793 by our own Act.   In doing so we made over to you valuable rights, which up to that time were vested in the State, but we carefully reserved the rights of the cultivators.   We shall now ascertain and define the rights of the cultivators ; and we shall settle your relations with them on the basis of those rights.'

"The result was embodied in the famous Land Laws of 1859, which divided the cultivators of Bengal into four classes :—

"1. Tenants who had held their holdings at the same rent since 1793, and whose rents could not be enhanced on any ground whatever.

"2. Tenants who had held their holdings at the same rent

for twenty years, and were, therefore, presumed by law to have held since 1793. The rents of such tenants could not be raised on any ground unless it could be shown that they had not held since 1793, in which case they belonged to the next class, namely—

"3. Tenants who had held their holdings for twelve years. Such a tenant enjoyed what are called the 'occupancy rights,' that is to say, he had a right to occupy his holding so long as he paid the rent ; and his rent would only be raised by a suit at law. In such a suit it must be proved, either that his holding measures more acres than he pays for, or that he pays a lower rate than other occupancy tenants in the neighbourhood, or that the productive power of his land, or the price of the produce, has increased without any effort on his part. In short, the rent of an occupancy tenant could, by the law of 1859, be raised only if he held at rates proved to be unfair either to the landlord or to the neighbouring tenants of the same class.

"4. The fourth class of cultivators, according to the code of 1859, were those who had held for less than twelve years. In these the law recognised no rights, and left them to make what bargains they could, by leases, or as tenants at will. . . . Further experience since 1859 has taught the Government that even these provisions are inadequate to avert the wholesale enhancement of rents in Bengal. It accordingly issued a Commission in 1879 to inquire into the questions involved ; and the report of the Commission has just reached England.

"The Commissioners, like the legislators of 1859, have arrived at the conclusion that a substantial peasant right in the soil exists in Bengal. They accordingly confirm all the rights given to the peasant by the Land Code of 1859, and in some important respects they propose to augment them. The cultivators who have held their land at the same rent

z

since 1793 can never have their rent raised; and those who have thus held for twenty years, are still presumed to have held since 1793. The cultivators who have held for twelve years have their privileges increased. Their occupancy rights are consolidated into a valuable peasant-tenure, transferable by sale, gift, or inheritance; and it is proposed that all increase in the value of the land or the crop, not arising from the agency of either the landlord or tenant, shall henceforth be divided equally between them. This provision is a very important one in a country like Bengal, where new railways, new roads, and the increase of the people and of trade constantly tend to raise the price of the agricultural staples.

" What political economists call the 'unearned increment' is no longer to accrue to the proprietor, but is to be divided between him and the cultivator, so that landlord and tenant are henceforth to be joint sharers in the increasing value of the land. This is an important step; but the great changes proposed by the Rent Commissioners refer to the husbandmen who have held for less than twelve years, and whom the Land Code of 1859 admitted to no rights whatever. It left them to make the best bargain they could with the landlords; and this bargain has been such a very bad one as to cause widespread distress.

" The Commissioners declare that the competition for land, if unchecked by law or custom, reduces 'the whole agricultural population to a condition of misery and degradation,' and they have resolved, so far as in them lies, to arrest this slow ruin of Bengal. They enunciate the principle that ' the land of a country belongs to the people of a country ; and while vested rights should be treated with all possible tenderness, no mode of appropriation and cultivation should be permanently allowed by the ruler which involves the wretchedness of the great majority of the people, if the alteration or amendment of the law relating to land can by

itself, or in conjunction with other measures, obviate or
remedy the misfortune.' Strong doctrine this; and very
stringently do the Commissioners apply it. In their draft
code they propose a system of compensation for disturbance
the thorough-going character of which contrasts strongly
with the very mild Irish Bill which the House of Lords
rejected last Session.

"The Bengal Rent Commissioners would accord a *quasi-*
occupancy right to all tenants who have held for three years.
They propose that such a tenant shall not be evicted, except
(*a*) for non-payment of rent; (*b*) for the breach of some condition in his lease for which the penalty of eviction was
stipulated; or (*c*) the refusal to pay an increased rent. If
the landlord demands an increased rent from such a tenant,
and the tenant prefers to leave rather than submit to the
enhancement, then the landlord must pay him—first, a substantial compensation for disturbance, and second, by a
substantial compensation for improvements.

"The compensation for disturbance is calculated at a sum
equal to one year's increased rent as demanded by the landlord. The compensation for improvements includes payment
for buildings erected by the tenant, for tanks, wells, irriga-
tion works, drainage works, embankments, or for the renewal
or improvement of any of the foregoing; also for any land
which the tenant may have reclaimed or enclosed, and for
all fruit-trees which he may have planted. The operation
of these clauses will be that before the landlord can raise
the rent, he must be prepared to pay to the out-going tenant
a sum which will swallow up the increased rental for several
years. The practical result is to give a more or less complete degree of tenant right to all cultivators who have held
their land for three years or upwards, that is, almost the
whole agricultural population of Bengal.

"The analogy of the situation in Bengal to the agrarian agitation in Ireland is in some respects a striking one. In both countries a state of things has grown up under British rule which seems unbearable to a section of the people. In Bengal the peasantry have fought by every weapon of delay afforded by the courts; in England the Irish representatives are fighting by every form of obstruction possible in Parliament. In both countries we may disapprove of the weapons employed, but in both we must admit that these weapons are better than the ruder ones of physical force. In both countries I believe that the peasantry will more or less completely win the day, for in both, the state of things of which they complain is repugnant to the awakened conscience of the British nation.

"But the analogy, although striking, must not be pushed too far; for, on the one hand, the Irish peasantry has emigration open to it—a resource practically not available to the Bengal husbandman. On the other hand, the proprietary right in Bengal was a gift of our own as late as 1793—a gift hedged in by reservations in favour of the peasantry, and conferred for the distinctly expressed purpose of securing the welfare of the people. The proprietary right in Ireland is the growth of centuries of spoliation and conquest. It may, perhaps, therefore, be found possible to accord a secure position to the peasantry of Bengal without injustice to the landlords.

"But the Irish difficulty is a more complex one, and demands a higher order of statesmanship for its solution; for the problem in Ireland is how to get rid of a national inheritance of wrong with the least cost to the nation and with the least infringement of vested proprietary rights."

From Mr. Hunter's second lecture I give

three extracts, one from the beginning, one from the middle, and one from the end :—

"On Tuesday I endeavoured to place before you the real meaning of the poverty of the Indian people. This evening I shall ask your attention to some of the difficulties which that poverty gives rise to in the government of the country. Men must first have enough to live upon before they can pay taxes. The revenue-yielding powers of a nation are regulated, not by its numbers, but by the margin which exists between the national earnings and its requirements for subsistence. It is because this margin is so great in England that the English are the most taxable people in the world. It is because this margin is so small in India that any increase in the revenue involves serious difficulties. It may seem a contradiction in terms to say that the English, who pay at the rate of 40s. per head to the Imperial Exchequer, besides many local burdens, are more lightly taxed than the Indians, who pay only at the rate of 3s. 6d. per head to the Imperial Exchequer, with scarcely any local burdens."

"You will find the natives of India the safer guides with regard to the wants of India. I hold in my hand a petition lately presented to Parliament by the British Indian Association. That petition sets forth the native programme of reform. It asks for a larger and more independent share in the legislative councils of India, and it is certain that at no distant date such a share must be conceded to the Indian people. It urges the necessity of military retrenchments, and the injustice of dealing with the Indian finances in the class interests of England rather than in the sole interest of the Indian taxpayer. Well, at this moment, retrenchments to the extent of, I believe, £1,500,000 are being proposed

by the Indian Army Commission; and there is no doubt
that Indian finance has been sometimes dealt with with
an eye to English rather than to Indian interests."

"You must realize that the responsibility for India has
passed into the hands of Parliament, and through Parliament to the electoral body of Great Britain. You must
realize that if through ignorance or indifference you fail to
discharge that responsibility you are acting as bad citizens.
You, must therefore set yourselves to learn more about
India. You must act in a spirit of absolute honesty towards
the Indian finances, and you must deal with Indian questions which come home for your decision, not in the interest
of privileged classes or of political parties in this country,
but in the sole interest of the Indian people."

The administrators of the Poor Laws in Ireland are another source of serious evil. As we
have said before, the land agent is generally
the Chairman of the Board of Guardians, and
the guardians hear but to obey. They are for
the most part struggling shop-keepers, who dare
not speak, and who are treated with contempt
by their masters. No doubt in some places the
Poor Law Guardians are manly and independent; but when the agent is a terroriser, they
generally for fear, if not for profit, prefer to
submit. The land agent can generally secure the
co-operation of subserviency. Even on the bench
he can secure the silence and co-operation of
some J.P., for whom he has obtained the coveted
dignity, because the recipient of the favour may

have risen from a very humble position. A guardian may have a son who wishes to be promoted to some post of social importance and monetary value. The very few who could, or who might speak, are not only carefully bribed to silence, but they are also made useful tools.

The difference between English and Irish Poor Law is briefly this :—

" 1. Union rating obtains in England, electoral division rating (for out-door relief) in Ireland.

" 2. In England the able-bodied are entitled to out-door relief :

    (*a*) In any case of sudden or urgent necessity.

    (*b*) In any case of sickness, accident, or bodily or mental infirmity affecting either themselves or any of their family.

    (*c*) For the purpose of defraying wholly or partially the expenses of the burial of any member of their family.

" In Ireland out-door relief cannot be granted (supposing the workhouse not full or infected) unless the head of the family is himself disabled by sickness or accident, the only exception being in case of persons evicted.

" 3. In England out-door relief may be granted to a widow with one child ; in Ireland she must have two or more.

" 4. In England out-door relief may be granted :

    (*a*) To all widows for six months.

    (*b*) To the families of persons confined in gaols or asylums.

    (*c*) To the wives and children of soldiers and sailors.

(*d*) To children of non-resident persons, if the
mothers reside within the Union, thus making
provision for families deserted by their natural
heads. No corresponding powers to the above
are conferred upon Boards of Guardians in
Ireland.

And yet, from the suppression of manufactures
in Ireland, and the absence of all *Government
employment* the poor are dependent on Poor
Law help.

Mr. Fox, in his valuable pamphlet says:—

"Some modification of the existing Poor Law system is
obviously necessary. The adoption of the principle of
Union rating, as in England, would have a most beneficial
effect, inasmuch as it would tend to promote an extension of
that out-door relief so sorely needed, yet so much more
restricted in Ireland. And if a number of the local clergy
were admitted to seats at the Board of Guardians, in virtue
of their office, their presence could scarcely fail to diffuse
amongst that important body somewhat more of kindly consideration for the sad misfortunes of the destitute and deserv-
ing poor.

"The smallness of the amount of Poor Law relief distributed in Ireland, as compared with England, is not generally known. In 1878 85,000 persons only were relieved
in Ireland, at a cost of £990,000; while in England
748,000 persons were relieved, during the same period, at a
cost of £7,688,000. Taking the population of Ireland at
one-fourth of that of England, it will be seen that the Poor
Law relief distributed in Ireland, the poorer country, is not
one-half what it is in England, the richer country. (P. 36.)

The resources and wealth of the Empire are freely given for English undertakings, whilst a trifling loan is denied to Ireland to construct a railway, improve a canal, or to form a dock for shipping purposes. Within some twenty years past upwards of five millions of public money have been spent on English harbours, including Alderney; whilst a sum of £40,000, not the one-hundredth part, was all but refused to Ireland to improve her harbours, and was opposed by Lord F. Cavendish, brother to the "Liberal Whig" Marquis of Hartington, and son of the Duke of Devonshire, who owns large estates in Ireland and draws from them a princely revenue. A Parliamentary paper has just been issued (Sept. 1880) from which it appears that, in addition to this, coast defences have cost the country, within a few years, £7,413,346, and that the whole of this, except £194,000 spent on the convict establishment at Spike Island, was expended on English harbours, making together upwards of twelve millions of the public money. Of the latter expenditure, Portsmouth alone received £3,067,991, about twenty times the amount expended on the whole of Ireland.

The Rev. John Boylan, P.P., says :—

"The great evil of this country is the want of employ- ment for the energetic and industrious; and it has been

Ireland's misfortune, for centuries, to be divided almost between two classes—the few rich and the multitudinous poor
—the landlords, as a body, sitting there, from year to year,
watching for their rents instead of opening up our industries
by the investment of their capital and giving employment to
the people in grand public works of permanent utility."

Yet, even in the Famine every possible difficulty was put, again and again, in the way of
having relief works opened.

The London correspondent of the *Freeman's
Journal* writes :—

" It is pretty manifest that the Government are afraid, in
face of the General Election, to publish the list of the loans
which have been demanded and those which have been
granted. A more shameful transaction in this connection
has come under my notice. The scheduling of.Unions has
been delayed, through the red tapeism of the Board of Works,
until they have been deprived of the benefits of the Act.
This is bad enough, but there is a greater grievance to come.
The Parsonstown Union was duly and legally scheduled,
but on application for loans for farmers, who have been
absolutely ruined by unprecedented floods, the answer from
the Public Works Office was, that all the funds granted by
Government, at the low terms, had long before been applied
for and exhausted. It is hard enough that Unions which
were scheduled only at the last moment should be rejected;
but it is perfectly scandalous that sufficient provision should
not have been made for loans for all the Unions which had
complied with the requirements of the Act."

Mr. Bright gives the following reason why
there is so much pauperism in Ireland :—

"But one of the results of this system of insecurity is this, that tenants will not cultivate their lands according to the best of their knowledge or according to the best of their capital ; for to improve their cultivation is followed too often by the increase of rent. I met the other day a gentleman, one of the most extensive and intelligent farmers in this country, who had been over the island, and who had passed through some of the discontented and suffering counties. He said, ' The land is soaking with water, the cultivation is slovenly, and the farmers do not obtain more than half what ought to be obtained from it.' He says, as to the insecurity, that a man hardly attempted to put on a good or new coat, for fear it should be discovered that it was a sign that he would pay a little more rent (applause)."

Mr. Tuke says :—

"I have been told over and over again that the dread of having an increased rent to pay constantly prevents improvements in the land. On the other hand, I am frequently told that this is an imaginary fear and that the thing is rarely done. Be this as it may, the above instances go to prove how very real the fear is, and that it operates to a most mischievous extent. It is, I am persuaded, very largely at the root of the wretched cultivation so common here, and the cause of much of the bitterness of feeling existing between landlords and tenants.

"' I met a little farmer,' said one of the party, ' who was returning from England with £11 for his summer's earnings, who told me that he would never go to England for wages, if he was free to stay and reclaim the mountain-land he held in addition to the small quantity of arable land cultivated.' ' Free,' that is, from the fear of having to pay an increased rent for improvements solely effected by himself."

Of course the landlords deny it. They say
the people are lazy and wont work. Again I
quote Mr. Tuke :—

"A turn in the road brought us to the house of Dr.
Thompson, the Protestant Rector of Glencolumbkill, who is
working most zealously for the people. On the road and
around his house we saw a number of men very busily at
work in spite of the rain. They received either 9d. a day
wages, or 6d. where the families received an allowance of
meal. Dr. Thompson represented to us the great willingness of these men to work. 'They will crowd for it at 6d.
a day.' When they came up for their small pay we saw
them receive it with the greatest thankfulness."

Honest John Bright says, in his recent memorable speech :—

"I believe, as much as I believe anything, that it is possible to frame a measure of legislation which will satisfy the
great bulk of the Irish tenant farmers, and will, before long,
withdraw them from the influences of men who would lead
them into calamities not less than those of which they complained of and now endure (cheers). What they want is
this—some mode by which when a man has his house over
his head—built it himself probably, or built by some preceding member of his family, and has his little farm around
him, he should not incessantly be taught that he may any
day have notice to quit, and be turned out of his farm and
home, and that the rent should not be constantly added to
until even going out of his farm is a less evil than remaining in it. He wants some security from the constant torture
and menace which he feels hanging over him, and he wants

a'so that there should be some broad and generous and complete system established by the Government, which landowners who are willing to sell—of which there must be many now (laughter)—that landowners, who are willing to sell, and there are many at all times, and where tenants are able and willing to buy, that through the instrumentality of this Government Commission you may gradually, year by year, add rapidly to the number of proprietary farmers in Ireland (cheers). Another point is worth mentioning. In the year 1847, in January of that year, I recollect hearing Lord John Russell, in the House of Commons, explaining the objects and intentions of the Government with regard to some provision for the famine that was then overtaking the Irish people, and one of the proposals was this—to take into the hands of the Government, through some managing power and authority, waste lands in Ireland which were capable of being profitably cultivated, and by some arrangements finding homes, and farms, and employment for a considerable number of people. Now, Ireland contains about twenty millions of acres. I do not know the number of acres that may be called waste lands. I have heard it put at two millions and more, but I will assume, for the sake of my illustration, that there are one million of acres in Ireland that are capable of cultivation, and would repay the cultivator; and that it would be as wise to cultivate as the average portion of the Irish land that is now cultivated. Well, what would a million acres do? It would make not less than 40,000 farms of 25 acres each. It would be possible, probably, to bring over from those extreme western parts, where the climate is precarious and the land so stoney and so poor—it might be possible to invite little farmers, peasant occupiers from those districts, and to place them upon waste lands thus divided and thus cultivated. What is a million; what is five millions; what is ten millions to

this country to pursue to a successful issue a great question
like this? (Cheers.) We hear that the Afghan war
certainly has cost twenty, and good authority says before all
the accounts are made up, and everything is settled, that it
will have cost thirty millions (hisses). I will assume twenty
millions ; that is a large sum—a sum that trips glibly off the
tongue, but of which none of us has the slightest idea how
much it is. If there be anything to be done in Afghanistan
or in Zululand, if there be some very foolish ministry picking
up quarrels in the East of Europe, they can bring you thousands of men from Bombay to Malta (laughter), spite of Acts
of Parliament and spite of constitutional usages. Is it conceivable that an English Government and an English Parliament, omnipotent within a great Empire, cannot come forward,
and by a strong will, and strong hand, and strong resolve, do
whatever is necessary to be done with regard to the condition
of Ireland? (Loud cheers.) The general results may be stated
in figures. I stated them here in figures not long ago ; but
they are so startling and so impressive that in one sentence
I shall place them before you again. The proprietors of
land in Ireland are few in number for a country so large,
and among them are those who hold estates, properties
which, or a part of which, they can let—I mean estates of
80 or 100 acres ; over that I suppose there are not more
than 12,000 or 14,000 owners in Ireland. One-third of Ireland is possessed by 292 persons ; one-half of Ireland is
possessed by 744 persons—I suppose about as many as are
in that gallery at the other end of the hall ; and two-thirds
of the whole island are in the possession of 1,942—perhaps
a little more than half the persons that are present now in
this building. But, on the other hand, there are more than
500,000 tenants. There is a great fact—500,000 families,
having at least from two and a half to three millions of
persons dependent upon the soil, competing with each other

for the possession of a farm, having no variety of occupations, as there are in England, having, of course, only one way, and that only the way out of the country, to escape from the difficulties in which they find themselves. These 500,000 tenants are living, as they allege, for the most part in a condition of continual insecurity. The rent may be raised half-a-crown an acre this year, and another half-a-crown next. If the farm passes from the father to the son, or from the widow to the son, or from the farmer to his brother, or to another farmer of a new family, there is an occasion when it is easy to propose some addition to the rent. The addition may not be so large as to shock the farmer and to drive him to cease from any attempt to enter upon the farm. By little and little rent is added to, the irritation of the tenant becomes greater and greater; he sees the end to which he is being driven. He cannot live upon the farm, and he must give it up, and he must find himself homeless in his own country, and thus there has grown up in Ireland—and of course most in the poorest districts— there has grown up an irritation and a discontent which is the notorious and the universal material on which social or political insurrections are generally based. We must not forget that in Ireland men who hold the land hold the homes and the lives of the people (applause). It matters not disguising it, or putting it in language less unpleasant. . . . I have seen something of Irish farmers in travelling for weeks in that country. I have heard of them from many people, some not of the political opinions which I hold. I have lately had the opportunity of discussing with men connected with the making of railroads in. Ireland, engineers, contractors, and persons eminent in that way, and yet I am bound to say that I have heard on the whole nothing but a good opinion, a sympathetic opinion, of the general character of the Irish population with which they were connected.

The farmers are, in the main, industrious and honest. There has been no country in Europe, no part of the United Kingdom, in which rents have been more generally and constantly and fairly paid than in Ireland, until the recent troubles (hear, hear). The Irish farmer is an economist. He saves even to penuriousness. The great object of his life is to enable him to give a small portion to his daughters on their marriage (hear, hear). The Irish people expatriated to the United States have sent millions and millions of money to Ireland to help their poor relations to make the voyage thither."

"It has been said by the same high authority that I before quoted (a laugh) that a great part of the troubles of Ireland came from its being surrounded by a melancholy ocean (great laughter). Well, I believe all islands are surrounded by some kind of an ocean (great laughter), and all oceans that I have yet seen wear at times a very melancholy aspect (renewed laughter); but it is not that the soil of Ireland is not green enough, or that the ocean is not prolific enough in fish; in fact, there is nothing in the geographical condition of Ireland that in the slightest degree accounts for the trouble which Ireland has been to itself and to this country, with which it is now politically allied. But we find that, as a consequence of a policy which we all now regret and condemn, Irish patriotism, as apart from what is called patriotism in this country, has consisted to a large extent in hatred of Protestantism, hatred of landlords, and hatred of England. If the English people had been informed, if they had been capable within the last two centuries of judging fairly of these matters, there cannot be a doubt that—if in addition to this the Government had been merciful and just to Ireland—Ireland would be as closely welded at this moment to England as Scotland is (applause), and it would be as difficult to raise the flag of insurrection or discontent in Ireland as it would be for Prince Charlie again to appear with his flag in Scotland (applause).

The difference between the *status* of the tenant in England and the tenant in Ireland is briefly this :—

1. In England a yearly tenant can only be evicted on a year's notice, which must expire on the anniversary of the taking.

2. In Ireland a yearly tenant may be evicted on a three month's notice.

3. In England the out-going tenant is entitled to receive compensation for all unexhausted improvements.

4. In Ireland the tenant could be evicted without receiving any compensation whatever up to the year 1870. In that year an Act was passed giving him compensation, except in cases of non-payment of rent. The landlord takes advantage of this deceptive legislation, raises the rent beyond what the tenant can pay, ejects him, and thus obtains possession of the improved land without compensation—an injustice the more flagrant as the improvements are generally made by the tenant and not by the landlord. In this act of injustice he is assisted, to use Mr. Gladstone's words, by an army of soldiers and constabulary,

But there is more than the bare *legal* difference. In England there are few landlords indeed who do not take a personal interest in their tenantry. At Christmas and Easter special help is given to the very poor, the sick, and aged. Free gifts of coals and blankets are in the smallest English villages liberally distributed amongst the people. In Ireland, with rare exceptions, nothing of the kind is done, and the only intercourse between landlord and tenant is the " stand and deliver " process of getting the rent.

If English statesmen will not protect the rights of Irish tenants at least they might give them the trifling means of encouraging Irish fisheries and reclaiming waste lands. If some of the millions spent on useless wars were expended in this way, England would gain more than Ireland.

God help the poor patient fishermen, driven even to mend their boats with brown paper in their earnest, honest desire to work ; and God forgive the men who live on their toil and sweat and then taunt them with idleness.

Mr. Tuke says (p. 32) :—

"At Mackery a little in-shore fishing is carried on. Coracles are the boats employed, and during the stormy winter many of these frail craft had been damaged and rendered 'useless. One poor man had just been up to the Rectory to beg for some *brown paper* to mend his boat with. A more enterprising man, the Rector told us, had built for himself a good wooden boat, and had done extremely well ever since, and was much better off than his neighbours. The harbour, or bay, is safe and sheltered, and the Rector (Rev. S. E. Burns) thought that if funds could be got for a few good boats, which could be built by the men themselves, it would be of great and permanent benefit to them."

The whole history of Irish fisheries is a history of the pitiful struggles of hard-working, honest men against every possible disadvantage.

We give a few extracts from this year's current report :—

"GENERAL REMARKS."

" So far, I think the Act of Parliament affording loans to fishermen has proved a success, and an impetus has been given to fishing operations. It is to be regretted that they are not carried out on the west coast on an extensive scale, instead of the uncertain, spasmodic attempts that are made by the poor people living near the coast. This class of persons is unsuitable for large undertakings by themselves, though they might be made useful to others who would enter into the enterprise, which, to command success, must be carried out by the personal superintendence, labour, and active exertions of the principals themselves. Until such people are found it is well to foster the industry of the poorer classes who now follow fishing on the west coast, and who at seasons are enabled to bring additional supplies of food into the country.

" Without the loans, I have no hesitation in saying that many of them would have been obliged to have abandoned fishing long ago. I should like to see the loans extended to the other maritime counties where they are not now available, and where they would be a great boon to many.

Not so. The fisheries in and about Kenmare were ruined in the famine year, and I have in vain implored the noble owner of vast estates here to do something to restore them.

" LISCANNOR STATION.—From Spanish Point to Cancapple.

" Bream, cod, and ling, are the principal descriptions of fish captured ; canoes only employed. Lobsters and crabs were taken in a small quantity this year. They abound on the coast, but the difficulty of getting them to market is the great drawback to any improvement. No steps have been as yet taken to remove the rock which is so dangerous at the mouth of the Liscannor Harbour. Unguarded—about twelve miles.

" The fishermen in the whole division are reported to be peaceable and orderly.

"WATERFORD DIVISION.—It is reported that off Bonmahon more mackerel, bream, cod, and whiting were seen, but the take was not large owing to the want of proper gear for their capture.

" The fishermen are reported to have been orderly and well conducted.

"KILLYBEGS DIVISION.—The boats, however, in this district are too small for successful fishing, and the gear requires to be better in order to enable the fishermen to pursue their avocation at a greater distance from the coast.

" BALLYSHANNON STATION.—Bundoran to Eske River,
Donegal, about thirty miles; unguarded nearly the whole
coast.

" Herrings, mackerel, cod, ling, plaice, whiting, and bream
are the fish taken. Small shoals only of herrings and
mackerel appeared this year a quarter to two miles off the
shore. No quantity was captured. Lobsters and crabs
were captured in good quantity at Kildoney and Bunnat-
roohan. At the latter place the harbour requires something
of improvement to afford shelter for boats. At present it
is in a bad state of repair and a great loss to the fishermen,
being their only place of refuge on this part of the coast.
The fishermen complain also that they are not allowed to
reap any of the advantages offered to fishermen in the neighbouring county by loans for repairs of boats and providing
suitable fishing gear.

" In the whole division the fishermen are peaceable and
orderly, and no conflicts.

" BELDERRIG STATION.—From Brandy Point to Glenul-
dra, about thirty miles; unguarded about sixteen miles.
Mackerel is the principal fish taken, and large shoals appeared in August and September about two miles off the
shore, but there were no adequate means for their capture.
Fishing only very partially carried on on this coast.

" PORTACLOY STATION.—The same remarks as the former
station apply equally to this, save that at Portacloy a large
quantity of lobsters were taken.

" PULLENDIVA STATION.—Easkey to Dunmoran, about
thirteen miles. Herrings, mackerel, and pollock are the
principal descriptions of fish taken, but herrings in the
largest quantities. Several large shoals of mackerel appeared in June and July off Dromore, and herrings in
September, but very few were taken in consequence of in-
sufficient gear. A very fair catch of lobsters took place.

They were sent principally to the Dublin markets. It is reported that there is plenty of fish along this coast, but the people have not the means to procure boats and gear.

What need to say more. Everywhere the men are reported as peaceable and orderly, anxious for employment, repaying thankfully, even in the worst times, the miserable loans made to them.

And yet we are told the Irish are lazy and will not work, and that it is no use to do anything for people who will not help themselves. Waste Fisheries! Waste Lands! It is a wrong record of national injustice. If English fisheries were destroyed or injured by the visitation of God, public subscriptions would establish them again, even if Government failed to do so.

Waste Lands!

At the lowest computation there are two millions of acres in Ireland, or one-tenth of the available area of the country, capable of reclamation, but utterly unreclaimed. Will any one believe that this state of things would be allowed to continue in England? where, as a matter of fact, seven millions of acres have been reclaimed since the time of George III. But, does anyone believe that there is the smallest chance that either a Liberal or Conservative Government will take up this question in earnest, as the Irish people have a right to expect?

"Mr. Brett is of opinion now, as in 1847, that public employment should take the form of the reclamation of waste lands, together with the encouragement of a better system of husbandry amongst the small farmers; and I understood it to be his intention to report to this effect to the Government, by whom he is employed on special service in Mayo at the present time. His facts and figures are of paramount importance just now, since even a Land Bill, fashioned upon the lines of the most pronounced reformers, could not bring any immediate accession of prosperity to a population wanting 'elbow room,' so to speak, and suffering from chronic starvation in consequence of such want. Speaking of the waste lands, he observed, that there are at least four baronies in the West which might afford scope for an early experiment in reclamation, not only without pecuniary loss, but with infinite economic gain, to the State, viz.:—

			Average value per acre.	
Erris (Mayo)	...	232,888 acres ...	1s.	1d.
Boylagh (Donegal)	158,517	„ ...	1s.	3d.
Ballynahinch (Galway)	194,584	„ ...	1s.	4d.
Ross (Galway)	...	98,000	„ ...	1s.	5d.

Mr. Brett, whose long connection with Public Works in Ireland lends the weight of practical experience to his opinions, is clearly convinced that the whole of this enormous acreage, which includes neither deep bog nor mountain top, is capable of complete reclamation. And, moreover, he can point out, he says, "numerous instances in the Counties of Mayo and Sligo, as well as in Wicklow and Waterford, of reclamation effected at considerable expense, where the produce of the lands in two years defrayed the entire cost of outlay."

It is a weary record. What need to give details or to enter a statement of what every one knows.

The Rev. P. Logan, Kilcar, writes :—

"The fishermen had no boats and no tackle; little work was given (except the making of one road), and there was no harbour to protect the boats or fishermen, Much work might be done if means were forthcoming; at the best of times they cannot *live* on their present small holdings, but there is plenty of waste land which wants cultivating and which they ought to have, as the land is for the people."

Let me turn to a pleasanter theme, to prove that if the mysterious "capitalist," of whom we hear so much and see so little, would only come to Ireland, instead of talking about coming, Irish people would be only too thankful to avail themselves of such openings.

I have been in correspondence with the managers of the principal Irish industries—the Belleek Potteries, and the Bessbrook factories. Let me first give Mr. Tuke's report of the province :—

"We had the great pleasure of seeing the Belleek China Works and meeting the intelligent and enterprising owner and manager, Mr. Armstrong, who, with his partner, has put £40,000 into these works. The "water power" of the outlet of the lake, the felspar, which constitutes 73 per cent. of the china turned out, and the cheapness of labour, were the inducements twenty years ago for establishing the works here. They are now giving employment and good wages, from 9*s.* to 40*s.* or more a-week, to a large number of people, representing 1,000 persons in all, and these works prevent the town of Belleek from being on the relief list. In addition to the many pretty little articles of Belleek ware familiar to all, the great turn-out of the place is now in sanitary ware of all kinds. Jenning's and Tylor's sanitary ware, and Maw's inhaling bottles, &c., are made here. Mr. Armstrong is a most ingenious and energetic man, and it did one good to find one man really solving the question of Irish misery and discontent by giving full employment at good wages, and combining with this a strict and intelligent oversight of his people. Whilst we were going over the works, a man came up to show him some work he was modelling. "Yes," he said, "as good as I could wish it ; it is perfect." And, as the man went off, Mr. A. said, " Seven years ago that man came to me at 5*d.* a-day, and, now he is earning 35*s.* a-week, and on the 1st of April will earn £2 a-week."

The pottery works at Belleek began thus :—

Some twenty-five years ago, it was observed that the cabin of a tenant on the estate of John Caldwell Bloomfield, Esq., of Castle Caldwell, had been adorned by an unusually brilliant coat of white-wash. On being spoken to on the subject, the peasant explained that he had lighted on an old lime-pit, or a supply of "naturally burned lime." Mr. Bloomfield, taking an interest in a production of nature, had

the spot examined ; and, in consequence of what
‾he' found, had borings made in different parts
of his estate, which disclosed the existence of a
wide stratum of fine white earth. On chemical
examination at Dublin, this earth proved to be
a species of Kaolin—a felspathic clay, similar to
that which forms the " bones," or interior, infu-
sible, portion of Chinese porcelain. Other materials, Mr. Bloomfield was informed, were necessary ·to be procured, in order to establish a
manufacture of pottery from this china-clay ; but
it proved, not unnaturally, that the description
of felspathic earth which *is* fusible, and which in
China, under the name of *pet-un-ze*, forms the
|"flesh " or·flux of the porcelain, was also to be
found on his estate, together with many other
valuable minerals.

This china-clay and the felspar were sent to
·Mr. R. W. Armstrong, then residing in London,
with the view of having them practically tested.
After the lapse of a few years, during which
time Mr. Armstrong repeatedly visited Castle
Caldwell, and had a number of trials, and articles made from the clay, felspar, white quartz,
&c., at the Royal Porcelain Works, Worcester,
by the zealous co-operation of Mr. W. H. Kerr,
who was then one of the proprietors of the
Worcester Works.   That gentleman, as an

Irishman, entered fully into Mr. Armstrong's desire of having the quality of the Irish material tested and tried in every way, with the ultimate object of establishing an Irish pottery, if such could be commercially done. These trials and testings were afterwards submitted by Mr. Armstrong to his friend, Mr. D. M'Birney, of Dublin, a merchant of standing and well-known enterprise, who ultimately, in 1857, embarked with Mr. Armstrong in the practical trial of producing first-class ceramic goods in Ireland, composed largely of Irish materials, and made *by Irish labour* on *Irish soil;* and these gentlemen are now owners of the Works, trading under the firm of D. M'BIRNEY & Co.

[In the interior, the factory bears all the appearance of business and bustle. Enormous grinding-mills, in which the raw material is prepared for the hands of the artisan, rumble and roar, driven by the irresistible and constant power of a large water-wheel; the furnaces of the great ovens, in which the moulded clay is baked, hiss and scream, as if striving to undo the noble work for a time committed to their care; while, when we leave turmoil and din and turn into the workshop, the lathes and turning-plates whiz noiselessly round, as the soft, putty-like clay is being deftly moulded by the skilled

workman into many beautiful designs. To
minutely particularise the numerous operations
carried on in this factory would be simply to
describe the various details of the potter's art,
from the time the china-clay and felspar are
brought intó the factory in their raw state, until
they leave it, in the form of porcelain, china,
and stone-ware, of the most exquisite and
⁓chaste patterns.]

" Within easy distances are to be found very
fine and promising indications of lead, copper,
all the felspars, orthoclose, oligoclose, quartz,
various micas, albite, syenite, sphene rock,
schorl, soapstone, serpentine marbles, as well as
fossil encrinite and black marbles, sulphate of
barotes, and, near the felspar districts on thè
Castle Caldwell Estates, molybdenite, in the
oligoclose veins near Garvary."

We now turn to another class of industry
which has not been less successful.

Bessbrook, near Newry and Rostrevor, in
the north of Ireland, has long been famed for
its factories established by Mr. Richardson.

The number of its inhabitants is now nearly
4,000, and there has never been any house for
the sale of intoxicating drinks. It is, perhaps,
the oldest place in Ireland connected with the
flax spinning and weaving trades, and at the

present time the people mainly depend on this industry for support. The head of the firm, to whom the mills and factories belong, is John Grubb Richardson, an eminent member of the. Society of Friends, and a strong supporter of the Temperance movement. He is the owner of the surrounding property, and under his fostering care the place has grown from a few huts to its present size and interesting character as a *model town.* It is a quiet, isolated spot, and has made its mark in the history of the Linen Trade.

Every family in the place has one or more of its members engaged in the mill, which produces family linens, damasks of the best designs, pocket-handkerchiefs, and many other articles into which linen yarns can be woven.

It is said that no town in Ireland below 10,000 of a population can support a book-shop. In Bessbrook one exists, of no small importance, which, combined with a lending library, fulfils a useful purpose, and is very well supported.

Undisturbed by the evil consequences of *strong drink,* more care is bestowed on the quality of goods produced ; and this, while repaying the proprietors for their paternal oversight, is indirectly of advantage to the purchaser also. The Bessbrook linens have long borne the highest repute in the best markets of the world, and can be relied on as genuine when the engraving of the Works with the word ." Bessbrook" is printed on the band.

The Bessbrook damasks have earned the reputation of being the finest ever made by machinery. In this branch of manufacture the people of Bessbrook stand unrivalled, and have succeeded in weaving table-cloths, by power-loom machinery, equal to the finest made in hand-looms.

Large employment is also given in the working of granite quarries, the stone being of a special quality, and largely used in public buildings.

Thus we see that when factories *are* established in Ireland they succeed, and when fisheries *are* helped ever so little they prosper. It is time, then, to have an end of all idle talk about Irish laziness, or about this wonderful capitalist who is always coming, and never. comes.

The two capitalists, Mr. Richardson, of Bessbrook, and Mr. Armstrong, of Beleek, who have come, have succeeded even for these interests, and they claim and receive the thanks of a people always grateful, when they have even the least solid cause for gratitude.

APPENDIX.

No. I.

Report of the Trials

OF

GERARD O'CONNOR, Rev. ANDREW O'SULLIVAN, JEREMIAH O'CONNOR, And WM. M'CARTHY,

AT THE KERRY ASSIZES,

Held at Tralee on the 18th October, 1832,

FOR CONSPIRING TO RESIST THE PAYMENT OF TITHES AND EXCITING THE PEOPLE TO THAT EFFECT, WITH THE SPEECH OF

MR. O'CONNELL

IN DEFENCE OF THE TRAVERSERS.

THE traversers were arraigned on Thursday, 18th October, upon an indictment, containing twenty counts, charging them, in various forms, with having conspired to resist the payment of tithes in the parish of O'Dorney, as well as in the whole of Ireland, with having incited the King's subjects to enter into illegal combinations against the payment of tithes; and with having incited the subjects not to pay tithes either to the clergy of the Established Church or the lay impropriators. The Traversers pleaded *not guilty* to all

B 2

these counts, and tendered a traverse *in prox.* A lengthened discussion now arose between the counsel on both sides as to the right of the prisoners to traverse. Several authorities were cited by Messrs. O'Connell, Gibson, and Pigott. We profess not to give a report of the argument on this point, so uninteresting to all but professional persons, and we accordingly insert the rule of the Crown book, inserted upon his lordship refusing to allow the traverse.

His lordship, upon refusing the application, was moved by the learned counsel to take note of the objection, and soon after a note to the following effect was filed with the Clerk of the Crown :—

The traversers, Gerard O'Connor, the Rev. Andrew O'Sullivan, Jeremiah O'Connor, and William Stack M'Carthy, having been called on to appear, and the indictment having been read, and upon hearing the same, and upon view and inspection of their several recognizances (*prout*), they tender a traverse *in prox* to the whole of said indictment, and two sureties for each of them to appear and abide tr.al according to such tender of traverse, which traverse the Court was pleased to reject ; and thereupon said traversers tender a traverse *in prox* to each count, *seriatum*, of said indictment, and two sureties for each of them, to appear and abide trial according to such last-mentioned tendered traverse, which last-mentioned traverse the Court is pleased to reject, and thereupon said traversers plead *Not Guilty* to the whole of said indictment, and tender a traverse *in prox* to the whole of said indictment, and two sureties for each of them, to abide trial according to said last mentioned tender of traverse, which last mentioned traverse the Court is pleased to reject ; and thereupon the said traversers tender a traverse *in prox* to each count of said indictment, *seriatim*, and two sureties for each of them to abide trial, according to said last-mentioned tender of traverse; and which said last-mentioned traverse the Court was pleased to reject."

The following gentlemen were then sworn on the jury after three changes by the Crown :—

Dominick Rice,	William Hilliard,
James M'Carthy,	Francis Twiss,
William M. Chute,	John Hilliard,
William Blennerhassett	Alexander Elliot,
Robert Hilliard,	Jas. Wm. Raymond, and
Kean Mahony,	William Collis, Esqrs.

Counsel for the Crown—George Bennett, Stephen Woulfe, and J. Rutherford, Esqrs.

Counsel for the traversers—Daniel O'Connell, John Gibson, and D. R. Pigott, Esqrs.

Messrs. Daniel Supple and Maurice Leonard, Agents.

Giles Sullivan, sergeant of police, cross-examined by Mr. O'Connell—Is sergeant since the formation of the police ; could not help being a regular and excellent reporter ; Jeremiah O'Connor advised the people not to violate the law : did not recollect this when on his direct examination because he was not asked ; remembered the varnish, shins, and marrow, but not this ; took no note only what struck him ; said nothing in his information about it ; the magistrates instructed him to tell everything contrary to law, what he thought treason, and not to mind telling them anything but the treason—(a laugh)—the magistrates were Colonels Stoughton and Crosby, Rev. J. Chute, and Oliver Mason ; swore three minutes ago through mistake that "he recollected nothing else ; is sergeant of police ; five policemen were in O'Dorney ; saw cows at Ballyduff ; they were not sold ; the magistrates swore him to tell the truth so far as the informations ; got a message from Colonel Stoughton to go to O'Dorney ; thinks, but is not positive that M'Carthy advised the people to keep the peace ; never heard the cow was a widow's cow; was examined more than once; was sworn twice; recollects not whether examined three times; was sworn a third time; remarked to J. O'Connor that M'Carthy said nothing offensive at Ballyduff; advised O'C. not to use insulting language; did not swear about the 3rd at all.

Adam Firrell, a policeman, sworn — Saw Jeremiah O'Connor on a grey horse at Ardfert, followed by about 150 persons; heard him say the password of every man should be "down with the tithes," and advise the people not to fight among themselves; saw him parade with a brand five inches long, several persons following.

James Godfrey, a policeman, being sworn, said—About three hundred persons were assembled on the 16th July at the tithe meeting; saw Gerard O'Connor there; heard him make a speech, in which he advised the people to stand heart and hand together, and that no person should bid for cattle distrained for tithes; saw the Rev. Mr. O'Sullivan there; heard him tell the people not to pay tithe, but to allow their cattle to be sold, and that none ought to bid; heard J. O'Connor desire the people from the platform to allow their cattle to be sold, and to hold no conversation with the pound keeper of O'Dorney for not giving up the cattle for tithe, if he did not excuse himself; heard him also advise the people not to drink, and not to violate the peace; heard M'Carthy advise them not to pay tithe; J. O'Connor held up a tumbler and said it contained water—("that's a conspirator," observed Mr. O'Connell); did not drink the entire of the glass (laughter); Mr. M'Carthy desired the people to assemble on the 25th; witness saw him on the 21st at O'Dorney; he (Mr. M'C.) told the people to take care of Paddy M'Kews; "here," said he, "are the cattle, but where are the bidders?"

Cross-examined by Mr. O'Connell—Recollects hearing

Mr. M'Carthy say to the people, "it was not by holding illegal meetings in the solitude of night, but by constitutional meetings only they would succeed." (Mr. O'Connell read this passage, among others of Mr. M'Carthy's speech, from the *Tralee Mercury*, to refresh the memory of the witness.) Witness admitted the delivery of these words was followed by the cheers of the meeting; he swore informations before Captain Bowles; did not include these words; did not recollect them until reminded of them now; has been serjeant of police for nine years; was formerly a private in the Miltown Yeomanry or dismounted cavalry; was in the Miltown corps when the three Murphys offered to fight the whole corps (great laughter); was not afraid of the Murphys; is very fond of boiled Murphys (a laugh); is now a serjeant; would not like that any one should call him a corporal (a laugh); did hear some threats offered to one of the traversers at the sale at O'Dorney; O'Connor, the policeman, threatened one of them.

J. Coffee, policeman, swore he was present at the meeting at O'Dorney on the 15th of July; from two to three thousand persons were there; heard J. O'Connor describe to the people, in Irish, what the tyrants' carriages were composed of—that the springs were made of the sinews of their limbs and the paint of the sweat of their brows; by tyrants were meant those who enforced the payment of tithes; heard him say Paddy M'Kew was at hand. This witness being cross-examined, said Serjeant Godfrey was at O'Dorney on the 15th; O'C. desired the people to keep the peace and not violate the law.

E. Sullivan, policeman, swore he heard J. O'Connor say he was the first to oppose tithes, and that he had a number at his back; that the people should be as a bundle of rods; when Mr. O'Sullivan observed the parsons would not give up their livings as easily as the people thought, O'Connor

said they (the parsons) should give them up; witness saw
W. S. M'Carthy at the meeting; he (Mr. M'Carthy) used the
words "large letters of blood;" something was said about
parsons' children, such as "weeds of a garden, or devils out
of hell;" can't remember half what was said.

D. O'Connor, policeman, gave the same testimony as the
preceding witness; there were from two to three thousand
persons present; that J. O'Connor advised the people not
to oppose the laws; that Mr. O'Connor being a classical
scholar witness could not translate what he said; J.
O'Connor also preached peace and temperance; said he
was one of the first who opposed tithes, and he thanked
God he had a great number that day to back him; that the
people should stick together like a bundle of rods, and that
they could be put down (the carriages, with their appur-
tenances, saying as above), saying their enemies were about
them; witness heard M'Carthy warn the people of two
baronies to attend on the 25th, adding "who'll purchase?"
This witness was not cross-examined.

The evidence for the prosecution having closed, the
Court consented, at the request of counsel on both sides, to
adjourn to the following day. The jury were in the meantime enlarged.

"MR. O'CONNELL—Gentlemen of the Jury, I say with the
most perfect confidence, there is not one particle of evidence
in this case on which to ground a verdict of *guilty* against
the Traversers. This I undertake to demonstrate. I say,
suppose every word true that was sworn by the witnesses (a
position which I will not admit), you could not legally or
conscientiously find a verdict of guilty. Two things are in-
dispensably necessary upon which to ground your verdict—
credit and accuracy; the accuracy of a witness is just as
important to find a verdict on as his credit, without both you
cannot as conscientious men find a verdict of conviction.

Good God ! are we in Algiers ? are we in a region of slavery ?
I arraign this prosecution—I arraign the Anglesey Administration—

" Judoe Moore—Mr. O'Connell, I must not—

" Mr. O'Connell—My Lord, I reiterate it, I arraign this
as a base and audacious attempt to put down public opinion,
and trample in the dust such as dare be free. I will venture
to say, there is not one man in that jury box, be his com-
prehension ever so limited—but must acknowledge from the
argument of yesterday, the right of my clients to traverse in
prox, not to postpone their trial to another assizes. But
that right I do not rely on ; I fling it overboard, I rest on
the plain indisputable fact, that there is not an iota of what
was sworn which *can* be tortured into legal evidence against
the traversers. Mr Bennett was pleased in his truly able
speech to pass an unmerited eulogium on me ; I do him full
credit for his kind opinion, not from the vanity of supposing
I deserve it ; but from the private friendship which I have
ever entertained for him. The learned gentleman says he is
not a politician, notwithstanding his political, powerful, but
at the same time, as was his duty, his most artful and insinu-
ating speech.—Yes, gentlemen, I maintain in that speech he
urged topics that did not belong to such a prosecution—
topics he was not entitled to use—and as an Irish Barrister,
he should not use. In this able and powerful address, many
things were stated in explanation of the object of this prosecution. Among other things it was put on public grounds.
This is a mere delusion ; I say the object is not the protection of property, but the destruction of liberty ; it is a foul
conspiracy, not a protection —conspiracy by those whose
fixed determination appears to be, to trample on the rights
of the subject. How can a series of meetings, independent
of, and unconnected with each other, amount to conspiracy ?
The learned gentleman mixes up tithes with rents, *claims* of

Individuals with individual property, talked of convulsions, volcanoes, eruptions, infant torrents and huge precipices. The object of his statement was to shew that this prosecution was tending to tranquilize the country. I deny it! to put an end to disturbance and disaffection in this country! Where is the disaffection; where the disturbance? Are the means of obtaining constitutional redress, the prerogative of the subject, to be misconstrued into disturbance and disaffection? No man can be deemed guilty of disturbance, or disaffection, who loudly exclaims to his oppressed fellow-countrymen, "Rally, my friends; show that your country is tranquil, shew perfect submission to the laws, and put not yourselves in your enemies' power!'" Was not this the very essence of the meeting, for which my clients are now arraigned? did they not show perfect submission to the law? Remember, Gentlemen, that the meeting which was to have taken place on the 25th of July, *never took place:* not *one* meeting was held after the 15th! Why? because Gossett's letter was circulated through this country on the 16th, in the *Tralee Mercury:* that was the first intimation of the illegality of those meetings which this county had, and it was met by perfect submission; not one meeting since! What stronger argument can be adduced to disprove the intention of conspiracy, and show a determination of obedience to the law? Yes, but it is said the law was outraged before the 16th. Suppose *that* for argument; our plea is, we were ignorant of the law; some of the heads of the government were the same. If the mind be not disposed to evil, there is no crime —'*Non est reus si mens non est rea.*' Here the strongest popular feeling was allayed, and sunk in perfect obedience to the law.—Nay, more, according to Godfrey's evidence, the people gave up their meetings, *which were held to petition, to petition the legislature,* cheerfully and readily. Mr. Bennett said that this prosecution was to protect private as well as public, property: "if tithes were abolished, rents could no longer be recovered." This I also deny; emphatically deny;—there is no analogy between them. For rent a person will get some value, sometimes, indeed, very little—especially from the grinding agent of an absentee landlord—but, yet, *something* is given; but *no* value for tithes. He wished you to confound the sacred rights of private property, which men enter into society to protect, with the property of a corporation, which has been altered by the legislature before, and which may be so again, whenever the necessities of the State require it. Let me put a case; suppose Catholicism the established religion of this kingdom. In a parish in this county there are 12,498 Protestants and 50 Catholics, even those 50 not regularly attended by their pastor, who visits them only in the shearing season, for the purpose of fleecing the flock. There you see the majority are Protestants, (though the fact is *vice versa*). Now, I ask, when those Protestants felt they derived no benefit from their Popish rector, who discharged his sacred duties, perhaps, by deputy; who gave no value, except by importing English dairymaids, to make bad butter—(a laugh)—I ask you, gentlemen, would not this great Protestant majority be justified in combining to get rid of such a system? For my part, I never will voluntarily pay tithes; such, my determination, shall never be shaken by a side-wind prosecution of this kind. I make this declaration fearlessly. I canvass the freeholders of this great county, on the principle of this my avowed hostility to the tithe system. You, gentlemen of the jury, have a high duty to perform; you have to exercise your judgments, I hope, unbiassed by prejudice, upon the guilt or innocence of the traversers. Oh! the blessings attending that bulwark of the liberty of the subject, THE TRIAL BY JURY! In former times, what miseries have been consequent on the want of this most excellent system! The want of

knowledge of the juror, formerly, *alone*, caused a most righteous judge, nine times, to turn back a jury—for what? because they would not convict a person arraigned for having
published a· pamphlet, recommending to the people of
Ireland the use of Irish manufactures. And yet, the trial by
jury, though the great safeguard of the liberty of the subject,
has its defects: one prejudiced man may prevent a *good*
verdict; but one *honest* man may prevent a *bad* one. I dare
say, there are many conscientious men in Spain, who wish
to see the inquisition, the horrible inquisition restored.
There are many honoured men in this country, who hold it
as their conscientious opinion, that things should undergo
no change; others of a different opinion; but each man in
that jury-box is responsible to his God, and the prejudice of
one is counteracted by the *honesty* of the other. It *is not*
illegal to look for the extinction of tithes. How can it be
so, when that sentence is pronounced already against them
by government? I speak in the spirit of that feeling which
swells my bosom as the representative of this great county.
I address myself to freeholders; claim their votes, and assert
it is the essence of political honesty to agitate any question
tending to the extinction of this odious impost, and *still*
agitate until it be totally abolished.

"But when I say this, 1 do not mean to say, I should
ever advocate the depriving the many worthy men who have
devoted their youth to study, their lives and energies to
preaching the gospel, of the means of subsistence. God
forbid I should advocate such a system. No! I would give
them full compensation. Never be it said I should advocate the spoliation of the tender wife, the friendless children,
and drive the wretched father forth to a merciless world, a
prey to poverty and biting indigence. No! I would have
their situation rendered even more comfortable than it is.
I would place them so as that they may be enabled to

devote *more* of their time to their sacred duties, to remove
their thoughts and feelings from the passing interests of temporal, to the higher, and to them more natural walks of spiritual avocation. Indeed, the *Globe* of last night, the organ
of the Ministry, declares, that there is something in contem-
plation for the extinction of tithes. The government, however, appears to be under the influence of two antagonist
principles, one of good, and the other of evil. They have
revived the system of the Manicheans, who worship their
God of justice and of injustice. At one time they bid us
'agitate, agitate, agitate,' and then turn round on us for
doing to-day what they themselves recommended yesterday.
Mr. Bennett dwelt on agitation and conspiracy. My learned
friend read from a newspaper, sentences importing to be the
opinions delivered by Baron Smyth. Now, my conviction
is, that Baron Smyth never said a word of what that paper
attributed to him. More absurd propositions were never
uttered. I will read this passage from Lord Plunket. (Here
the learned gentleman read a passage from the speech of
3rd July, contained in the *Southern Reporter*.) Now here
is an article published in the name of the Lord Chancellor
of Ireland. Thus, it is not illegal to assemble, not illegal
not to pay tithes ; and, yet, we have these spies of magiste-
rial inquisitors parading the county, and military marching,
until pigs and cows are frightened at the very name of a red
coat. In England, no popular candidate comes forward
without pledging himself to advocate the extinction of tithes.
To say then that a whole nation had conspired, must be
considered an absurdity. Why, no change of any grievance
can take place without inquiry. For the sake of argument,
we will take the circumstances of the Reformation. How
can the principle of the Reformation be defended, if church
property be inalienable ? The English transferred that property from the Catholic clergy to the Protestant, because

they preferred the latter. This would never have occurred if they could get a jury to send to gaol those that would advocate the protection of public property, and so deprive the people of England of that right. But, perhaps, it may be argued, that the law is not to be disputed in England, though it might in Ireland. Can you, gentlemen of the jury, say, individually or collectively, that tithes are not a fit subject for alteration in both countries? If you decide so, if the right be not recognised, then the Rev. Mr. Denry should hand over his tithes to Dr. M'Ennery. This was the system a few years past, when unjust laws against Catholicism prevailed, commonly known by the name of the *Penal Laws*, when you, John, could be metamorphosed into Giles. When, if a Catholic was in possession of £20,000 by filing a bill of discovery against him, a Protestant could deprive him of it. If the Attorney-General could then put down the people who dare exclaim against this most abominable law —if a struggle was not then made to rescue the people from this gross oppression—if police scraps and patches of evidence were then admissible, what would have become of the liberty of the subject? Oh! let every man forget such principles; let each man devote himself to the cause of justice; let not the voice of a nation be smothered, that ought, that can, and that shall be free. The scissors of the Attorney-General, forsooth, lops off those means of one reformation by which another has been effected. The means by which the Reform Bill was carried in England, cannot have escaped your minds. When 300,000 men were ready to march to London, where was the Attorney-General then? where the Colonel and the Police? The Colonel asked me to tell what was bad—'Tell only what you thought was treason,' says the Colonel. I appeal to all men of sense, to gentlemen, to Christians, if such a proceeding was not opposed to reason and justice. Oh! let me not find you

forgetting that you are independent, conscientious men. Let
it not be said that you found a verdict against the traversers,
because there was some little Protestant prejudice existing
among you.

"Before I come to canvass the credit and accuracy of the
witnesses, let me once more premise to you, there is not one
particle of legal evidence. It is not unknown to you, that
Kerry was the last county in which these meetings were
held. You have them in Kildare, in Meath, Kilkenny
and other counties, with their deputy lieutenants, their
magistrates, their police, and their Paddy M'Kews to boot.
Kerry is the last. Government allows them to go on—
sanctions them. Be not the tools, then, of those persecu-
tors, who would employ when they want you, and turn you
off when they have done with you.

[Here the learned gentleman read a part of lord Plunket's
speech, of the 3rd of July.]

"Shall you, gentlemen of the jury, be coerced to-day that
that was a crime which the Lord Chancellor declared was *not*
a crime? Let any person, with two ideas, answer this question. Did government know those meetings were illegal or
not? Our case is, we were ignorant. Did Mr. Blackburne
know they were illegal? If not, and that I had the tithe-
brand, I would brand *ignorance* on his forehead; and instead
of six inches long, it should be nine. But they knew it—
they allowed it to go on—they entrapped the poisonous ver-
min, and now call upon you to put them even to death!
Gentlemen, a spy can never be but despised, and particularly
a spy before a crime. He who employs a spy, instigates to
crime, and then calls for punishment. Do the jury smile?
No; they agree with me. The meeting was peaceable. Did
they use a stick, stone, fist? Yes, one—there was a threat
held out to one of the traversers—carry that into the jury-
box with you. Good God! Do I stand in Kerry? Are

twelve men to be found so degraded as to find a verdict
against persons peaceably meeting to discuss what they consider a grievance?   There is no indictment for words—we
are not indicted for a libel ; for sedition.   Hearken, gentlemen, to a trial which took place in the time of Dean Swift.
—Oh, the value of trial by Jury !—the check which a jury is
to a judge who wilfully mistakes the law ! We have in the
' Life of Swift' an instance of the valuable check a jury is to
a corrupt government.   In 1720, this great man published a
tract relative to Ireland, entitled, ' A Proposal for the universal use of Irish manufactures.'   The use of Irish manufactures ! there could be no offence in that.   Of this pamphlet, and its consequences, he gives the following account, in
a letter to Pope :—' I have written,' he says, ' in this kingdom, a discourse, to persuade the wretched people to wear
their own manufactures, instead of those from England.'
This treatise soon spread very fast, being agreeable to the
sentiments of the whole nation, except of those gentlemen
who had employments, or were expectants ; upon which a
person in great office here immediately took the alarm.   He
sent in haste for the Chief Justice, and informed him—(of
what, gentlemen? ' of a seditious, factious, and virulent
pamphlet, lately published, with a design of setting the two
kingdoms at variance.'   A seditious, factious, and virulent
pamphlet, for recommending the use of Irish manufacture !
In twenty or thirty years hence, we'll hold the present proceedings in the very same light that we now hold this
' seditious, factious, and virulent pamphlet.'   Oh, the inestimable value of trial by jury ! Well, let us proceed—
' Directing at the same time that the printer should be
prosecuted with the utmost rigour of the law !' The
utmost rigour of the law ! ' Prosecute,' says this person in power, the Arimanes of this Manichean government—prosecute Jerry O'Connor, Gerrard O'Connor,

William M'Carthy, and the priest torn from the sacred duties of his altar, and prosecute all with the utmost rigour of the law. 'The Chief Justice has so quick an understanding, that he resolved to outdo his orders,' This person in power resolves to outdo his orders. 'The grand juries of the county and city were effectually practised with'—(the jury was effectually practised with!)—'to present the said pamphlet with all aggravating epithets, for which they had thanks sent them'—(you, no doubt gentlemen, will have a vote of thanks sent you from Dublin, signed C. Boyton, secretary) 'and their presentments published for several weeks in all the newspapers. The printer was seized and forced to give great bail. After his trial the jury brought him in *not guilty*, although they had been *culled with the utmost industry.*'—Though culled with the utmost industry, these honest, upright jurors, though cautiously culled, men of principle, brought the poor printer in *not guilty.* 'The Chief Justice sent them back nine times, and kept them eleven hours, until, being perfectly tired out, they were forced to leave the matter to the mercy of the judge, by what they call a special verdict.' Oh, if I had been the barrister who defended the printer, they should have incarcerated me ere I would allow that judge to send back that jury *once* after their verdict. Kept that jury in eleven hours after their verdict! Atrocious judge! Oh, that Heaven would put in every honest hand a whip to lash the rascal naked through the world. Astonishing, that the very stones of the street did not rise to proclaim his disgrace, and tear the ermined robe from off the miscreant's back! 'During the trial the Chief Justice, among other peculiarities, laid his hand upon his heart, and protested *solemnly*, that the author's design was to bring in the Pretender.' Aye, gentlemen, 'Popery, slavery, brass money, and wooden shoes.' To bring in the Pretender!—(laughter). How analogous to our present proceedings. That pamphlet was just as much a design to bring in the Pretender, as our crime here was conspiracy. There is no indictment for words—for libellous words—for seditious words—for exciting persons not to purchase at tithe sales— no count for threatening those who should buy—(if I be not stating facts the counsel at the other side should stop me)— take the evidence in the strongest sense, there is no count in the indictment to found a verdict on. Is the jury of this high, independent county to be made the base instrument of the government, to send in a perjured verdict? I do not blame the skill of the prosecutors ; the law has not conjectured such a crime. I fearlessly assert there is no count in the indictment, on which to ground a verdict. Let us look at the law of conspiracy as defined in Chitty's Criminal Law : we find it here defined, '*vagum et incertum ;*'—here we find the law of conspiracy '*vagum et incertum,*' loose and uncertain. Now where there is a doubt on the minds of a jury, the prisoner is entitled to the benefit of that doubt. In Rome the law of one of the tyrants was so *equitable,* that, when he chose to create victims, he caused his proclamations to be printed so small and posted so high, that it required the very best eye to read them—as telescopes or spectacles were not invented in those days. The hissing in a theatre is here adduced as authority for expounding the law of conspiracy. This is contemptible and foolish, the opinion of an old woman, than whom there was not a greater on the bench, than he who pronounced it, Sir James Mansfield—a weak judge, a well-meaning man, but no authority. But does this opinion constitute law? Who is to make law? Judges say, they cannot make law : Coke's opinion is that judges have made law ; and we have evidences of it, when we hear every idle briefless barrister, who has nothing else to do but reporting what judge such-a-one says, on such a subject, not analogous to the one then under consideration. Hearken to what

Hawkins says :—'It seemeth certain, *ut videtur*,'—now,
seeming precludes certainty. (The learned gentleman here
quoted Hawkins, Blackstone, Chitty, and other lawyers'
opinions of the law of conspiracy ; in particular he dwelt on
Chitty). 'Few things so doubtful in law as the point at
which combination becomes illegal.' This authority cannot
be doubted when it is quoted by the other side (here Mr.
O'Connell referred to 13th East. 230, King and Turner).
Here you see, *false et malitiose* is a necessary ingredient in
the crime of conspiracy. King and Ecles, in the case of certain poachers combining to meet at night, to poach, not considered conspiracy. If the traversers have combined, so have
the Quakers ; that exemplary and respectable class of Christians, have been conspiring for the last 200 years Whoever
among that respectable class is guilty of paying tithes, that
person is read out of meeting—nay, they go farther, and say,
whoever takes the surplus of what is sold for tithes, is read
out of meeting. Who ever heard of their being indicted for
conspiracy ? There is no conspiracy to resist tithes in Ireland—I fearlessly assert it. My lord Plunket has said the
same : he having laid his view of the law, dare we dispute
it ? The public at large are not injured ; the injury is only
to individuals. This comes precisely under the case of King
and Ecles. Let us come to the evidence. There are six
witnesses, Giles Sullivan, Adam Firrell, J. Godfrey, J. Coffe,
E. Sullivan and D. O'Connor. Not one of all these could
prove a breach of the peace. Note that I pray you. I call
upon you to note, not one could prove a blow, except the
three made to one of the traversers—no breach of the peace.
This was at the meeting of the 10th—the next meeting was
on the 15th. On this day the Rev. Mr. O'Sullivan first appears, and no one can say that what took place that day, is
evidence as against him. I'll spare my breath with respect
to him. I shall throw overboard the opinion of Sir J.

Mansfield, a government-influenced judge. We have instances, gentlemen, of judges having been influenced."

Judge MOORE.—Mr. O'Connell, this is too much. I really cannot suffer an imputation which I feel I do not deserve.

Mr. O'CONNELL.—My lord, I was but commenting upon a quotation concerning the opinion of Sir James Mansfield, which fell from the learned counsel at the other side.

Judge MOORE.—I am sorry I mistook you, Mr. O'Connell, I thought you meant——

Mr. O'CONNELL.—I meant what I said ; but my lord, I would rather go to the dock, or pass my life in a gaol, than suffer the interests of my clients, or my privilege as an Irish barrister, to be frittered away by any judge. I am here to advocate public liberty, as well as private right—the basis of a nation's prosperity. I stand here between the peaceable inhabitants of my county and their oppressors. I assail the Attorney-General for having brought this paltry prosecution without evidence, in the very teeth of reason and justice.

Mr. BENNETT.—The Attorney-General is not here, Mr. O'Connell.

Mr. O'CONNELL.—It is not my fault that he is not here. *He is here by his prosecution—I assail that prosecution.* This jury is not to try a petty civil bill—a petty question, the upshot of which is a month's imprisonment. No I they are here to protect their country from the grossest wrong—to protect their liberties—their right of meeting to establish their country's welfare by constitutional means. One of the counts is—inciting not to pay tithes in O'Dorney ; another, inciting not to pay tithes all over Ireland. As to incitement to conspiracy, I look upon it that is a new law.

Judge MOORE.—Mere incitement is not indictable.

Mr. O'CONNELL.—The first in the parish of O'Dorney and another all over Ireland. Now, there is not a particle of the existence of tithes in O'Dorney; whether it pays now, or not, does not signify : we have no legal evidence of the payment of tithes in the parish of O'Dorney; on the contrary, we know it to have been a mitred abbacy; and my learned friend will admit that the principle of *ecclesia non decimat ecclesiam*, prevailed in those days; and I warrant that the abbots of O'Dorney looked well to their rights, and paid tithes to no man, neither lay nor clerical. If I am to have law, let me have law. We are indicted for conspiracy to prevent the payment of tithes all over Ireland. Not one particle of evidence is there extending the conspiracy farther than the two baronies; but, remember, this conspiracy must be a criminal conspiracy—it must be a conspiracy to act in co-operation for an illegal purpose. The witnesses have not proved the entire of any one discourse : is this evidence of what has been said? The witnesses picked out what was *bad*, and not until their memory was jogged by me, could they remember one thing that was *good*. If they had sworn that nothing else but *that* was said, then indeed it might be considered evidence : but was there nothing said to explain or qualify? We are triumphant in the qualification—every one of the witnesses admitted the qualification. It is not from parts of sentences that we can collect a whole—the principle I thus arraign is no less repugnant to the spirit and letter of constitutional law, than it is irreconcilable to common sense, to general morality. If it were not so, Atheism could be proved from the Holy Scriptures. "'There is 'no God,' is written in your Bible," exclaims the Atheist triumphantly. "True," says the Christian, "but it is set down as the language of a fool : 'the fool saith in his heart there is no God.'" Now let us see Gerrard O'Connor's speech.—(Here, the learned counsel read that gentleman's speech from the *Tralee Mercury*.) "It is not by holding illegal meetings in the awful solitude of the night you can rid yourself of

an oppressive law. No ; but by assembling in the open day,
before the face of Heaven and the world—by using argu-
ments instead of force—by wielding the pen instead of the
dagger or the sword—by substituting the exercise of moral
power for a display of physical strength ; in a word, peaceably
and constitutionally assembling as you have on this day—by
proclaiming to the world the wrongs and injuries which you
suffer, and by petitioning the legislature of your country for
redress : it is by these means—*and these alone*—you can ever
effect any benefit for your native land." This was the language of Gerrard O'Connor : but all this was suppressed,
withheld by those worthy, creditable, and accurate witnesses,
until by mere chance I have been enabled to draw it from
them. This, remember, was cheered by the meeting, the
attending at which forms the subject matter of this prosecution.

Gentlemen of the jury, bear this in mind, I entreat you,
that there is no continued chain, but partial portions of isolated evidence relied on to convict my clients ; a means of
procuring the oppression of the subject by the mockery of
justice, the semblance of legality—one of the never-failing
resources of bad and tyrannical governments, and their
creatures. It was by means such as these, that in former
times the illustrious Russell was made the martyr of public
liberty. A jury was packed for the occasion by the infamous
Jeffries ; and from a discourse on theoretical liberty found
among his papers, such particular portions were selected as,
by a forced interpretation, procured at once the object of
the accusers and the conviction of the accused. The noble
Russell was convicted upon such evidence as that : his an-
gelical lady attended his trial, and supplied him with notes
of the evidence, and when she saw her husband foully mur-
dered by the sentence of a corrupt judge, and the verdict of
a packed and ever infamous jury, she stilled her throbbing

bosom, and the angelic heroine repressed her breaking heart, but that she might teach her infant son to tread in the footsteps of his father, that she might devote him on the altar of the British Constitution, and swear him there never to disgrace the name of Russell; and one of the first acts of a British reformed Parliament—the first Parliament that ever met after the glorious Revolution of '88, restored the name of Russell in lustre and purity, to the admiration of all England; and that same act condemned and denounced the infamous modes resorted to to convict him—the choosing out garbled and isolated passages from his writings, and suppressing all that could qualify or explain them. In modern times we have Smith, the missionary, for advocating the liberty of the gospel, persecuted the same way. No man can indict me for saying, "I never will pay tithes;" such a stretch of the law was never contemplated. Gentlemen, had I not an interest in thus pressing you, I should not put this proposition half the number of times to you. Bear well in mind, gentlemen, you are bound to give the traversers the benefit of every doubt; every shadow of rational doubt must have vanished before you can convict. This county was never yet disgraced by any verdict against a traverser on which a doubt hung, and I assert that my clients are as entitled to an acquittal as any traversers that ever stood in this court. As to the words imputed to the Rev. Mr. O'Sullivan, of "parsons giving up their tithes;" and "here are the cows, but where the purchasers?" there is a decided difference in the evidence of the two witnesses, O'Sullivan and Connor, which impeaches the accuracy of both: what then becomes of their veracity? one must be wrong, that creates a doubt as to which, and a doubt acquits. I must grind this into your minds—you cannot reconcile the evidence of Giles Sullivan, and that of Daniel Connor. There is a plump contradiction, a direct and emphatic contradiction. What do you think of this man who could not remember "the thousandth part of what was said ;" no certain swearing as to a chairman ; there was no chairman. You may, gentlemen, remember to-morrow what you heard to-day—(a laugh). You will find it hard to remember the entire of it though you heard me say I would not pay tithes. You could swear to a great deal of what was said ; you would still have a greater difficulty in a week, still more and more in a month. But, what will you say, when I tell you the informations were not sworn against the traversers for two months after the alleged offence. When I asked one of the worthy witnesses why he did not tell the recommendation of D. Connor, and the others to the people to keep the peace. 'He said he did not at the time recollect that,' did not remember one particle of what by chance I got out of him by the assistance of a newspaper. Some of the witnesses could remember a number of words, a ludicrous tale of marrow-bones, shins, parsons' children, weeds of a garden, devils out of hell or something.' This puts me in mind of a ridiculous affidavit filed in one of the courts above :—it was in the case of a landlord moving the court for leave to bring an ejectment. The affidavit set forth—that he, this deponent, called on the said so and so, for the rent and arrears of rent then due to this deponent, as such landlord, and the answer which this deponent then got from the said so and so, was, *botherum boo*, or words to that effect. This is a State trial, a trial which is to put down Whiteboyism ; we who meet together to discuss our grievances ; constitutionally to meet and address parliament by petition, compared to Whiteboys. I assert that this very political agitation is the most powerful instrument to put an end to Whiteboyism. There was no political agitation in 1819, and look at the atrocities committed. I aided constitutional agitation, and Whiteboyism ceased ; when constitutional agitation commenced, Whiteboyism vanished. In a word, gentlemen, when I consider those scraps and patches of evidence, these inaccuracies snatched up, and relied on as evidence, no indictment inciting not to buy, no evidence of tithes in O'Dorney. I rest in full reliance on your verdict. The entire county looks to you; the spirit of Kerry men exists in you; we have fled to the integrity of a Kerry jury from those wrongs which party zeal has accumulated on us. There may be some among you possessed of your prejudices; but you are Christians. I call on you then for that verdict which will give the Court satisfaction and reflect honour and glory on yourselves."

The priest, Mr. O'Sullivan, was acquitted. There was, in fact, no case against him, as he had advised peaceable agitation. Jeremiah O'Connor and W. S. M'Carthy were fined £10 each, and imprisoned for a month. Gerrard O'Connor was fined £10, and a fortnight's imprisonment.

To-day, the son of this gentleman, the Rev. M. O'Connor, P.P., is one of the principal promoters of the Land League in Kerry. So does history repeat itself. He remembers but too well the events of his father's most unjust imprisonment; but he also has lived to see the tithes abolished, in consequence of the determined resistance of the Irish people.

APPENDIX.
No. II.

No. 1.—OUTRAGES.

TO the last moment of going to press we note the persistent efforts of the English papers to publish "outrages" which have never happened and which have often been contradicted *some days before* in Irish papers; *e.g.*, the *Graphic* has a terrible outrage in its issue for December 4—a man who had both his ears cut off in Kerry. This story which never existed, except in the imagination of the inventor, was contradicted several days previously in Irish papers.

English readers, when they see accounts of Irish outrages in the English papers, take it for granted that they are true; if they would take it for granted that they are *not* true for the future they would be nearer the truth. They should also be very careful not to believe sensational letters about the state of Ireland, written to

English papers by Irish landlords. The object of these gentlemen is simply to prevent English people from legislating fairly for Ireland, and to enable them to continue oppressing their tenants. The Irish people only ask for just laws from England; why are they to be denounced for this? But as they would not be heard otherwise they have been obliged to form a great national strike to obtain justice. In a strike there must be demands made by the whole body, such as fixing Griffith's valuation as a basis for rents until the strike is settled.

From careful investigation I find that not one in ten of the outrages, either on men or animals, is true. As a witty friend of mine said, they should be taken *cum grano salis-bury*.

2.—Oppressive Rules of Estates and Magisterial Decisions.

The following speaks for itself. It cannot be too widely known that "excessive rent" is not the only burden which weighs down the Irish tenant. At a meeting of the Land League, in Dublin, Mr. Egan made the following report :—

"The property he referred to was situate at Ballinamore, near Balla, in the county Mayo, and belonged to Mr. Anthony Ormsby. He would only give the names of six townlands, and he did not know whether they represented the entire property :—

Townland.			No. of Hold-ings.	No. of Per-sons.	Government Valuation.	Present Rents.
Laragan	..	..	12	77	£65 19 0	£108 0 0
Ballinamore	..	..	16	96	108 9 0	169 15 0
Ballintaffy	..	...	9	62	127 6 0	171 0 0
Durphy	..	..	13	89	108 6 0	170 15 0
Comderra	..	..	8	72	47 19 0	77 5 0
Carrindyne	..	..	15	108	137 0 0	227 10 0
			73	504	£595 19 0	£924 5 0

Almost the entire of these lands consist of mountain slopes, and were all reclaimed by the tenants, without any aid from the landlord. In addition to the above exorbitant rents, the tenants are obliged to pay the entire taxes—not even getting the usual allowance of half poor-rates. They were also obliged to discharge 'duty work,' or free labour, themselves and all the members of their families, with their horses and donkeys. Tenants must get landlord's consent to their marriage, or the marriage of their children, and if they omit to do so are mercilessly fined. Thirty-five tenants were evicted off Laragan townland, and seventeen tenants off the townland of Durphy, after they had reclaimed the land. One tenant on the latter townland, Pat Walshe, had his holding twenty-two years ago at £3. The rent is now £11 10s.; the valuation is £4 10s.

"One of these was fined 10s. for one stone on the top of the gable not being whitewashed to the landlord's liking; 2s. 6d. for stopping at home from duty work to bury his child; 2s. 6d. for his pig rooting on his own farm.

"John Ruane was compelled to change from where he lived, and build a new house on some waste land in order to have it reclaimed. When he had the house built the landlord compelled him to throw it down and to build it ten yards further in. When he had reclaimed the land he again

compelled him to leave the place and go live on the
mountain. The poor man lost his life and died.

"Pat Walsh, a mason, worked at a building thirty-five
days, but would not get paid for fifteen days. When he
grumbled at this treatment he was made throw down the
wall and to build it without payment, and as soon as he had
it finished he turned him out without compensation.

"Thomas Cavanagh was compelled to throw down his
house and build a new one. When he had lived there a few
years he was forced to change to a bog, where he had to
build again. When he had reclaimed the bog he changed
him again for the third time, and wanted to change him the
fourth time. When the man refused he turned him out
without compensation. He had to go to the workhouse,
where he and his wife died. Each time he was changed it
cost him from £40 to £70.

These particulars had been supplied to him from what he
believed to be the most reliable source in the district.
Almost the entire of these lands consisted of mountain slob
reclaimed without any aid from the landlord. On the property a system of fines existed, of which he would give a few
specimens:—

"John Gormley was changed from his holding in the
middle of winter, and had to build a new house, which cost
him £10, on a swamp near a spring. The house was so
damp that the cattle got sick, and some of them died. The
family had to remain up at night all winter to keep fires lit.

"Thomas Conlon, who lived three miles away, was
ordered in to work duty work three days in the week. He
worked two days and remained away the third. He was fined
5s. for not attending.

"Pat Delany was fined 10s. for his cattle straying on a
bog road nearly a mile from the main road. He was fined
5s. for the top of his chimney not being whitewashed

according to the landlord's liking, and 5s. for stopping away from duty work.

"John Carney was fined 5s. for repairing his own mearing without the landlord's consent; 10s. for taking a stone from an adjoining farm, which was unoccupied; and £1 for cutting a few whitethorn bushes.

"Michael Conlon was fined 12s. for being seven days late in whitewashing his house; 10s. for some quicks which were pulled near the main road some distance from his house. Nine years ago he was compelled to go mowing to the landlord, and was fined 7s. 6d. when he did not make a drain in his holding at the same time. He was fined 12s. 6d. for repairing his own window (laughter). He was forced to spend twenty days mowing hay at 10d. per day, while he might have earned 8s. per day at that time. He was also fined £2 per annum for life for not going to work while his hand was sore. He was also fined £1 for burning scutch grass on his holding.

"Pat Hyland, of Ballantuffy, was obliged to build a new house which was often visited by the landlord when building. After it was built he did not like the appearance of it from the road. He made him throw it down and rebuild it. He (the landlord) promised him £7, compensation for windows and doors, but refused to pay it. When the house was finished he made him throw a portion of it down for the second time, and raised it eighteen inches. He also compelled him to cut a hill in front of his house.

"A little girl named Shearon was fined 5s. for looking through a fence on the road side, while a travelling show was passing. Mr. Ormsby chanced to see her (laughter).

"The following tenants were evicted by Mr. Ormsby, in order to enlarge his demesne :—

Thomas Walsh, Martin Quinn, Widow Moran. Widow Shearon, Thomas Kilray, Pat Shearon, Pat Kelly, Michael

Early, Thomas Begley, Pat Kelly, Edward M'Donnell, Peter M'Donnell, John Ruane, Thomas Quinn, John Hearn, Patrick Reaney, Patrick Ruane, Daniel Duddy, Patrick Duddy, Roger Halligan, Patrick Halligan, Edward Ruane, Martin Ruane, Edward Mulligan, and John Connelly.

"Phelim Brennan was fined 12s. 6d. for his cattle being found on the road.

"Anne Nolan, a servant, was fined 5s. for going to see her mother in her illness. She was also fined 7s. 6d., because she could not make the cows produce as much milk as they did in summer. Ormsby measured the milk night and morning for three years. Most of the tenants on the property have been changed from one place to another, as it pleased the landlord.

"John Jennings of Laragan, was fined £3 for getting married without the landlord's sanction, which was proved in open court at last Quarter Sessions, at Swinford.

"Mr. Brennan—I hope the Government will take that list of outrages into consideration when they come to consider the suspension of the '*Habeas Corpus.*'

"Mr. Egan—I have only to say that these particulars came to me, as I consider, well and thoroughly vouched. If Mr. Ormsby can disprove any of the statements made in that document, we here, at this League, will give him every opportunity of vindicating himself."

I have omitted many particulars to save space. There has been no contradiction published.

The Rev. John Magee, P.P., Stradbally, writes of the "Office Rules" on the Marquis of Lansdowne's Queen's County Estates :—

"1st.—That on the Marquis of Lansdowne's property in

the Queen's County, in addition to all its other exactions, an office rule (one of those silent office rules) required that no bachelor could dare to take the girl of his choice in marriage till first he presented himself at the office and obtained from the famous agent, or quasi Vicar-General, Mr. Trench, a canonical licence to marry.

"2nd.—That any tenant bachelor disregarding this edict or rule of office was liable to be fined one year's rent."

A case was tried at Tralee, in March, 1880, from the report of which I extract the following:—

"Denis O'Brien was next examined—He deposed he got possession of the farm from Mr. Chute; there were some arrears of rent, but he could not say how much it was; there was no arrangement between my father and myself about the land, but there was an arrangement between Mr. Chute and myself.

"Mr. Wall—What was the arrangement?

"Witness—That I was not to get married without Mr. Chute's consent.

"His Lordship—And are you to bring the girl to Mr. Chute to see her? (laughter)."

Mr. Marmion, J.P., in giving evidence before the Land Commission, has said that, eleven years ago, he gave 300 leases on the Castle Townsend property, the term of each farming lease being sixty-one years, and of each building lease 300 years. They were given, on an average, at fifteen per cent. above the Poor Law

Valuation. For the next five years, Mr. Marmion avers, that there were more improvements made on that property than for the half century previous, and he never had any difficulty in getting the rental. In this case both landlord and tenant were therefore materially served by security ; and he (Mr. Marmion) received the warmest acknowledgments from one and the other.

He next gives an example of a very different kind :—" I hand you," he says to the Commissioners, " a lease, called Richard G. Campion's Compound Form . . . The rent is £23, the valuation £9 10s. I know another, held under the same agent's management," he adds, "where the rent was £16 16s. Mr. Campion sent the tenant a lease to execute, raising the rent to £30. The tenant refused and protested, and what was Mr. Campion's reply? That if the lease was not executed before ten o'clock next day the rent would be raised to £40."

Mr. Marmion deposed that he knows estates where the rent is double the valuation. He declares that he has raised, in local banks, £100,000 for tenants, and has had only three defaulters, one of whom is a magistrate of the county.

At a meeting where the Rev. P. Waldron, P.P., Killerin presided, he detailed the dealings

of Mr. Henry with his tenants, whom he fines a
guinea each if they go to England to work.
The tenants pay double Griffith's Valuation, and
land for which they give him 18s. an acre is so
bad that a curlew would not alight on it.

During the distress in Ireland, Colonel King-
Harman, writing to the *Times* said :—

"There is, no doubt, a certain amount of imposition and
of seeking after unearned food, instead of honest work,
among a few of the idle and worthless, who must always be
found in any community, and who will be found in Ireland,
as elsewhere. As a rule, however, I say boldly that our
people in the West are making a brave fight, and are generally found asking for work, and not clamouring for charity.
I could tell of instances of families who are getting relief
meal, at the rate of half-a-pound per head per diem, helping
their neighbours. Is this demoralization?"

III.—ORANGEMEN AND THE LAND QUESTION.

One of the most important of the Irish land
meetings was held in Ulster. It is generally
supposed in England that there is no land
agitation in this part of Ireland. On this
occasion there were no less than five Members
of Parliament present, a number of gentlemen,
members of Orange lodges, and a number of
the Catholic clergy. The significance of such a
meeting cannot be over-estimated. It was held
in the Town of Monaghan on the 22nd Novem-

ber, 1880. The M.P.'s present were Messrs.
Given and Findlater, Mr. Litton, M.P. for
Tyrone, Mr. Richardson, M.P. for Armagh,
Mr. Dillon, M.P. for Dungannon. The chair
was taken by Mr. William Anketell, J.P., and
the meeting lasted four hours. Mr. Henry
Overend, an Orangeman, spoke first. Canon
Smullen, P.P. of Clarus, seconded the resolu-
tion.

" Mr. Henry Overend, of Farney, Carrickmacross, moved—
"' That the Ulster Tenant-right Custom does not afford
sufficient protection to tenants against capricious evictions
and unjust rents.'
" A regiment going into the field thought it a great
honour to be put into the front of the battle. He had been
put into the front that day to move the first resolution.
What had the Ulster Custom done for the people of Ulster?
" Voices—' Nothing.'
" Mr. Overend—' Office rules' came in and made it of no
effect. He travelled there that day from Farney, and along
with him was another Orangeman (cheers). He had a
Roman Catholic J.P. along with him, and also a sound
Farney priest. They could take arm in arm on the Carrickmacross railway platform, and were not ashamed to say
what they were. He went to church on Sunday and the
others went to Mass on Sunday, and they were glad to shake
hands when they met (cheers). Let them do all that there
—stand up for the cause boldly (cheers). Don't be
ashamed or afraid of their landlords. He believed there
were lots of Orangemen there (cheers). He could see them."

Mr. Findlater spoke strongly on the neces-

sity of breaking up the great London Corporate
Estates and selling them to persons who are
living in Ireland and who spend their money
there.

The *Times* of Sept. 28, 1880, had an article
which may well be quoted in connèction with
this subject, and which said on English authority that Ireland is not over populated. How
painful it is that English writers are so perpetually stultifying themselves by their extraordinary inconsistency when writing on the
Irish question.

"There appears to be much to support the views of those
who maintain that these poor and populated parts of Ireland are plague-spots upon the face of the earth, only to
be cured by getting rid of most of the population, and
who say that those who would give security of tenure to
those people, or who in any way try to mitigate their condition while keeping them where they are, are only perpetuat-
ing an unmixed evil.

"But there is a great deal to be said on the other side.
To begin with, if these people are crowded together on a
miserable soil, not fit properly to support them, that is not
their doing, but ours. It is the British colonists who have
driven these Celts from the better part of Ireland till,
hemmed in between the Saxons and the deep sea, they have
taken refuge among the bogs, mountains, and rocks, where
they now are. In the circumstances, they do not so much
deserve blame for living so miserably as credit for having
lived at all. If their cultivation is not so good and tidy as

it might be, what could we expect of serfs who have so long lived without any rights of property?

"After all, low as the condition of these people is when judged by modern standards, this is but primitive man as he has existed ever since he was turned out of Paradise. And even in the exceptionally disadvantageous conditions under which he has lived and multiplied in the West of Ireland, his physical type has not degenerated. On the contrary, we know that, unkempt and undeveloped as are the seedling plants in this human jungle, as soon as they are cultivated and cared for they are found to be very fine specimens of humanity, as fine as exist in the world. There is no better or more prolific nursery of the human race.

"Looking from the point of view of our own interests, we may well hesitate much, before we cut of these sources of fresh virgin humanity. Does not history show that when nations cease to derive fresh blood from their sources they begin to decline? We have already dried up one of our best sources in the Scotch Highlands. Shall we be wise to destroy the Irish source also? It is like cutting the national tap-roots by which sustenance is drawn from the lower soil. Who was it who, when tired and sodden by the affairs and the luxuries of the world, used to return for a season to the savage tribes from which he sprang, and to come back fresh and re-invigorated? Seriously, I do believe that our country would not be what it is without supplies of fresh blood. How many of us are there whose not very remote ancestors were raised in Highland cabins little better than those of the Irish, and had the inestimable advantage of freedom from shoes and stockings?"

IV.—LANDLORDS AND LAND AGENTS AS MAGISTRATES.

I have elsewhere expressed a strong opinion

on the subject of land agents and landlords acting as magistrates. I believe it to be the source of innumerable evils, and of evils of a class which cause special disaffection to English rule. The land agent's social power is simply unlimited ; if you add to this legal power he is omnipotent. Landlords are always calling out for coercion, and for repressive laws, and enactments for the people. Hence, when they act oppressively towards their tenants, whether socially or magisterially, they are simply acting on the one principle which they consider the only way to govern Ireland. The almost unlimited power of a land agent or landlord, however, must be judicially supported, by at least sufficient co-operation from others. But this is easily secured, especially in remote districts. It is not difficult to get a J.P. appointed who will quietly acquiesce in the rulings of the great man—above all if the person so selected belongs to a lower class in life, and is struggling up to "gentility," the unwise ambition of too many in Ireland. The gift of some place in connection with the many offices needed on a great estate will sometimes transfer a " patriot" into an humble follower, and thus the rule of the agent is quietly and safely established. In such cases, even if the agent is obliged, in common decency, to leave the bench where his own tenants are in question, he is sure that his wishes will be carried out all the same.

But, in most cases, the land agent is quite ready to adjudicate cases where his tenantry are concerned. The following extract, from the *Freeman's Journal,* is one of many such cases, and shows the urgent necessity for having magistrates who will be impartial judges, or who, at least, may not be suspected of acting either from personal interest or to please a powerful land agent or landlord :—

"THE MISSING CHILD—EMILY WALSHE.

" Monasterevan, Saturday Evening

" This evening, the woman Walshe, who carried away the child she claims as her own, was arrested in Waterford, and brought back with the child to Monasterevan. She was charged before Mr. Harvey, J.P., Lord Drogheda's agent, with taking away, by force, a child not her own. Mr. P. Daly, Solicitor, appeared in favour of Mrs. Walshe, and, as a preliminary matter, submitted to the consideration of Mr. Harvey, in whose house, I may remark, by the way, the investigation was held, that, in a case of such importance, the presence of some other magistrate was desirable. Mr. Harvey sent, not for the local Catholic magistrate, James Cassidy, Esq. J.P., but for his employer, the Marquis of Drogheda. The case then proceeded. A Mrs. Wall swore positively that the child in question was her child. This seemed quite decisive to the magistrates, who ordered the child to be given up to Mrs. Wall. In vain Mr. Daly urged that the woman Walshe was prepared, if she got the opportunity, to swear that the child was hers, and that, in any case, as the matter might be said to be involved in some degree of uncertainty, the child ought to be put in independent custody pending the settlement of the question of the child's identity. The magistrates refused to entertain that view of the case, and persisted in giving the child to Mrs. Wall. Strange to say, too, though the crime of a poor mother seizing on a child whom she honestly believed to be hers does not seem to be a great one, the magistrates refused bail, though bail was offered to any amount required, and remanded her till Monday next. The Catholic people here have no disposition to prejudge the question of the child's identity, but they feel that a fair trial has not been given; that as Lord Drogheda's lodge-keeper was implicated in the matter, he and his agent were not precisely the judges that good taste would have selected, and, above all, they feel, and justly feel, that to give up the child to the parties against whom there is at least an implied charge of conceal-ing Emily Walsh, from a writ of the Queen's Bench, was not exactly the best measure to secure the interests of justice. They hope, however, that there is some unprejudiced authority in the land that will take care that the child, who-ever she be, will not be spirited away till the matter shall have been thoroughly investigated."

But it is not only in land cases that I believe such persons to be utterly unfit for the Commis-sion of the Peace.

The following case, which has just been brought to my notice, has caused no little bitterness, and I fear such cases are by no means uncommon.

Who is to make them public? Certainly not those who are the actors in them, and the voice of the poor can rarely, indeed, make itself heard.

The following letter has been addressed to me, and it is in every particular .correct, as I have learned from personal inquiry :—

"MADAM,—I most respectfully beg leave to state.that my son, Daniel Harrington, a child ten years old, was sentenced to one month's imprisonment, on the 6th day of September last, at a petty sessions held at Kenmare, the justices being John T. Trench and Daniel O'Brien Corkery, Esqrs.

"The cause arose out of he and a boy, double his age, throwing stones at each other across a stream, and my little boy striking the other with his stone, and on the day of trial it can be shown that the small scrape inflicted on the injured boy was healed, only three days having elapsed. I am, Madam, your obedient servant,

"JOHN HARRINGTON.

"Toormore, 3rd December, 1880."

I have seen the child—a singularly frail, delicate lad, smaller even than his years would suppose him to be. He was kept in solitary confinement, picking oakum during the whole time. The case is too painful for comment. The boy was neither wild nor vicious, nor had he ever committed any previous offence. How would gentlemen who inflict such sentences on the poor like to have their own children treated thus? Is there ever to be one law for the poor and another for the rich?

And yet, so capricious are the sentences of the same magistrates, that for violence and assault a far lighter punishment has been given.

VI.—Promises.

Landlords are constantly complaining of their tenants, because, as they say, they do not trust them. Now, if Irish landlords are such benefactors to their tenants, if their government is as wise, and just, and kind as they say, why do they object so vehemently and noisely to have laws made by England for the relations between them and their tenants?

This is a consideration which most assuredly ought to weigh with every impartial person.

In the famine year landlords blamed their tenants bitterly, because they refused "employment" offered by them. But the unhappy truth is, that from long years of too painful experience, Irish tenants have learned to distrust their landlords utterly. They always find that "leaving things to the landlord" ends in taking from themselves what is justly theirs.

Again, let it be asked, Why do Irish landlords fear English law so much if their dealings
with their tenantry are fair?

But we can scarcely open a paper without
seeing some complaint of unfair dealing, and too
often of treachery, of which an honest man
should be ashamed.

The following has been addressed to Earl
Fitzwilliam :—

"CLONEGAL, Co. CARLOW, *November* 18.

"MY LORD,—It has been suggested to me that it would
be well to draw your lordship's attention to a fact connected
with the management of your property, which you may not
personally be aware of. Last spring I waited on the Shil-
lelagh Board of Guardians, and asked them to schedule the
union under the Seeds Act. In reply I was told that your
lordship would give your tenants seeds, free of all cost, and
Dr. MacCabe, the Local Government Inspector, who was
present, hearing the announcement, drew my attention to
the fact that sixteen electoral divisions belonged to your
estate. This statement was also made in the public Press
at the time. During the last three weeks, I have been told
by different persons on your property in this parish, that it
is your intention to make them pay for these seeds, which
they thought, and the public were led to believe, was a free
gift, and that tenpence on every five shillings' worth will be
charged as interest. If this report be untrue, I think it is
greatly to be regretted that one of exalted rank, high position and character, should, at a time like the present, be
misrepresented. Hoping your lordship will pardon this in-

trusion, and begging the favour of a reply, I remain, your
obedient servant,

"JAMES F. DELANY, C.C."

We have already given instances of how
landlords actually took advantage of the famine
to add to the rents and burdens of their tenants,
while professing in England to be doing acts of
charity for them.

VII.—FISHERIES.

The following is one of many instances lately
before the public of the perpetual difficulties
put in the way of Irish industries :—

"TO THE EDITOR OF THE FREEMAN."

"Arklow, *29th November.*

" DEAR Mr. EDITOR—Now that your journal is pleading
so ably the cause of the tenant-farmers of Ireland, I beg
you will bring under the notice of our rulers and our local
lords the cause of another class of her Majesty's subjects—
the poor fishermen along the coasts of our country. The
fishing in general these three past seasons has been a
failure. The condition of our piers and harbours, particularly along the eastern coast, is a disgrace to any civilised
nation. The month of November now past was usually the
fisherman's harvest. He had no fruit to gather this season.
How, I may ask, are these brave men to pass the winter?
We have been promised over and over again by the late and
present Government a grant and loan for the improvement

of our harbour here at Arklow. Now or never, I would say, is the time to fulfil these promises. Over 1,200 brave men belonging to this town are living by the sea. They are after spending the past year along the coast, north and south, but without success. They are not idlers. It is no fault of theirs that they did not bring bread to their families. At this moment 3,000 human beings are in imminent danger of starvation. The only remedy I could suggest is to at once set the works of a new harbour afloat. That will be giving labour of a kind these men can be employed at. It is with very great difficulty even in good weather the smallest boat can cross the bar. On Tuesday night last a boat called the James was wrecked in attempting to enter the harbour; the crew of five men were nearly lost. One poor man named Cullen was part owner. He is ruined for the season. We hear and see several losses of the same sort each year. Having tried every other means, locally and otherwise, and not succeeding in bringing this question of the Arklow harbour to any successful issue, I now throw myself on public opinion; and I call on the Press and our Members of Parliament to bring forward this matter in such a way that the Government of the country will at once bring succour to 3,000 people.—I am, Mr. Editor, yours very truly,

"JAMES DUNPHY, P.P., Arklow."

VIII.—MR. CHARLES RUSSELL'S LAND SCHEME.

The following sketch of a scheme of land law reform for Ireland has been published by Mr. Charles Russell, Q.C., M.P. :—

"I say emphatically that no patching up, no extension, no

modification of the so-called Ulster custom will avail. The action of the landlords themselves in Ulster, especially since 1870, has shattered the confidence of the people in the efficacy of that custom. It needs little consideration to see that a right in the tenant to sell his interest in his holding cannot long have a healthy existence side by side with a power practically uncontrolled in the landlord to raise the rent. That power, exercised by small gradual increments of rent, stealthily but surely eats into the very vitals of the custom. Further, I feel confident that no system which contemplates a future periodical revaluation of rents will be found effective or satisfactory either to landlord or tenant. If, therefore, the plan known as the "three F.'s" contemplates, not a rent fixed once and for all, but periodic revaluation, I believe it would prove an endless source of ill-will and discontent. I know no sound automatic arrangement by which rent may equitably be made to rise and fall. If the only alternative were between periodical readjustments of rents and its permanent fixture at what the tenant would now consider an excessive rent, I think he would prefer the latter because of its certainty. What is now to be done ought to be done with a view to a permanent settlement—as far as there can be permanence in the shifting conditions of human society. I may therefore at once say that, in my opinion, the direction which the settlement of this question should take is, so far as it can be done, to turn the occupiers of agricultural holdings in Ireland into a peasant, or, as I prefer to call them, occupying proprietors, securing them meanwhile in the possession of their holdings at rents justly ascertained and fixed now once and for ever. I shall presently point out the modes by which I think these results may be attained.

"It must be obvious from what I have already written that in many instances in Ireland to stereotype the existing condition of things in the case of small and poor holdings would not be to secure comfort to the tenant. A reduction to what even the tenant would consider a fair rent would not mean the difference between want and plenty. But it is wonderful upon how little some Irish tenants can live, and what a change even a small accession of means can effect. Even in the case of the very small and poor holdings (which I should hope to see gradually disappear), I have no doubt that perfect security, prompting the tenant to unstinted exertion would enable him to take much more out of the land than he does at present, and thus better his condition. Still, it is clear that there will yet remain cases—probably many—in Ireland which no scheme of fixing a fair rent, or of converting the tenant into a proprietor will meet, and in reference to which the remedy must be either migration or emigration. The clearances effected in the famine years and since have devoted to sheep and cattle large tracts of fertile land capable of sustaining many families in decent condition, but it does not seem possible to formulate any plan by which Parliament can undo the work so effected. The desired changes must be brought about by the gradual action of time and progress. But I have pointed to the vast tracts of waste lands capable of reclamation, which lie side by side with that which the tenants have already reclaimed. I believe that the waste but reclaimable lands in Ireland have been estimated at some millions of acres, exclusive of the enclosed lands, the productive capacity of which could readily be doubled. If these were properly dealt with, and, where advisable, added to the existing holdings, the cases would be comparatively few in which there would not be land sufficient (under the new energy which the sense of security would give) to support the existing tenants and their families in at least rude comfort. But, to carry out such a plan as I suggest, the necessity is clear for the creation of a strong and permanent land commission, which shall have functions of a judicial, an executive, and of a ministerial character. At these I shall presently glance.

"With this preface I shall state in outline my remedial suggestions.

"1. I would abolish every system of settlement or entail which can interfere with the sale or dealing with land absolutely at any given moment. In other words, I would require that there shall always be a person with absolute dominion over the land able to sell and make good title to it. Let the proceeds of the sale of the land be tied up or settled in any way you please, but leave the land itself free to be dealt with.

"2. In all cases where land is held by middlemen (that is, lessees intermediate between the owner in fee and the occupier) I would give to whichever of the parties had the major interest in the holding the right to buy out the other on payment to him of such sum as might be agreed on, or failing such agreement, then in payment of such sum as the commission should award; and I should give to the owner of the minor interest a corresponding right to purchase in the event of the owner of the major interest failing to purchase for six months after he had been served with notice calling on him to elect to purchase or sell.

"3. I would declare every tenant of an agricultural holding in Ireland who, at the date of the passing of the proposed Act or at any subsequent date has been, by himself or by his predecessors in title, say ten years in occupation of his holding, entitled to demand from his landlord a fee farm grant or lease for ever of his holding, at a rent to be fixed at the date of such demand once and for ever, subject to a right on the part of the landlord to appeal to the commission and show special circumstances which should equitably disentitle the tenant to the grant. The rent should be fixed, if possible, by agreement between landlord and tenant, but, in case of disagreement, to be fixed by or at the instance of the commission referred to. Probably the services of the judges of the county courts could be utilised for this purpose. When fixing the rent, all improvements made either by landlord or tenant should respectively be taken into account; also any special circumstances pointing to probable prospective increase in value affecting the particular holding. Every such fee farm grant should be in a form to be prescribed by the statute, and of the shortest and simplest kind. Each such grant should by statute simply imply covenants by the tenant to pay the fixed rent and keep the premises in repair, against waste, against subleasing, subletting, or subdividing without landlord's consent, but no covenant against charging or selling his interest, mines and minerals to be reserved to the landlord. On breach of any covenant the landlord to have a right of sale, with right of pre-emption, two years' arrears of rent to be a first charge upon the proceeds. For any greater arrear landlord to rank with ordinary creditors.

"4. Wherever it could be proved that at the date of the passing of the Act the rule had been on any estate to allow a hanging gale or gales of rent for an uninterrupted period of say ten years, I should declare such gale or gales as absolutely irrecoverable, and as for all future rent I should declare that any rent beyond two years' rent should be a mere personal debt due by the tenant, and should as against the land or the proceeds of the tenant's interests rank with other creditors.

"5. I would allow each tenant who had obtained his fee-farm grant to buy at any time, at 25 years', or at any lesser number of years, purchase that might be agreed on, his rent, or any part of his rent, not being less than £1. In order to obviate any inconvenience to the landlord from having payments made in sums too small for advantageous investment, I would provide for interim payment of such moneys to the land commission, securing the tenant meanwhile his yearly rent reduction. The land commission might be empowered to issue land bonds, even for small sums, which I feel sure would be a popular investment for the small savings of the country. I regard some such provision as this as of the highest moment.

"6. I would give the land commission power to insist upon the sale of corporate estates, and of all estates mortgaged beyond a certain proportion of their value—say 75 per cent. But in this latter case, unless by the consent of the owners, no more of the estate need be sold than would be needed to pay off the incumbrance.

" 7. The land commission to have statutory powers to buy and deal with (a) all the waste lands in the country; (b) the estates above referred to at No. 6 ; (c) all other estates as to which the legislature might consider it right to give the commission the compulsory powers of purchase ; (d) all such estates as may be voluntarily offered for sale.

" 8. On any purchase of an estate being made by the land commissioners they should pay the owner by land bonds with Government security, bearing interest at 3 per cent., redeemable at par. The owner should be entitled to receive so much in bonds as at the current price of the day would represent the full purchase money of the estate.

" 9. The lands so purchased should be sold by the commissioners to the tenants to be held in fee-simple, such sales to be in consideration of such cash payments and annual instalments in discharge of principal and interest, and thrown over such number of years, not exceeding fifty-two, as to the commissioners would seem best, provided, however, that all calculations for the payment by annual instalments should be based on the assumption that not less than three per cent. interest should be secured to the State on all money due by the purchasers. So long as the tenants remain debtors to the State for any part of the purchase money, such tenants to hold upon the terms and subject to the restrictions substantially as they would as to fee-farm grants under head No. 3.

" 10. I would appropriate the balance of the Irish Church Surplus as a guarantee fund to indemnify the State against possible loss in these transactions.

" 11. The land commission should keep a set of registry books, divided into counties or into poor law unions, in which all dealings with lands which pass through the hands of the commission should be entered, such entry to be the only registration to be recognised as effecting such lands. This would but inaugurate a system of local registration like that in France, and would tend to simplify and cheapen the dealings with land. It might easily be adapted in course of time to cover all dealings with land.

" 12. I would authorise the commission to expend such sum as they might consider judicious within certain limits in planting such portion of the waste lands purchased by them as could not be profitably reclaimed for tillage, but which might with ultimate profit be converted into plantations, or otherwise enable them to utilise such lands.

" 13. I would throw upon the land commission all proper expenses of valuation of titles and of conveyancing in connection with all estates dealt with by them, and such examination of titles and conveyancing should as far as possible be carried out under the direction of the land commission, and should not be referred to any other court.

" After all, the legislature is on these suggestions only asked to do on a larger scale what is every day done on a small scale. Where the public need of a road, or a railway, or other work of general utility requires the compulsory expropriation of a particular man's rights, they are expropriated. He has to give way to the needs of the community in which he lives. He is paid, not what he may consider the value of that which is taken from him, but the full compensation which the appointed legal tribunal awards him."

"IRELAND AND ROME."

Translated from the "Aurora" of the 12th.

"After having written of the origin and of the present state of the Irish question, we come to treat of its solution. In order to apply a remedy with any good effect we need to have a thorough knowledge of the disease. From what we have written it appears manifest that the Irish peasant is at the mercy of a landlord, who can at any moment evict him, and thus become, without any expense, the owner of all the improvements made by him on the soil, and even of his cabin. The tenant cannot find in the great manufactures, which in Ireland have no existence, any refuge from the cruelty and avarice of his landlord. For he has not even an escape in the justice of the law, whose verdicts, too often returned by the landlords themselves, are either most expensive to obtain, or, when obtained, not quite impartial. A stable and radical reform of the agrarian laws, excepting those which are right and just, would then be the first remedy. The introduction of new industries and the development of the old throughout the whole island would be a second remedy. The purchase of the land from the few landlords and the sale of it in small allotments to the peasantry, giving them all possible facilities for repayment, would be the third.

"Of these three remedies which offer themselves spontaneously to the mind of every one who knows Ireland and its present condition, which has the English Government tried? Not one. It has confined itself to the creation of commissions, consisting of landlords who have interests different from those which they, as commissioners, are bound to protect. If it had had a desire to remedy efficaciously so many grievances, the British Government should have listened to the protests of the Irish members against the absence of a tenant farmer on these commissions. The present agrarian laws need to be modified in such a way as to secure the tenant on that land which he has watered with the sweat of his brow, or, if not, all the obstacles which prevent his becoming owner should be removed. And the latter, in our opinion, if not the only, is at least the most practicable remedy sanctioned by experience in other countries. On the soil of every land the people who inhabit it should be able to live. Now to whom does the soil of England and Scotland and Ireland belong? Does it belong to the 32 million inhabitants of the United Kingdom? No; it belongs solely to 7,000 proprietors. Consequently the lives of 32 million individuals are at the disposal of seven thousand persons, who at any moment may evict the tenants, and without having expended a coin in improving the land may directly or indirectly rob them of the capital and of the labour which they have expended in rendering it productive. Now until this land will become the possible property of all, until the barriers be removed which prevent the peasant from becoming if it pleases him, or if he is able, by easy and just means, the owner, the agrarian question in Ireland will never be settled. This system by which property freed from landlordism is rendered accessible to the purse of all, is the system which has given property to Belgium and Prussia, and which renders the states where it has been long in force powerful. Let us take for example Prussia, where by means of a general and peaceful reform the question was systematised at the beginning of our century. On the 9th of October, 1807, a decree issued by Stein, Prime Minister, took from the nobles the exclusive faculty of possessing land. To the prolotarian were extended the rights of every free nation, and every Prussian was recognized as qualified to own, to vote, and to bear arms. Eight years after Hardenburg completed the work of Stein. The ancient tenures, for the greater part uncultivated and as extensive as provinces, became the property of the Government, which divided them into small farms of twenty acres each. So the lands of Prussia, which were first in the hands of some thousands of privileged proprietors, are now in the hands of two millions and a-half of peasants. When a person wishes to-day to buy a farm in Prussia he has only to go to one of the many Government offices in his district, offices more numerous than police-stations in Ireland, and there ask for the topographical plan of the lands for sale. When he has found what suits him, he pays a twentieth of the total price, and he is recognized as proprietor. From the supreme tribunal he receives a paper, with a document of the nineteen successive payments, with their respective dates, and the interest of the money up to the last payment. This document, a kind of temporary agreement, is given by the Government to the former owners of the soil, who can negotiate it like any other value, the Government being responsible for the exact payment. When the peasant has made the other nineteen payments he becomes proprietor without any of the formalities or law expenses which elsewhere are multiplied to infinity. This system should be adopted in Ireland. What was done with the Church lands by the law known as the Church Temporalities Act ought to be done for the whole of Ireland. Then, whoever has the wish and the money to make a first payment may become master of the soil. The land of Ireland would become fertile if the tenant were able to work it with the conviction that he would not be torn from it, and then the country would become one of the richest agricultural countries in the world. The effect of this reform is easily foreseen. The new tillers of the soil would have more money, they would be fed better, would dress better, and would give their children a better education—a matter entirely neglected to-day through poverty. When the peasant, by means of his industry, would have rendered the land fruitful, he would not be afraid of the landlord coming and increasing his rent, and he would be able to supply his necessaries and procure himself reasonable comforts. The tradesman and the professional would be thus stimulated in their occupations, and the prosperity of the agricultural classes would be increased, and the Irish would not be obliged to give their labour to a master. too often without faith and without heart. And what an increase of general prosperity for the entire kingdom! It is well known that in the last twenty years almost three million persons were obliged to flee before starvation and other scourges. Where did they go? Unaccustomed to everything but tilling the soil, they overflowed the large cities of England and Scotland looking for employment, and, being forced by hunger, they offered their services for a price much lower than that demanded by the English and Scotch workmen. Thus they have contributed to lower the standard of wages, and to fatten with their tissue the already wealthy capitalist, rendering, at the same time, the condition of the honest and intelligent artizan much more trying and difficult. Here, then, is the best solution of the great problem, according to the wisest opinions. It is true, we confess, that it strikes right to the heart, and through the most delicate fibres, the pride of the powerful aristocracy. If England will find courage to make the great sacrifice, and find wisdom and energy in her statesmen to carry out such a peaceful revolution, the

world would once more render homage to British good
sense and equity. But if a contrary policy will again
triumph in Westminster Palace, will we see poor Ireland
patiently await in the generous help of her distant sons the
bread which is to save her from famine, or shall a cry of
war from Donegal to Cork warn us that the patience of
nations, like that of individuals, has its limits? We anticipate for generous Ireland a just and peaceful solution of
these difficulties, an efficacious remedy for her wrongs; and
for the sake of Old England we do not wish that she should
add to her long and complex list of enemies of to-day this
glorious and noble island, which can supply the British lion
in the most critical moments with soldiers like those named
Roberts and Garnet Wolseley."

I appended to this an extract from a speech
of Mr. Sexton, M.P. :—

"Mr. Sexton went on to say how glad he was that the
labourers themselves were not to be hoodwinked by this
equivocal anxiety for their well-being. They knew well
enough that the only gifts they had ever received from the
landlords were the rent collector and the sheriff. He would
also draw their attention to the cry now raised against the
league that they were favourers of outrage, because some
factious "voice" in the crowd chose to be humorous. Not
one of those who made such charges but knew well enough
that outrages were not countenanced by the Land League.
The best proof of this was before them to-day in the presence of their venerated priests, whose mission it was to
teach them the truths of religion and the beauties of a truly
Christian morality. This was the function of their zealous
clergy, and he did not think that speakers at public meetings were bound to be continually lecturing the people

against crime, thereby implying that the people were pre-
disposed to outrages, and required perpetual cautioning to
keep them from shedding the blood of their fellow men.
All sympathy with murder has been disavowed by the Land
League, and he would not insult the morality of our virtuous
people by preaching to them (applause)."

PUBLICATIONS

OF

P. J. KENEDY,

Excelsior Catholic Publishing House,

5 BARCLAY ST., NEAR BROADWAY, NEW YORK,

Opposite the Astor House

Adventures of Michael Dwyer.................	$1 00
Adelmar the Templar. A Tale................	40
Ballads, Poems, and Songs of William Collins	1 00
Blanche. A Tale from the French.............	40
Battle of Ventry Harbor.....................	20
Bibles, from $2 50 to........................	15 00
Brooks and Hughes Controversy.............	75
Butler's Feasts and Fasts..................	1 25
Blind Agnese. A Tale.......................	50
Butler's Catechism.........................	8
" " with Mass Prayers...........	30
Bible History. Challoner...................	50
Christian Virtues. By St. Liguori..........	1 00
Christian's Rule of Life. By St. Liguori....	30
Christmas Night's Entertainments...........	60
Conversion of Ratisbonne...................	50
Clifton Tracts. 4 vols.....................	3 00
Catholic Offering. By Bishop Walsh.........	1 50
Christian Perfection. Rodriguez. 3 vols. *Only complete edition*...........................	4 00
Catholic Church in the United States. By J. G. Shea. Illustrated......................	2 00
Catholic Missions among the Indians........	2 50
Chateau Lescure. A Tale....................	50
Conscience; or, May Brooke. A Tale.........	1 00
Catholic Hymn-Book.........................	15
Christian Brothers' 1st Book...............	13

Catholic Prayer-Books, 25c., 50c., up to 12 00

☞ Any of above books sent free by mail on receipt of price. Agents wanted everywhere to sell above books, to whom liberal terms will be given. Address

P. J. KENEDY, Excelsior Catholic Publishing House,
5 Barclay Street, New York.

1

Christian Brothers' 2d Book	*$0*	*25*
" " 3d "		*63*
" " 4th "		*88*
Catholic Primer		*6*
Catholic School-Book		*25*
Cannon's Practical Speller		*25*
Carpenter's Speller		*25*
Dick Massey. An Irish Story	*1*	*00*
Doctrine of Miracles Explained	*1*	*00*
Doctrinal Catechism		*50*
Douay "		*25*
Diploma of Children of Mary		*20*
Erin go Bragh. (Sentimental Songster.)		*25*
El Nuevo Testamento. (Spanish.)	*1*	*50*
Elevation of the Soul to God		*75*
Epistles and Gospels. (Goffine.)	*2*	*00*
Eucharistica; or, Holy Eucharist	*1*	*00*
End of Controversy. (Milner.)		*75*
El Nuevo Catecismo. (Spanish.)		*15*
El Catecismo de la Doctrina Christiana. (Spanish Catechism)		*15*
El Catecismo Ripalda. (Spanish)		*12*
Furniss' Tracts for Spiritual Reading	*1*	*00*
Faugh a Ballagh Comic Songster		*25*
Fifty Reasons		*25*
Following of Christ		*50*
Fashion. A Tale. 35 Illustrations.		*50*
Faith and Fancy. Poems. Savage.		*75*
Glories of Mary. (St. Liguori.)	*1*	*25*
Golden Book of Confraternities		*50*
Grounds of Catholic Doctrine		*25*
Grace's Outlines of History		*50*
Holy Eucharist	*1*	*00*
Hours before the Altar. Red edges		*50*
History of Ireland. Moore. 2 vols.	*5*	*00*
" " O'Mahoney's Keating	*4*	*00*
Hay on Miracles	*1*	*00*
Hamiltons. A Tale		*50*
History of Modern Europe. Shea.	*1*	*25*
Hours with the Sacred Heart		*50*
Irish National Songster	*1*	*00*
Imitation of Christ		*40*

Catholic Prayer-Books, 25c., 50c., up to 12 00

☞ Any of above books sent free by mail on receipt of price. Agents wanted everywhere to sell above books, to whom liberal terms will be given. Address

P. J. KENEDY, Excelsior Catholic Publishing House,
5 Barclay Street, New York.

www.ingramcontent.com/pod-product-compliance
Lightning Source LLC
Chambersburg PA
CBHW020447270326
41926CB00008B/517